Modes of
Creativity

Books by Irving Singer

Modes of Creativity: Philosophical Perspectives

Mozart & Beethoven: The Concept of Love in Their Operas with a new preface, The Irving Singer Library

Meaning in Life trilogy with new prefaces, The Irving Singer Library

The Nature of Love trilogy with new prefaces, The Irving Singer Library

Philosophy of Love: A Partial Summing-Up

Cinematic Mythmaking: Philosophy in Film

Ingmar Bergman, Cinematic Philosopher: Reflections on His Creativity

Three Philosophical Filmmakers: Hitchcock, Welles, Renoir

Sex: A Philosophical Primer, expanded edition

Feeling and Imagination: The Vibrant Flux of Our Existence

Explorations in Love and Sex

Sex: A Philosophical Primer

George Santayana, Literary Philosopher

Reality Transformed: Film as Meaning and Technique

Meaning in Life:
The Creation of Value
The Pursuit of Love
The Harmony of Nature and Spirit

The Nature of Love:
Plato to Luther
Courtly and Romantic
The Modern World

Mozart & Beethoven: The Concept of Love in Their Operas

The Goals of Human Sexuality

Santayana's Aesthetics

Essays in Literary Criticism by George Santayana (editor)

The Nature and Pursuit of Love: The Philosophy of Irving Singer (ed. David Goicoechea)

Modes of Creativity

Philosophical Perspectives

Irving Singer

The MIT Press
Cambridge, Massachusetts
London, England

For information about special quantity discounts, please email special_sales@mitpress.mit.edu

This book was set in Palatino on InDesign by Asco Typesetters, Hong Kong. Printed and bound in the United States of America.

Library of Congress Cataloging-in-Publication Data

Singer, Irving.
Modes of creativity : philosophical perspectives / Irving Singer.
   p.   cm.
Includes bibliographical references (p.   ) and index.
ISBN 978-0-262-01492-2 (hardcover : alk. paper)
1. Philosophy 2. Creation (Literary, artistic, etc.) I. Title.
B945.S6573M63   2011
128'.3—dc22   2010020603

10   9   8   7   6   5   4   3   2   1

To my grandson Theo in the hope that, long after he learns how to read, he will read this book, and go beyond it

Contents

Preface

This book is a sequel to my book *Feeling and Imagination: The Vibrant Flux of Our Existence,* which itself developed out of my earlier efforts in *The Harmony of Nature and Spirit.* As with most of my writing, these works are attempts to deal with unresolved issues in relevant explorations of mine that preceded them. The concept of creativity as I approach it in these chapters arose from my intervening ideas about imagination, idealization, consummation, and the aesthetic as well as my recurrent analyses of love, sex, and compassion. In one way or another these all intersected with inchoate speculations of mine about human affect in general. Only after having lived through the prior investigations was my thinking sufficiently advanced for me to undertake the further questionings in this book.

The idea of creativity is nevertheless different from the concepts with which I grappled in my other writing. In contrast to them, it has recurred in almost everything I have undertaken as a philosopher and student of human values. In preparing the new prefaces that I recently wrote for the reprinting of my trilogies on the nature of love and meaning in life, I was struck by the many occasions on which I talk about creativity and the nature of what is or is not creative. I noticed how often the contexts of my remarks yearned for greater analysis and further insight, which I constantly seemed to shy away from. In fact, at the time I was writing those books, the subject was too difficult for me to do much of what I would have liked to accomplish.

The subtitle of the first volume of *Meaning in Life—The Creation of Value*—was suggested to me by an astute and talented editor. I remember feeling at first that this title was too grandiose, too daring and presumptive on my part. I finally concluded that it was just right for what that volume tried to do. Everything in it centered around the way in which human beings create the values by which they live. Since I knew that more was needed to explain the creativity being discussed and displayed, I could not escape the feeling that what I had written was still inadequate.

In attempting to overcome that sentiment in subsequent books and now in this one, I have intentionally avoided any assurance that a rigorous definition of the relevant terminology can truly elucidate this aspect of our existence. Eminent theorists in psychology and the philosophy of science have held out the assurance of finding an all-embracing formulation, but in my opinion their theorizing is most profitable when it issues into fruitful distinctions or empirical discoveries that are independent of any proffered definitions. The former is what still matters most to me.

I relish the remark of the poet A. E. Housman, who rejected a request that he define the nature of poetry. As he put it, he could not do so any more than a terrier could define a rat. In my own writing as a whole, and above all in the current venture, I draw upon a methodology entailing concrete analyses

that seek to locate the meaning of a concept worthy of philosophical attention by placing it within a range of relevant
insights about experiences and human interests to which it
pertains. These are generally humanistic, literary, and, as it
were, anecdotal of human consciousness rather than being
conclusive or strictly scientific. My approach is pluralistic
rather than abstract, dogmatic, or putatively objective. With
respect to the varied and panoramic phenomena that I try to
explain, I am convinced that this kind of orientation can be
very useful for scientists as well as humanists.

In my pluralistic approach, I concentrate upon the diversity
of types of creativity and the alternate ways in which it appears
in our species, across and within all the arts and sciences, and
throughout the ordinary living of life as we know it. I offer a
gamut of reflections that amplify but do not seek to duplicate the
investigations that issue out of related studies in cognitive
science or neurobiology or psychology. I wish to fortify their
thinking and discoveries about creativity by aligning them to
the aesthetic, affective, and phenomenological framework of
experiential behavior that permeates the human quest for
meaning.

At the same time I must confess that even in the later portion of this book, including the pages on creativity in science,
mathematics, and technology, I bypass to some extent the excellent research that recent workers in those fields have begun
to do. From their own perspective, neurobiologists, for example, have provided splendid studies that are largely empirical
but occasionally theoretical as well. In what I hope will be the
sequel to this book, I look forward to mining the philosophical
implications of their findings. I lay the groundwork for that
possible effort in my concluding remarks after chapter 10—

which itself demands further elaboration and development—as well as in the notes that supplement the individual chapters, together with the list of substantive references appended as a note to this preface.[1]

Creativity is cultivated and even worshipped by humankind because it instigates, while also augmenting, productions whose meaningfulness we cherish in themselves and in their vast utility for attaining the good life and a properly examined one. Within that framework, creativity belongs to a family of interwoven responses that comprise imagination, originality, inventiveness, and novelty in what we do or feel or believe. In common parlance these are often presented as bolstering each other. For instance, we speak of creative imagination, to which nineteenth-century Romantic authors like Samuel Taylor Coleridge devoted a great deal of thought. But also some people refer to "imaginative creation," as if creativity can possibly occur with or without imagination. My own linguistic intuition tells me that this interpretation is incorrect. Imagination is subsidiary to creativity and a necessary condition for it.

In *Feeling and Imagination* I approached imagination as the entertaining of possibles, which place it in a domain that is quite different from the past, present, and coming actualities that constitute what we envisage as the real—which is to say, the ordinary—world that we inhabit. Yet that world would have no meaning to us apart from the possibilities that we always and relentlessly entertain. Extending what the character in Shakespeare says: We are of imagination all compact. In my attempt to explore our entertaining of possibilities, I distinguished among the logical, the empirical, the technological, the moral, and the aesthetic or fictional variations predicated upon *im*possibilities. That analysis was too skimpy, as I now realize, but of greater importance is the fact that I failed to examine adequately what the nature of possibility is in itself. I surmised that it had a role in the creativity of animals like us, but only more recently did I discern how greatly interwoven are the imaginative and the creative.

Something similar applies to the relationship between creativity and inventiveness, novelty, and originality. By themselves none of these is necessarily creative. What is invented may have little of the usefulness or permanent importance that creativity involves. Nor do novelty or even originality entail any guarantee of this sort. On many occasions they may each be lacking in the consecutive and highly valued ability to make radical changes in oneself, in one's culture or environment, and conceivably in the world at large. Nevertheless they can all be necessary conditions for the existence of creativity. Throughout my text I frequently refer to them in that capacity, without seeking to invoke the rigor—which can often turn into rigor mortis—that more formal definitions might yield.

By concentrating instead on modes of creativity, I wish to articulate a *Weltbild*, a world-picture, that reaches beyond the creative, the imaginative, the inventive, the novel, or the original. All these belong to pervading patterns of existence and concerted relations between the cognitive and the affective that require philosophical insight and explication. The comprehensive portrait that I construct is designed to make our ideas clear about the interactions of these phenomena. The optimal clarity, assuming it is attainable, can have very broad ramifications for scientific and technological pursuits, as well as those that are explicitly artistic. Ideally the desired harmonization between technical disciplines and the humanistic focus upon moral and aesthetic bases of meaning and happiness may fortify eventual modes of creativity that are themselves novel and inventively productive. That is the goal toward which all my literary efforts are directed.

In working on these issues, I normally avoid jargon of any sort and I introduce new terminology as little as possible. One exception is my use of the word *transformation*. In chapters 1 and 10 I discuss its origin in other books of mine and seek to strengthen my employment of it in this book. Readers will notice that it crops up at several points in the text. It is meant to convey the manner in which creativity of every kind issues from previous realities that are altered dynamically, and often radically, while also being salvaged in some respect. Creativity does not occur in copying or mechanically reproducing whatever prior being it engages with, or by eliminating it completely. I deploy the concept of transformation to indicate how the raw materials of what will somehow become creative are changed in the process of being used or reconstructed or merely valued and enjoyed.

That is a recurrent theme throughout my discussions of the different modes and vast disparity of creative occurrences to be found in human life. The concept of transformation needs more analysis, which the sequel might awaken in me, but my lick and promise here may suffice for the parameters of this endeavor. In its overall structure the book contains two fundamental parts. One of them begins with chapter 1, on the need to reverse misconceptions about creativity, and ends with chapter 5, on aesthetic creativity. While these chapters examine many different topics related to creativity as a whole, they are also designed to anticipate the remaining discussions in the book, which deal with specific modes of creativity that overlap with the aesthetic in one way or another. Toward that end, chapters 1–5 make preliminary statements about the major theses that are central to my pluralistic views about the nature of creativity: my claim that the human preoccupation with what is creative devolves from the biological, psychological, and social bases of our material being; that creativity is not limited to any single aspect or activity in human existence; that it inheres not only in the mainly aesthetic goals to which fine and useful arts are dedicated, but also in components of science, technology, mathematics, moral practice, and ordinary, daily, experience that embody notable elements of the aesthetic.

Chapters 6–9 address particular problems within these general categories. They lead to chapter 10 on creativity as it is related to our species' feelings and conceptions about "reality." In lieu of any definitive finale, the reader will then find concluding remarks in which I discuss further research that others, as well as myself, may deem worthy of consideration.

Though scientists are much concerned with creativity in their chosen pursuits, their actual theories about it have been fairly scarce and rarely systematic. For humanists the creative is widely recognized as the golden thread that binds their disparate studies of values and life-enhancing qualities in all artworks generically, together with the impact of art upon society as a whole. Nevertheless, aesthetic practitioners today sorely need the unique perspective that philosophical works have traditionally provided in former centuries, but much less often in our period. As an example of what analytic philosophers can do, the appendix to this volume consists of a talk by Moreland Perkins, professor emeritus of philosophy, University of Maryland, who delivered it to a gathering of lower-school teachers. In form as well as content, its method is quite unlike my own. I welcome it as a supplement and separate resource that complements the peripatetic philosophizing that is predominant in the chapters that I have written.

During the years I was struggling with the many drafts that eventuated as this book, I taught a seminar at MIT on the nature of creativity. As in all my teaching there, the enlarged self-education that went into the subsequent manuscript issued from the teaching activity itself. Having such excellent students enabled me to formulate ideas I had never considered before. Week after week, I learned from the process of teaching the course what I could and should believe in this area of philosophy. I am grateful to those who participated with me in this rewarding experience and thereby served as co-producers of my work. Others whose encouragement, advice, and criticism were extremely valuable to me were Josephine F. Singer, Moreland Perkins, Thomas E. Stone, Jane L. Philbrick, Kathleen A. Caruso, and the anonymous outside readers to whom the press sent for their approval one of the later drafts.

I. S.
May 2010

1

Prologue: Reversing Mistakes about Creativity

Traditional and Modern Misconceptions

This preliminary chapter will seek to present a framework and a foundation for the progressively more constructive thoughts in the remaining chapters. Trying to sweep away the detritus of several past and recent perspectives in philosophical theories of creativity, I limit my polemical attack to the minimum that most readers require to see where I am coming from and will proceed hereafter. In the development of this chapter, I also sketch some ideas about the quest for creativity as a means of coping with the sense of dread and often desperation that resides generically in the human condition, and that the joyful access to creativity is capable of overcoming.

To begin with, I suggest that we who were born into the orthodox ideologies of our culture have inherited deeply engrained, but retrograde, assumptions about creativity. We have been taught that it reflects a spiritual domain that exists apart from our natural condition, that in human beings creative ability is an approximation of the infinite and eternal power of a deity that created nature as a manifestation of its own pure spirit. This Supreme Creator is thought to be the defining model for any creativity that may be available to lesser beings like ourselves. In the last two hundred years the Romantic views that permeated the Western world, and more recently much of the entire world, have modified the religious dogmas by identifying creativity with the having of extraordinary experiences without which this highly desired value would not exist. And finally, as a derivative from these two perspectives, creativity is often believed to be inherently good, albeit always liable to notorious misuse by weak or evil people.

I will be contesting these and related ideas of creativity at various points, but in a fashion that differs from some other thinkers who have also found them unacceptable. Within traditional Christianity of the Middle Ages there occurred a constant and never fully resolved debate about the relation of God the Creator to the world he brought into being. Though church doctrine ordained that the deity is outside of time and space, and therefore beyond the realm of matter, various thinkers who considered themselves devout Christians affirmed the unending presence of God in everything he had created with endless love and wisdom. Reformists like Luther or Calvin, just to mention two of them, believed that human beings are by nature thoroughly depraved, but both of these theorists retained the conviction that God's love infuses all existence, descending into the world for various purposes and then returning to its sacred origin.

Medieval pantheists who interpreted this notion as indicating that God and nature are really one and the same were considered heretics, and even executed in some cases. By the nineteenth century, however, their outlook was often quite acceptable. It arose triumphant in the romanticism that served as the dominant attitude within much of the religious and secular philosophy of that period. In Hegelian metaphysics, which reigned in academic circles for a hundred years, God (or "the Absolute," a more technical term sometimes used) was thought to re-create the world continually in a pervasive search for the complete and ultimate form of spirituality. Through ideals that remaster and overcome the moral limitations of materiality, the divine spirit was taken to imbue nature with ever greater achievements that are truly valuable and give more and more meaning to life. God was by definition the Absolute inasmuch as his sheer essence totally explains each aspect of the natural order while also signifying the final destination for which everyone, and everything, yearns without always realizing how much such striving seeks to reach this metaphysical terminus.

Much of twentieth-century philosophy was a reaction against Romantic and Hegelian "objective idealism." Nevertheless there arose a school of thought, loosely referred to as "process philosophy," that sought to reject the extensive dichotomy between nature and the divine while retaining at the same time some of the Hegelian inspiration. In general, the new mindset remotely resembled Friedrich Nietzsche's teachings but also differed from them. Its basic thrust focused on the concept of creativity as related to ideas about universal freedom, in contrast to any externally imposed determinism that might cause events and experiences to be what they are. All entities or moments of consciousness, it held, come into being as instances of self-creation and thus self-determination. Thinkers who contributed most to this type of philosophizing were Charles Sanders Peirce, Henri Bergson, Alfred North Whitehead, and Charles Hartshorne. In defiance of the logical empiricism that has been dominant in English-language philosophy, they all formulated theories that are metaphysical and even theistic speculations about the role of what they considered to be cosmic creativity. Since in this book I will be trying to reverse the influence of that kind of thinking, I will summarize only briefly some of its major theses.

As usually interpreted, Whitehead's philosophy is especially pertinent because of its effort to unify scientific studies of nature with metaphysical views about creativity as a way of explaining reality in general. Having affirmed a distinction between Being and Becoming, Hegel had argued that the empirical world is an all-pervasive struggle to transcend creatively its temporal and imperfect "Becoming" by progressively approximating the oneness that constitutes the underlying "Being" of reality. In repudiating this approach, Nietzsche argued that Becoming is the *only* Being we can imagine. Whitehead's tactic is significantly different from that of either Hegel or Nietzsche. He claims the creativity that characterizes, and even unites, all reality underlies not only the Becoming of what exists but also its transcendent Being.

As Hegel conceived of it, the Absolute embodies the highest ideals and their perfect fulfillment incorporated in the Being of what is real. Whitehead repudiates this notion. In his alternate approach, he amplifies Bergson's conception of "creative evolution," which is to say, nature as it unfolds through the evolutionary processes explored by various branches of science. Suggesting that creativity is a constant within Becoming that also makes sense of what is meant by Being, Bergson sought to alter the common dogmas of Judeo-Christianity.

Instead of envisaging God as an infinitely perfect deity who then creates the world in an act of love that creatures can possibly emulate in their desire to reciprocate his bestowal of goodness, Bergson depicted the love that motivates the successive developments in nature, and that evolves creatively, as itself being God. The pantheistic love that Bergson portrays is not an emanation from a previously existent deity, but rather divinity itself coming into being through its temporal and nondeterministic immersion in nature. The very spirituality of God would then consist in his supreme creativity within the world as it develops by means of natural phenomena. In *The Two Sources of Morality and Religion*, Bergson portrays saints and ethical heroes as contributors to that progression, their own evolving creativity of mind and action thereby revealing the spirituality embedded in reality as a whole.

Bergson, whose renown peaked shortly before the outset of World War II, espoused naturalistic theories of evolution as scientific truth about the structure of the empirical world, while also insisting that nothing is totally mechanistic. Everything is motivated by the operation of inner and freely given creativity, he asserted. The title of *Creative Evolution*, Bergson's most famous book, manifests the synthesizing character of his philosophy.

Much of this approach was already present in Peirce's concept of what he called "agapastic love," which is likewise predicated upon the ideas of freedom and operative creativity. Since events in nature cannot be foreseen with certainty, Peirce concludes that an element of random chance must always be assumed. Universal creativity, as he views it, exists as the way in which an agent can unforeseeably effect some possible outcome. This kind of thought also reappears in Whitehead's philosophy, particularly as it was adapted by Charles Hartshorne. Writing about "Creative Synthesis," Hartshorne states:

"Here is the ultimate meaning of creation—in the freedom or self-determination of any experience as a 'new' one, arising out of a previous many, in terms of which it cannot, by any causal relationship, be fully described.... [Since] the motive or character [of a new experience] is *not* received from the past, it must be a *creation* of the present."[1]

Neither Hartshorne nor Whitehead—nor any of the other thinkers in this movement—denies that a great deal of the reality we are each familiar with is certainly not creative. They are instead referring to what they call the all-pervading "flow of existence" that supersedes the special individuality of any physical or mental manifestations of being. As Hartshorne says, a stone is not creative or self-determined, but its sub-atomic elements are. Their random and mainly unpredictable movements can only be charted in the probabilistic manner of quantum physics.

Pros and Cons of Metaphysics

All the same, we cannot surmise that process philosophy relies entirely on scientific theory and observation. It is explicitly a metaphysics, a seeing of the world that cannot be verified or falsified yet may possibly enable a sympathetic reader to perceive his life anew, and also the universe in which it exists. The philosophy seeks to provide aesthetic and valuational spectacles that can disclose qualitative aspects of reality that operate throughout nature as well as in our own experience.

Since I am not writing a thorough analysis of process philosophy, what interests me primarily is the fact that any metaphysics of this sort must be recognized as itself constituting a mode of creativity. In making its type of assertions about the basic creativity in everything, including whatever is clearly uncreative, it exemplifies the human inclination to imagine interpretations of the cosmos that are justifiable, if at all, only as conceptual works of art, or possibly art itself when it is sufficiently imaginative and capable of enriching what might otherwise be a barren, mechanistic attitude toward the world.

All these writers that I have just mentioned are at their best when they confront questions about how creativity occurs. In trying to answer those queries, Whitehead remarks: "Philosophy begins in wonder. And, at the end, when philosophic thought has done its best, the wonder remains. There have been added, however, some grasp of the immensity of things, some purification of emotion by understanding."[2] Whitehead's allusion to wonder is reminiscent of statements by Einstein that I will be quoting in this chapter and subsequently. Whitehead takes us a little further by attaching his speculation about the feeling of wonder to the ideas about creativity that he has been promoting as a metaphysician. In doing so, however, he confuses matters by suggesting that his work reveals "the immensity of things." That phrase does no work at all.

One might nevertheless argue that the latest findings in astronomy or subatomic physics support what Whitehead says. Thanks to these and kindred scientific developments, the world that our ancestors experienced as cozy and limited extensions of themselves in their physical surroundings could now appear to have an enormity that nobody would have imagined earlier. That may well awaken wonder that would not have existed before. But the metaphysical concept of what is considered cosmic creativity has no such grounding. It goes beyond any verifiable scientific observations. Being an aesthetic and creative artifact by virtue of its indigenous meaning, it may possibly inspire a sense of grandeur or even a kind of religious uplift—as the "Ode to Joy" in the last movement of Beethoven's Ninth Symphony does, to take only one example of what great art can evoke. Yet the notion of cosmic creativity alone fails to give us an accurate and authentic grasp upon either the nature or the being of the world's immensity.

And neither can Whitehead's theory be thought to provide any "purification of emotion by understanding." In painting its nonverifiable picture, process philosophy adds nothing to whatever we already know about reality. Instead it supplements the data in a metaphoric and unfactual manner, as artistic work often does. "Understanding" of the type that Whitehead seems to have in mind belongs to a special category, if only *because* it is metaphysical. Speculation about an ultimate creativity, seductive as such language may be, cannot yield knowledge that may or may not purify our emotions. In various places Whitehead states that creativity as he thinks of it "explains" why things are as they are. Without invoking causal reasons, he defends his doctrine by calling it an "introduction of novel verbal characterizations, rationally coordinated."[3] But these so-called characterizations are not capable of serving as *explanations*, any more than paintings by Monet or Picasso are.

Bergson as a Possible Exception

In some respects, and above all in the clarity of his writing, Bergson's statements about creativity are more convincing than Whitehead's. Having begun with the quasi-biological investigation that permeates *Creative Evolution*, Bergson's cumulative explication ends, in *The Two Sources of Morality and Religion*, with his discussion of creativity as the core of what he calls "dynamic religion." In the experience and behavior of mystics, mainly those that are Christian and Catholic, he finds creativity continually at work as the vital impetus (élan vital) that shows itself in love. In words that seek to unite scientific truth and religious faith, Bergson states his belief in mystical intuition: "Beings have been called into existence who were destined to love and be loved, since creative energy is to be defined as love. Distinct from God, Who is this energy itself, they could spring into being only in a universe, and therefore the universe sprang into being."[4]

In this bold conception, the physical, material and even mechanistic, components of ordinary life interact with its spiritual potentialities as the conditions needed for creative energy to exist in a world such as ours. Bergson's idea of God as belonging within empirical nature is immanentistic, much as Hegel's ideas about the Absolute were, and therefore neither otherworldy nor dogmatic in the manner that Western religion has normally envisaged. It is said that toward the end of his life, Bergson contemplated conversion to Catholicism but finally decided, as an act of solidarity, to remain a Jew in view of the Nazi occupation of Paris. His piety in making that decision can be applauded by Catholics as well as Jews. At the same time, Catholic theorists who were not themselves Bergsonian in their philosophy might well have felt that the pantheistic import of his metaphysics was alien to the teachings of the church.

As we will see later, Bergson denies that the ultimate problem of philosophy is why something exists rather than nothing. He argues that the very notion of absolute nothing-ness is meaningless, since the absence of something implies the substitution of something else. Mystical intuition resolves the issue, Bergson says, by displaying reality as filled with a sense of the creative and loving presence of God in the world: "God is love, and the object of love: herein lies the whole con-tribution of mysticism."[5]

The Seductiveness of Process Philosophy

What I find most intriguing about the outlook of the process philosophers is its persistent belief that all reality is creative in some way or other. This is a buoyant and affirmative view, though not one that coheres with my own experience of the world. I feel at times, as they do too, that the obviously chaotic occurrences in the universe—the tremendous explosions in every galaxy, the movements of matter over great distances of presumably empty space, the awesome number of light years traversed in such cosmological performances—that all this may be explicable in terms of completely mechanical and deterministic causation. Nonetheless, as process philosophers claim, there *might* be some inner freedom that matter mani-fests under these astounding circumstances.

That consideration may make us feel more at home in the universe: it tends to sustain what we experience as our own existence. But, then, we must also remember that we have no way of *knowing* about any such metaphysical possibilities, either pro or con. Science itself cannot pretend to answer ques-tions of this kind, and theorists who do are often presenting a prelude to the even more dubious imaginings of one or another theology. That is especially evident in the work of Hartshorne and, to a lesser degree, Peirce.

A Contrary Approach

My empiricist and pluralist perspective is designed as a buttress against the fanciful character of the lingering transcendentalism in process philosophies. The creativity that I investigate exists as an inborn capacity of the mind and brain that are prevalent in our species. There is no presumption that this dance of life, like the aesthetic as a whole, has any grounding in an objective and universal order beyond its own mundane occurrence. What I do feel confident about is the way in which animate creatures on this planet, above all ourselves, systematically adhere to the diverse forms of transformation that I will be discussing as modes of creativity. These are empirical phenomena that belong to the everyday structure of nature.

Speculations of mine along these lines began with a book entitled *Reality Transformed: Film as Meaning and Technique* (1998). In that work on applied aesthetics, I argued that cinema should be approached as neither a recorded reproduction of reality, which the school of realism maintains, nor as primarily an artful deployment of techniques, which the school of formalism believes. To show how films are both conveyors of meaning and vehicles of technical inventiveness, I tried to demonstrate that the two approaches ineluctibly coalesce. Cinema transforms reality through the formal devices that an accomplished filmmaker uses to express some vision of reality that he or she introduces as a creative artist.

In making these suggestions, I readily affirmed that all other arts rely on similar—though sometimes very different—types of transformational production. What I am now willing to entertain is the possibility that much, or even all, of life can be treated as one or another example of transformation. In that respect, we might extrapolate to the possibility that creativity of some sort resides in virtually everything that lives, and regardless of the ambiguities about reality that I address in chapter 10.

Though I present these ideas about transformation in as tentative a manner as I can, one may wonder nevertheless whether I am not myself open to the kind of criticism I have been leveling against the process philosophers. Can I truly deny that my asseverations are as unverifiable as theirs? Don't my reflections merely represent feelings of my own that I may possibly express creatively in this context? Shouldn't I admit that my personal outlook belongs to a philosophical genre that is comparable to those of these metaphysicians?

In the course of his work, George Santayana repudiated the idea that his writings should be categorized as "metaphysics." His culminating work was a speculative study in ontology, properly entitled *Realms of Being*, that is not truly empirical or scientific, and yet neither does it proffer dogmatic assertions about some ultimate and irreducible reality. At its level of abstraction, however, and in the a prioristic stance of its reasoning, I think that Santayana's ontology can be viewed as a variant of metaphysics. The same may be said about much of the conceptualization in the statements that I make about the nature of creativity. In pondering their merits and their shortcomings, the reader should always keep that in mind.

The Quest for Creativity

As a critic of the process philosophers and, in part, Santayana as well, I offer reflections—about creativity in art, science, and the rest of our existence—that may be formally similar but are significantly opposed to theirs. I suggest that whatever is tenable in this field must be located within a perception of human nature as pluralistically seeking creativity in the alternate ways that issue from our temporal condition. The spirituality for which people have hungered throughout the ages can only be appreciated as a reification of creative modalities that occur within our particular species. In itself, human creativity does not originate either outside of nature or as a transcendent power within it, but instead as a recognizable achievement in our biological condition that beings like us cultivate and improve if we can. Reversing in this fashion the more prevalent perspectives about the creative and the spiritual will have extensive ramifications.

My previous writings on the nature of love and sexuality, and on the philosophy of film, have led directly to my current thoughts about the nature of creativity. Several of my books, especially the *Nature of Love* trilogy and *The Pursuit of Love*, sought to develop my ideas about bestowal and appraisal as two types of valuation that constitute the creativity of affective choice and personal attachment. I characterized both as products of imagination and idealization that evince a particular kind of creativity. This book seeks to unfold and extend what is implied in these notions. I consider the transformational capacity of art to be paradigmatic of human creativity wherever it occurs. From this it follows that not only love in its different modalities and the passionate pursuit of knowledge, but also all other meaningful interests, have an aesthetic component within them that manifests their creative potentiality. I make my case in a cumulative manner, and without prior assumptions that might constrain the ongoing inquiry. If we can illuminate the diversified forms of creativity that are evident and accessible to us, we may find that the all-embracing definitions that many philosophers crave professionally are, in principle, hardly worth our consideration.

Before trying to clarify these broad intentions, however, I return to the misconceptions in the history of ideas with which I began this chapter. In attempting to get beyond them, I will first study their origination out of layers of our human consciousness about which we are often unaware, even though they permeate our daily thought and behavior.

Relevance to Creation Myths

In virtually all religions, and in many philosophical theories thus far, there resides a description of the beginning of things. Many people affirm that their version of this account is literally true; others accept even the cosmic story they believe in as merely a form of mythmaking, however compelling the myth may be for themselves. At present, I wish to put aside the question of truthfulness in order to give prominence to some other aspects of this phenomenon. First, the myths of creation, like all other myths, are tales that people tell and retell as expressions of their own experience or desires. They are not only imaginative transformations of what outstanding individuals have encountered in their lives but also demonstrations of personal aspirations. The prevalence of these myths about the origin of everything reveals the enormous curiosity that human beings have always had about their existence as inhabitants of a world order that constitutes whatever appears to be reality and whatever may transcend it.

Why should this mean so much in every culture that we know? Indeed the very concept of culture partly depends upon the prevalence of such mythmaking. If we came upon a group of homo sapiens who lacked this aptitude, would we not infer that they are creatures without any culture? Those who possess the appropriate form of imagination are assumed to have developed consequent arts and skills that are more or less similar in all societies and the product of some common attempt to imagine how the world about us could have originated.

According to the frequent, though not invariable, belief, the current state of things arose as the result of a single event, a primal act of creativity that started the clock of time-determined and observable existence. That primordial event is often thought to presuppose the progenitor whom I have mentioned and whose enactment of this awesome feat serves as explanation of all creation. The very idea of a causal being that is "supreme" in the cosmos, though possibly preceding it as well, is itself a part of the creative imagination of humanoids like us.

In many of the mythic presentations, the primal and definitive moment of creativity served as the making of something out of nothing. The creator who is the single source of everything is then depicted as a magnificent artist or wonder worker capable of accomplishments that exceed whatever mortals like ourselves can effect or even comprehend. Though our creativity might be only a refashioning or reconstructing of what has already occurred, the initial and infinitely greater example of creation may be seen as the filling of an absolute void, the changing of mere nothingness into concrete actuality.

To those who are not sympathetic with this type of language, its very formulation can seem ridiculous. Shakespeare capitalizes on this in *Twelfth Night* by having Feste (the Fool) masquerade as Sir Topaz the Vicar and pompously proclaim: "That that is is."[6] We laugh because we feel that anything else must be a logical impossibility. But also we believe, or suspect, that it makes no sense to think that what now exists could have come out of some previous nonexistence. We can know only something that is at present, or has been, or may be in the future. Even unformed matter would have to have had an explicit composition of its own peculiar kind. To that extent, Shakespeare's ridicule of metaphysical speculation would seem to be justified. The abstruse assertion is only a trick of language. However creation of the world may have happened, it must therefore have been enacted as a remolding or transformation of ingredients, chaotic in themselves perhaps, that somehow eventuated as the structured cosmos we see about us. What still remains, nevertheless, is the query that G. W. Leibniz posed: Why is there *anything* in the universe rather than nothing? He might well have repeated what King Lear says to Cordelia in his presumed resemblance to God at the beginning of the play and before he goes mad: "Nothing will come of nothing."[7]

The Sense of Dread and Its Resolution through Creativity

In relation to the explicit nature of creativity, we need to analyze the opposition between the two forms of thought:

creation arising out of nothing or else out of an earlier some-thing. These alternatives embody different ideas about cre-ativity. What underlies them both, however, is the fact that we human beings use the terms *nothing* and *nothingness* in ways that baffle our intellect. That alone can jeopardize our ability to feel or act coherently in coping with our predicament as finite and mortal creatures. In his soliloquy on suicide, Hamlet says that "the dread of something after death / The undiscov-ered country from whose bourn / No traveler returns, puzzles the will."[8] But all such references to death, and any conception of its meaning that we may have, would seem to compound our puzzlement about life itself. Is death an absolute negation of everything we have personally experienced in having lived? How are we to make sense of this possibility? What exactly can it signify?

For most of us, the dread and puzzlement of our will to which Hamlet alludes result less from concern about what will happen to us after death than from the repugnance and the horror that we feel in the prospect of being totally annihi-lated. The undiscovered country from which no traveler returns may therefore be interpreted as the uncharted and solitary condition in which each man or woman exists just in living under the circumstances that define our state of being. We are born into permanent ignorance, sometimes painful ignorance, about our personal reality as well as the reality of everything else. The neonate screaming frantically when it surges into the world cannot understand what is perturbing it, and most people take little note of the incomprehension about life and death that gradually becomes habitual to them. Yet it continues until they die, despite whatever beliefs they may have accrued about our existence.

In commenting on Hamlet's speech as I have, I may be stretching, even distorting, Shakespeare's use of the word *dread*. He might well have intended nothing but a high level of fear. If we greatly fear something that might occur after death, we may be said to have a dread of it. What I am talking about is not the same. I have in mind the vexatious questioning itself, the nagging and frequently terrifying sense of our inadequacy as self-conscious individuals who intuit that the nature of life and death can never be understood by us, and possibly not by anyone else whom we can imagine. Many of the problems we encounter in everyday experience can be solved, but we do not know, we cannot conceive of, what would yield a solution to this one. Our troubled response is more than just trepidation about death as either sheer destruction or else a transition to some terrifying afterlife.

I will be arguing for the possibility that our concept of creativity may help us deal with this situation. But first I need to clarify further the nature of our consternation. Our dread of death, and also our dread of failure or only relative success in life, bespeaks an underlying desire to possess and retain whatever goodness we may have achieved by having lived. Such dread reflects a residual feeling of hopelessness, a vague yet all-embracing kind of discomfort about reality. As we can say that anxiety is normally fear without an object, so too can we characterize this sentiment as anxiety that precludes any awareness of there ever being, or having been, a primal and all-explaining act of creation, whether glorious or not. In itself this can destabilize constructive involvement in life. It stuns us with an intimation that what we value and care about might have no true import at all.

When existentialists like Martin Heidegger or Jean-Paul Sartre spoke in their philosophies of what they called "dread," they claimed that queries about the absolute nothingness at the core of being were the most significant ones that probing thinkers could ask. On this view, Leibniz's question becomes basic in all philosophical investigation. I am not of that opinion, though I perceive how artfully the Leibnizian remark directs us toward the human difficulty I have been describing. If we are stymied by a petrifying dread that structures all ideas about life, death, and everything in reality, we cannot hope to find an answer to what Leibniz asked about the possibility of absolute nothingness. But if there is no formulatable solution to this type of problem, as there is in other matters, neither can there be an *authentic* problem. Instead of leading into reflections that one might call philosophical or scientific or even truly rational—as there would be for a valid issue within our comprehension—the most we can strive for is a mere accommodation that may help us to go on living but that tells us scarcely anything that has real cognitive value.

In that event, we must agree with Bergson in dismissing Leibniz's utterance as just a cunning though endlessly tantalizing locution that has no genuine significance. As David Hume would say, it belongs to metaphysical writing that should be committed to the flames. It can provide a modus vivendi, perhaps, but little more. Is that an acceptable view? And are we able to face up to the unwelcome malaise that may result from it despite any of our maneuvers to muster a brave demeanor and cheerful outlook?

I suggest that our desire to be creative, and our preoccupation with creativity, may be the key to a plausible reply. Those phenomena serve as a principal means by which we surmount whatever dread or discontent we have. By searching for what is creative both in us and in the world we inhabit, we meet the dreadful anxiety head-on. Instead of masking it through diversionary dogmas that are unverifiable, or else by recourse to what Pascal called the "distractions" of secular life, our creative longings, as well as our piecemeal advances in satisfying them, make life worth living regardless of the agonizing uncertainty that may still remain. The myths about the origin of the world either out of nothing or out of something earlier must thus be seen as manifestations of the questing, and itself creative, imagination that issues into our joint effort to overcome our inevitable limitations in this regard.

Instead of portraying human nature as something that will someday be destroyed without our having any inkling of what that entails, those myths about the beginning of everything contribute in themselves to a meaningful creativity that only we could have brought into existence. That may be a consummation of humankind as such, and apart from any notions about a spiritual domain that precedes and possibly rewards our efforts. Conversely, we may add that in its many varieties the nature of creativity itself reveals what true spirituality is and must be.

An Erroneous Image of the Creative Person

As a major misconception, and a part of our legacy from romanticism in the nineteenth century, we are all prone to think that creativity can be explained in terms of the personality, particularly the feelings or emotions, that artistically creative people have. We have inherited an image of the supremely creative man or woman as self-contained within his or her particular world view—as a driven artist or charismatic public figure devoted to some private vision, withdrawn to that degree from most people and often unappreciated by them, liable to great arrogance or hidden scorn toward pedestrian humanity perhaps yet also imbued with a passionate search for higher values that others may equally cherish, sometimes living in garret-like circumstances and on the edge of poverty, misery, painful alienation, and occasionally psychological disturbance.

Beethoven is commonly taken as an icon of this type, but any number of creative men and women could qualify as well. Though the image may not be wholly accurate about Beethoven or the others, they nevertheless have served as archetypes of creativity imagined by multitudes who are not geniuses or fervent leaders like them. At a rehearsal that Leonard Bernstein conducted, I once overheard two women in the row behind me giggling over the fact that the crimson lining of his jacket was torn. In their quasi-motherly way, they obviously deemed this a characteristic though lovable lapse that one must expect in dedicated and greatly talented persons like him.

For a complementary but slightly different illustration, one might cite the example of Mozart. In *Amadeus*, the play and film about the composer's life and death, his rival Salieri expresses astonishment at the pristine perfection of Mozart's manuscripts. It is, he asserts, as if Mozart was taking dictation from God. When theorists have likened aesthetic productivity to the gift of prophesy that the deity accords to an appointed messenger, they too are drawing upon the idea of geniuses being touched with fire from on high. Inspirational experience as a whole could thus link someone's creativity to the original, infinitely more exalted, occurrence when the God of Genesis creates heaven and earth.

Skeptical as we may be about such grandiose notions of what can happen in our species, there are related data that should not be overlooked. People who experience moments they and we consider creative often report having had a sensation of unmatchable intensity and elation that does not exist at any other time. They feel they are the instruments of an inscrutable power that is more than themselves, a force that has descended upon them as its conduit for some exceptional purpose beyond their understanding. Though possibly resulting from stimulants or a psychological condition that excites and masterfully activates the central nervous system, this afflatus engulfs those who undergo it as if their overwhelming creativity could not have come from a source within themselves. The metaphoric reference to the taking of dictation from God aptly expresses the servile yet elevated feeling that the exultant man or woman undergoes. How to explain it is the task that lies before us.

Artistic Creation as a Paradigm for Creativity

In trying to clarify this issue, I will recurrently suggest that artistic creation of one sort or another is paradigmatic of whatever creativity human beings can have. In other words, all creative activities, diversified as they may be, include aesthetic elements that make the attainments of their scientific or other originators similar to the productions of an artist who is totally devoted to the aesthetic. That was also the belief of Romantic thinkers throughout the eighteenth and nineteenth centuries.

It culminated in Nietzsche's assertion that the superman, who is preeminently creative, must be an exceptional artist, regardless of his chosen profession, and indeed that his greatest creation consists in living a life that is itself a work of art. Any action or production that is truly valuable would then justify our ascribing aesthetic creativity to its progenitor. In this vein, religious believers may infer that the God of Genesis is a superlative artist on a cosmic scale, like the demiurge in Plato's *Timaeus*.

When the Judeo-Christian God regards his handiwork after six days of labor, he calls it "very good," as any human practitioner of the arts might say in evaluating something he or she has accomplished. But human beings who are scientists or laborers or simply persons involved in the necessities of practical life can also be artistic within their diverse modes of creativity. Their aesthetic capacity shows itself in makings and doings that manifest the feelings, perceptions, intuitions, judgments, and behavioral tropes that belong to their individual type of interest. What establishes their analogous role as artists is the partial presence of aesthetic creativity in their work. But, as we shall see, that varies greatly among the different attainments of different people. In them all, however, there may be comparable patterns and forms of creation. Those need to be disentangled.

In this undertaking I make no attempt, as I have said, to give a definition of the word *creativity*, or of the concepts that flock around it. The portmanteau language that we all use in this area does the work of communication in too many scattered ways for us to think that any single, rigorous, totalistic statement of necessary and sufficient conditions can account for every instance alike. Though creativity in cooking may partly resemble creativity in playing tennis or in composing a symphony, none of these can be definitive for the others, and no artificial construction will ever enable us to discern a single something that exists in each as contrasted with the rest of life. What we need to clarify is how they may *overlap* and metaphorically *suggest* a resemblance to the creativity in one another. That can progressively generate a pluralistic portrait of this aspect in our existence.

Trying for anything else is unneeded, except in certain circumstances where the definition-making of mathematics or logic, for instance, serves a special function. In our attempt to elucidate creativity itself, this kind of exception would not take us very far—as I will argue in later chapters—and could easily misrepresent the individual and inherently distinct phenomena that are involved.

That is why I entitle this book *Modes of Creativity*. At the same time I do not wish to deny the possibility of a unifying structure among the many types. Any such denial would be unfortunate since they arise equally out of the human desire to attain values and fulfill ideals that matter to us as natural entities. All creativity derives from that impulse.

Einstein on the Sense of Wonder

Studying the implications of putting the horse of human creativity before the cart of transcendentalistic spirituality or Romantic ecstasy, instead of vice versa as happens in traditional and some modern beliefs, I turn to a statement in the writings of Albert Einstein that I find extremely fertile though not wholly satisfying. Describing his religious attitude, Einstein says:

The most beautiful thing we can experience is the mysterious. It is the source of all true art and science. He to whom this emotion is a stranger, who can no longer pause to wonder and stand rapt in awe, is as good as dead: his eyes are closed. This insight into the mystery of life, coupled though it be with fear, has also given rise to religion. To know that what is impenetrable to us really exists, manifesting itself as the highest wisdom and the most radiant beauty which our dull faculties can comprehend only in their most primitive forms – this knowledge, this feeling, is at the center of true religiousness. In this sense, and in this sense only, I belong in the ranks of devoutly religious men.[9]

Inspiring as these lines surely are, they are baffling to some degree. A sense of mystery and wonderment is different from the affirmation that what is impenetrable to us can be known as something that "manifest[s] itself as the highest wisdom and the most radiant beauty." How can these ideas be coherently joined to each other? The feeling of being rapt in awe that Einstein describes can be, and is, experienced by atheists and agnostics as well as theists. It may be fundamental to many, perhaps most, religions that differ in fundamentals. Einstein is, of course, free to specify this response as the basis for what he himself deems *truly* religious. But what he says about the experiences to which he accords prime importance tells us next to nothing about their contents. His second statement above is a non sequitur to the first.

The vagueness or ambivalence in Einstein's self-portrayal as a devoutly religious man makes his attestation of faith sound unduly romanticized and largely useless for appreciating the scope of his own, undeniably spiritual, devotion. That resided in his heroic attempts to decipher what is true and beautiful in the world. These attempts were vastly creative,

and so what Einstein asserts may possibly point us in the right
direction for explaining *his* type of creativity, as well as that of
others like him.

But even so, we cannot derive from Einstein's statement a
viable clarification of all creative experience or inspired action.
And neither can his utterance support the idea that creativity
is always commendable or good, rather than potentially harmful. When Einstein first made remarks like the ones I have
quoted, he was widely and rudely attacked by outraged Christians and Jews who rightly saw him as someone who did not
believe in the personal deity they themselves worshipped. The
fact that he often alluded metaphorically to God—as in his
saying that the deity does not play dice, for example—intensified their anger toward him.

In the passage quoted above, Einstein would seem to be
mollifying such critics by wrapping himself in a religious
mantle of his own. That does not trouble me. What I find re-
grettable is the limited usefulness for our purposes of what he
says. The following chapter discusses in much greater detail
the dimensions of the creative experience and its relation to
creativity as an integrated making or doing of something. That
theme then becomes prominent in the chapter on the creative
process and the behavior that issues from it. Questions about
whether the different modes of creativity are at least partly
aesthetic and always beneficial, uniformly moral to that extent,
or on occasion noxious, even immoral, must also be addressed.

2

The Creative Experience

Creativity as Original and Personal

With respect to the nature of creative experience, as in many areas of philosophical investigation, one does well to start with common occurrences that exemplify the subject being studied. Though creativity involves doing or making something valuable, many of those who write about it put the greatest emphasis on describing the experience itself. Unfortunate as this may be, it is surely understandable. Creativity results from collecting items in one's own experience and then transforming them in a practical manner that is personal to oneself.

In that vein, we can begin by discussing two kinds of lecturers. One reads from a previously prepared and carefully written paper, a technical article perhaps, but also possibly a literary essay that may convey his or her thoughts to a receptive audience. This lecturer might also slavishly follow notes that have been prepared for the occasion. We would generally say that such lecturing is limited in its creativity; at least that it is not a clear case of a creative experience. This is recognized in the joke about an American history professor who mumbles over a line in a yellowing page he delivers to his class year after year. One day a student raises his hand and remarks: "Please, sir, I couldn't make out how many tons of cotton you said were shipped up the Mississippi that year." The professor stares in consternation at the page, some of which has disintegrated, but then smiles and replies triumphantly: "It doesn't *say*."

The old fool may have shown some creativity in his way of handling the embarrassing situation in which he found himself, but no one would think that his presentation of his subject matter was creative. A little different is the procedure of lecturers I have known who memorize in advance the ideas or information they wish to impart to their audience. Others prepare themselves for a lecture by reviewing written notes they use as a means of giving themselves greater security in their act of communication. To the extent that it is spontaneous, the overall experience can be considered creative, but it will be less definitely so than one in which the speaker is fully immersed in whatever material has been newly minted and directed toward the individuals to whom it is being conveyed afresh.

The actual material to which I refer may not be original in itself or completely unlike similar communications at other times. It suffices that its *current* presentation will be unique in the sense of having arisen out of the particular moment in which it occurs. That in turn reflects the immediacy in time and place of one person, a lecturer in my example, making contact with other persons who are attuned to him or her as someone whose mind and personality are fully present to them. If the lecturer evokes a sense of the importance of what he or she has to say to this audience—at least enough importance to justify their joint relationship—the experience of each may be creative in some respect. Both parties are then mutually involved in an exchange that is *inter*personal, largely unpredictable, and more or less spontaneous.

While this eventuality is what most artists hope to attain, the condition of actors and other stage performers is especially instructive. We go to the theater with the awareness that these men and women who present themselves in various roles are trained to project a persona, an embodiment of humanity, upon which their artistic success depends. We know that the actors have their own personal existence as well as the ability to enliven and proffer to us the persons they enact as dramatic artists. We know that they have rehearsed their parts, often for weeks or months, but we also know that in any one performance they may vary their enactment in accordance with haphazard realities in themselves or in their moment-by-moment rapport with the audience and their fellow actors. Their possible creativity emanates from this responsiveness to that challenge in the context of having refined their techniques through prior training as it enables them to perform each night and disclose, indeed enhance, what their fictive characters would be like if they were alive like the man or woman who is on stage.

If the actor's conveyance of that imagined vitality is not properly reinvigorated at some performance, the creativity of the experience will be diminished at that time. If a performance is truly creative, the spectators will somehow feel that they have been in contact with the personal being of the actor as well as the human-like but fictive character portrayed in its own dimension as if it too belongs to what we call the real world.

In other media the situation is not exactly the same. A musician who has not wholly ingested the music he is playing, who does not identify himself with it, will surely impress us as less than fully creative. He might remain faithful to the notes in the score, but as long as he has not become one with the music they formulate, his interpretation will seem mechanical. At the same time, neither the simulation of spontaneity nor its reality is sufficient for the creativity that musicians, like other artists, yearn to attain. Their ability to infuse their idiosyncratic mood and individual perception into the fabric of a particular performance is essential. The creativity in their art requires them to feel and to express *through their medium* what they are experiencing in the act of transmitting the sonic realities of the music being played in this rendition.

There is no guarantee that such creative experiences will issue into artistic productions that are themselves creative. That will depend upon the talent and sensibility of the artist, as we will see more completely later in this book.

At this stage of the investigation, we may nevertheless assume that radiant moments of the sort that I have been describing can have some inherent bearing upon whatever creative outcome that may result from them. When the eventuality is scientific or otherwise impersonal in itself, as art can also be at times, the nature of the creative experience that preceded it may be hidden or less apparent. But as a prior condition, it will have had a similar effect.

Jean Renoir's "Italian Method"

Continuing what I have been saying about creative experience in the performing arts, I want to keep in mind something that

Jean Renoir said about his method of directing actors for the screen as well as on the stage. He called it "the Italian Method." Starting with this conception of his, we may come to appreciate not only *his* creativity in all his films and plays, but also the kind of creativity he tried to elicit from actors in both these art forms.

Renoir reports that for days or even weeks on end he asks his actors to sit around a table and deliver their lines by reading them aloud from the script as prosaically as possible. He cautions them not to register any deep feelings or expressiveness. As time goes on, they may avail themselves of superficial gestures but none that might indicate what their characters would be likely to experience as human beings. Before reaching that crucial ingredient in any performance, the actors had to amalgamate and embody the external circumstances under which their characters presumably exist. If the actors were told how to perform, or if they were allowed to act out their roles prematurely, they could not manage to get beyond commonplace assumptions about the characters, which they would have copied unawares, either from other performers or else from the received platitudes of their society. As they continued in the somewhat passive repetitions of the lines and nothing else, the actors were expected to find that their own imagination was silently and intuitively creating an affective identification with the personage whose separate being they were to offer in public.

Renoir emphasizes that he, as the master of ceremonies in this technical exercise, had no way of predicting when this breakthrough might occur. It would arise all of a sudden, unforeseeably, out of the depths of an actor's feeling of his or her own reality. The outer gestures could then be

supplemented by the inner affectivity that the actor has naturally as a man or woman but that remained beyond reach until
the cinematic/theatrical situation brought it to the surface
through this method. What finally occurs, the performer's
unique enactment of some character's personality, might then
appear. As such, it would in principle be authentic rather than
merely contrived.

Renoir's account of this mode of professional preparation
illustrates the nature of creative experience in general. It is a
systematic transformation of the inner and the outer world
that one inhabits but then changes radically in an action that
expresses one's individuality. As with all other experiences,
the value or utility of this depends upon the consequences to
which it leads. The example of rehearsing differs from the one
about lecturing that I mentioned, since Renoir's method exists
without the presence of an audience and is not itself a culmination. Renoir is there not for the sake of enjoying the spectacle but rather as a guiding spirit or official supervisor of the
procedure. The emergent creativity in the rehearsals precedes
the creativity that may later be achieved by the actors onstage,
when the characters will have been fleshed out and put on display for all to see and hear. The audience's creativity occurs, if
it does, as a respondent part of the final event.[1]

Communication between Artist and Audience

As a further illustration, I want to cite something that Jack
Lemmon said during a talk he gave at Harvard University that
I attended and have mentioned in an earlier book. Comparing
the difference between comedy in a film and comedy on stage,
Lemmon reported that he felt incapable at first of performing

the scene in *Some Like It Hot* in which he is lying in bed fully clothed in his female regalia after a night of dancing the tango with the dirty old man (Joe E. Brown). When the Tony Curtis character climbs in through the window and finds him writhing on the bed, the lines that Lemmon was supposed to utter were hilarious but somehow very difficult for him to deliver. In his discussion at Harvard, he explained this by saying that on the stage the playing of comedy greatly relies upon the reaction of the live audience. Acting before the camera is nothing like that since there is no audience except for a director and some workers on the set.

The problem was solved by the director of this movie, Billy Wilder, who suggested that Lemmon should use a maraca in each hand to punctuate his agitated remarks. That worked marvelously. As Lemmon explained, the action with these props gave him a sense of being on stage and communicating his feelings to an audience whose responses he could thus imagine. With this example in mind, I need only add that there are different kinds of audiences. Some are silent and rigidly static, and some are nonexistent (as in the canned laughter on televised family sitcoms). To that extent, the audience may not be creative at all. Nevertheless the theatrical ideal is predicated upon a communication between creative artists and an audience that is, at least potentially, creative, each inciting the responsivity of the other. I will return to this when I discuss communication theories of creativity, and also the difference between comedy and tragedy.

Appropriate variations on the theme I have been sketching apply throughout our existence. A sculptor has to learn how to live creatively with the clay he molds or the marble that he chips. His creativity relies upon his ability to marshall and to use the tactile feelings that he experiences, as well as the meaning to him of whatever materials he employs expressively. But the same is true of a laborer who creatively digs a ditch or builds a wall. What might otherwise be routine and even deadening to the spirit becomes a creative venture once the work issues from a feeling of oneself as a wholly engaged contributor to this activity that progressively elicits mental and personal involvement. If a course of behavior is imbued with a sense of its importance, the final output that occurs may possibly, though not necessarily, manifest creativity capable of justifying whatever effort was required.

Camus, Kekulé, and Archimedes

By extending these rudimentary reflections, we can readily reexamine some familiar ideas in the literature about creative experience. In his celebrated essay on the myth of Sisyphus, Albert Camus ends with the suggestion that the pitiful sufferer might one day suddenly change in his attitude toward his penal servitude. Instead of lamenting his endless punishment in pushing the boulder up a mountain, fruitlessly since it always rolls back down again, Camus' Sisyphus interprets his situation in another, and more inventive, light. He accepts his fate not only by submissively acquiescing in it, but also by realizing that it is part of the destiny that, in his case, he has freely brought upon himself. In that view it overtly defines his personhood as just the individual that he is. Though this resolution of his life problem evinces a Romantic bravado one may well find ridiculous, I nevertheless see it as the result of a creative attitude that reorders his further existence. It unites the misery of his travail to the actual man that he is and has become. This identification with one's "fate," and the recognition that it constitutes what one is as a person, does not apply to all instances of creative experience. But it serves as an essential component in the type that Camus envisages.

A totally different kind is present in two renowned discoveries in the history of science, both often treated as resulting from distinct and unmistakable experiences of creativity. In one of them the nineteenth-century chemist Friedrich August von Kekulé underwent a visual occurrence that revealed to him the structure of the benzene ring. Having had this experience, he was then able to reach revolutionary conclusions about the molecular structure of organic compounds as a whole. The other instance that I have in mind is the "Eureka" event of Archimedes when he suddenly realized, while taking a bath, a way to measure the volume of any object.

Kekulé had long pondered, but to no avail, the configuration of benzene molecules. He tells us that as he sat before the fire one evening he dozed off and saw a phantasmagoria of atoms dancing before his eyes. Among them there were long rows twisting about each other as if they were snakes. To his surprise one of the snakelike rows made a circle of its body by putting its tail into its mouth. This, I am told, is the classic alchemical symbol of transformation, the snake devouring itself (the ouroboros). Kekulé instantly awoke with the solution to his problem: benzene molecules were structured in a ring. His creative experience subsequently led to other of his important findings. But how does any of this support what I have been proposing?

At first glance, one might argue that Kekulé's dreamlike imaging does not involve an expression of someone's personhood or even momentary being. All the same, we have to wonder why it is that no other scientist, and not Kekulé himself despite his conscientious efforts, had come up with this elemental discovery. It is as if the approach of all the other scientists were comparable to the mentality of the stereotypical professor reading the same ancient lecture year after year. No one was able to depart from that mechanical mindset, perhaps because it somehow worked adequately in many instances. To deal with an extremely elusive problem, something else was needed. And that could only issue from a mode of thought that runs in opposition to our usual consciousness. Sitting in front of the fire, Kekulé put himself into a semi-unconscious condition; dozing off, he relaxed the intensity of his search in a way that allowed a possible breakthrough to arise and expose its secrets to his imagination.

Moreover, the metaphoric display of a chemical row resembling a snake with its tail in its mouth is so special that few theorists would have surmised its scientific import. Apart from any sexological overtones, this kind of imagery exhibits a highly individual and pervasively nonrational aspect of life that is foreign to doctrinaire scientific methodology. By drifting into that uncharted terrain, Kekulé was able to undergo an experience that henceforth changed the parameters of productive and eminently constructive work in his branch of science. Creativity always has a capacity of that sort.

The case of Archimedes may seem different because his explosive response took place in the more routine circumstance of taking his daily bath. But that, like nodding before the fire, is also a condition in which one's state of mind is peacefully relaxed and generally amenable to a redirecting of habitual activities. Also, Archimedes had been struggling with what seemed to be an insolvable problem, just as Kekulé had. The king wanted Archimedes to determine whether a crown he had been given was made of pure gold or secretly alloyed with silver and other lesser metals. Archimedes knew that the existence of a piece of gold could be verified if one already knew its weight and detectable volume, but he had no way of calculating what might be the volume of a crown, with its irregular shape and complicated design. When he stepped into his customary bath on that eventful day, he noticed something he had never thought of before. He observed that the water was displaced to a degree that was commensurate to the volume of his body as it was being immersed in it. That meant he might collect the displaced water in a receptacle that measures its amount in quarts or whatever. He could thereby estimate the exact volume of his body, and he rightly inferred that the same would happen with the immersion of a crown. From this he could learn whether or not it consisted of pure gold.

Legend has it that when Archimedes received his sudden insight he leapt out of the bath and ran naked through the streets shouting "Eureka!," which in Greek means "I've found it." He might as easily have screamed "I've had a creative experience!" Its creativity stemmed not only from his experience in the bathwater but also from his dramatic awareness of what he could learn from his body at that moment. As with all of us, we are normally oblivious of what happens when we step into water. We do not think of it as a substance that is similar to nonfluid objects. Nor do we focus on our own materiality as something that is operating within the same laws of physics that govern the displacement of water in a bathtub. The experience of Archimedes was creative because it drew upon this fact about our reality that enabled him to employ it for a transformational idea neither he nor any other person had adequately probed before.[2]

Creativity and Dreaming

In the example of both Archimedes and Sisyphus, whatever creative occurrences they underwent pertained to the realm of conscious life. They were awake when the real or fictional revelations happened. But since such remarkable moments of creativity are sometimes so bizarre and even alien to ordinary wakeful experience, they have often been likened to one or another state of dreaming. Their kinship to daydreaming is most obvious. The biographers of Socrates spoke of his self-absorption in a trancelike state when some pattern of thought, presumably creative, would seize him in the streets of Athens. Kekulé is said to have concluded the description to his colleagues of his remarkable experience: "Gentlemen, let us dream!"

Particularly when it is a question of absolute concentration upon cognitive issues—as in philosophy or science or mathematics—creative experience has sometimes been considered a withdrawal from the mundane preoccupations that fill our purposive existence. Since daydreaming is frequently considered to be an escape into a condition of fantasy and relative idleness when the workaday mind is operating either pathologically or at a low level of its ability, theorists often relate creativity to what occurs during slumber, and so to dreaming proper.

Kekulé's experience is a good illustration of that because it shows, presumably, how an important scientific discovery can originate in a moment of semi- or complete unconsciousness. I want to emphasize that dreaming of a snake with its tail in its mouth is not inherently or in itself an example of creativity. To determine its relevance to whatever was indeed creative in the thinking of Kekulé, we have to place his dream in the scientific context to which it belongs—the prolonged research that preceded it, the governing image that was applied not to the depiction of snakes but rather to our knowledge about the bonding of benzene molecules, and the resulting developments in chemical science. Having made that clarification, however, we still need to know how and whether the visual or possibly auditory phenomenon that most people experience while asleep every night provides a clue to the creativity we value so highly.

When theorists offer a general answer, they all too regularly revert to Freudian notions about "the unconscious." In a passage that I briefly discuss in *The Harmony of Nature and Spirit*, Bertrand Russell says that if he has worked very hard but fruitlessly at solving a problem he will occasionally put it aside, place it in his unconscious, and leave orders that the solution be found therein. When he returns to the problem after a number of months, he tells us, he often discovers that the job has been done.[3] To think of the unconscious this way is to duplicate the Freudian belief about a region or dimension of mind that differs from the one we know in consciousness and that functions in accordance with its own rules and operating principles.

Freud developed this conception by studying the dreams his patients reported to him in his office. As there is something miraculously creative about the solving of problems in the manner described by Russell, so too can one marvel at the inventiveness that appears in many of the dreams that occur during sleep. Freud thought he could organize, and explicate, that inventiveness in terms of the psychopathological theories he subsequently introduced.

At the same time, one must ask whether dreams are being glamorized and overly glorified by the belief that they are always, or systematically, the source of what we recognize as human creativity. Most dreams are extremely chaotic and devoid of the kind of lasting consequence that issued from Kekulé's highly productive one. When Freud encouraged his patients to tell him their dreams, he partly did so because the mere *telling* of such lively material changes the patient into a verbal artist, and therefore not just a passive client who suffers for whatever reason. Relying upon the graphic though piece-meal material in the quasi-visual experience of dreaming, patients become storytellers actively performing before a receptive audience in the person of the therapist. The dreams they relate attain a solidity and narrative design demanded by the sheer act of communication. Without being creative in themselves, they may elicit the creativity that goes into a patient's monologue about them.

I say this in order to explain why the fleeting and frag-mented contents of a dream need to be unified or reconsti-tuted by a deliberate reenactment and transformation. Even though they might have been just casual blips, now they become performative vehicles as well as tools that can be useful for psychiatric interpretation. The process of recalling them is an art form of its own, and patients who have a creative experience in the course of that process might derive personal benefits as would any other artist. To suggest that in themselves dreams are the source and archetype of human creativity is to misinterpret its nature.

Furthermore, the therapeutic telling of dreams is a collaborative effort. It is elicited and augmented by the talent of psychiatrists who lead their patients into creating a comprehensible formulation of meaningfulness in the dreams they talk about. At this point the situation borders on what accomplished artists do when they creatively pick up the threads of what they have experienced in life and then creatively weave them into presentations that others may find significant and aesthetically enjoyable. These nanobits of dreaming *become* creative only if some individual uses them imaginatively. For that reason also, the notion that dreaming belongs to, and even reveals, what is called "the unconscious mind" is untenable. Human beings don't have two minds, one conscious and the other unconscious. A better conception of mentality derives from seeing how consciousness and dreaming interweave extensively without being reducible to one another.

As a further entrance into this situation, the following passage from Arthur Koestler's book on creativity is worth examining: "The creative act, insofar as it depends on unconscious sources, presupposes a relaxing of the controls and a regression of the modes of ideation which are indifferent to the rules of verbal logic, unperturbed by contradiction, untouched by the dogmas and taboos of so-called common sense. At the decisive stage of discovery the codes of disciplined reasoning are suspended— as they are in the dream, the reverie, the manic flight of thought."[4]

This interpretation treats "the unconscious" as a separate domain in human nature and thus it neglects the extent to which the rules of verbal logic in ordinary consciousness do not need to be suspended or supplemented or combined with the alternate effects that Koestler ascribes to dreaming and the rest. If the brain is always active, always open and available for stimulation, as I believe, what happens in "the dream, the reverie, the manic flight of thought" is already present in normal features of the conscious mind, and explicable only in terms of its interaction with them. The dreaming effect occurs as an extension of consciousness rather than a deviation from it. To say that dreams belong to an autonomous region of mentality apart from logic or common sense misrepresents not only the nature of creativity throughout life but also how greatly that relaxation of conscious controls may further it.

This frequent confusion in recent theories, and in the Freudian doctrines that have influenced them, is apparent in Koestler's account of why Kekulé's dozing could have culminated in his grand insight. Koestler likens that seminal moment to the experience of a biologist who was able to continue his difficult research only after having had a disturbing dream about a young girl in it to whom he was sexually attracted and who seemed ready to reciprocate. The biologist feels a sense of guilt while having this dream, toward the end of which the young girl mockingly tries to calm his inhibitions by telling him that she is "all brains." When the biologist awakes, he interprets this as meaning that she is a "brain-child" of his, which leads him to take heart about a suggestive idea related to his research that he had previously tossed out in conversation but now begins to take seriously. What was before a passing notion became directly instrumental in the creative work that the biologist was then able to do.[5]

Neither this instance of creative experience nor the one about Kekulé indicates any defiance of rules of verbal logic or the alleged dogmas and taboos of common sense. On the contrary, in Koestler's anecdote the biologist relies upon the verbal logic, or rather linguistic structure, that operates in nondreaming life insofar as he uses it to move from "all brains" to "brain-child" and thus to an awareness of the possible validity in the undeveloped idea that lingered in his mind and warranted further attention. In each of the two cases of scientific discovery, Kekulé's and this one, the respective dreams do indicate a "relaxation" of a sort. But what matters more than the kind that Koestler alleges is an obvious relaxation of the organism itself. Dreams occur when people are asleep and therefore resting not only their physical musculature but also their brains and overtaxed minds. This facilitates productive thinking by helping us to mull and digest more calmly—and with greater comfort than when we are on our feet—whatever questions or preoccupations that have been besetting us while awake.

Sleep, whether peaceful or fitful, provides an ancillary mode of coping with problems that may be overly stressful in the course of the urgencies that fill our conscious struggle to exist. Far from being creative, the chaotic characteristics of most dreams reflect the multiple interferences that repress the consecutive and imaginative, but often tiring, ability to think effectively. By putting us in a restful state, it is sleep, and not dreaming itself, that renews our creative energy.

A more promising description of how dreams may sometimes lead to a creative outcome can be found in what Mary

Shelley wrote about the origin of her *Frankenstein* novel. In a note some years later, she tells us about a sojourn in Switzerland during which she and her husband were joined by Lord Byron. The weather having turned menacing, Byron ordained that each of them would write a ghost story. Day after day, Mary tried strenuously to do so but found herself completely uninspired. She nevertheless listened carefully to the intense exchanges between Shelley and Byron about scientific experiments that might possibly succeed in restoring life to deceased persons or some quasi-human composite of what had been parts of their bodies. During a storm that caused her to sleep badly, Mary had a nightmare in which some such monster is successfully made animate. Her dream frightened her immensely, but when she awoke she felt that she had surmounted the problem of the ghost story: "Swift as light and as cheery was the idea that broke in upon me. 'I have found it! What terrified me will terrify others; and I need only describe the spectre which had haunted my midnight pillow.' On the morrow I announced that *I had thought of a story.*"[6] Those final italics are crucial, for Mary proceeds to delineate stages of her actual writing, and how much more than just her nightmare went into her creating the finished product of her novel.

Koestler on Bisociation

Kekulé and the biologist were focused and conscientious scientists who worked at their relevant investigations diligently over a long stretch of time: weeks and even months. Their creative experiences came to a head in the dramatic events that we have been discussing. But the process went on, in their brains and in their minds as well as in the rest of their functioning bodies, persistently and without being noticed at all times. That is how our digestive system also works. In both cases, we apprehend the highlights only sporadically or in a sudden and unforeseeable outburst like the ones in some impressive dream. Those operate not as the originating of a creative experience but rather as visual and auditory performances that shock the participants in a dream—the dreamers, who are themselves their own audience—into an awareness of what has been churning up affectively as well as cognitively. The creativity is furthered by the entire process and not just by any single element in it.

Altering our approach in this manner, we need not discard Koestler's fruitful notion of "bisociation"—the conjunction of contrasting patterns of thought or behavior. I will return to that notion in a later context. It calls our attention to the way that creative experiences consist of some harmonization between ideas or inclinations that are usually thought to be contradictory. This kind of benign intersection may indeed be one among other clues to the nature of creativity. But it happens throughout human existence. And when it does appear in dreams, it serves as just a marker of what is going on throughout the entire organism, and not only unconsciously. In medical practice this occurrence of creativity is recognized by dream therapists—including those who are either Freudian or Jungian—who interpret the processed material that patients ascribe to their periods of dreaming. Only the overall theory that some of the therapists profess needs to be rectified.

Testimonies of Noam Chomsky and Bertrand Russell

In this regard there is an implied conflict worth mentioning between the views of Koestler and something Noam Chomsky is reported to have said about his own creative experience.

Having maintained that the rare and productive flights of creativity arise in the unconscious, and above all in dreaming, Koestler asserts that these bisociational syntheses are a kind of "thinking aside." He claims that their defiance of rational logic manifests a mode of thought that is *fundamentally* different from what ordinarily exists in our waking state. The testimony that Chomsky provides, in an interview published in 1970, describes his dreams at that time in another manner entirely.

Having been asked whether the problems he is working on reside in the back of his mind throughout the dreaming, Chomsky answers: "All the time: yes, I dream about them. But I wouldn't call dreaming very different from really working." When the interviewer questions whether he literally means dreaming, he replies: "Yes, I mean it literally. Examples and problems are sort of floating through my mind very often at night. Sometimes, when I am sleeping fitfully, the problems that I've been working on are often passing through my mind." After the interviewer then asks whether the form in which the examples and problems pass through his mind is the same as when he is awake, Chomsky says: "Yes, as far as I know, in exactly the same form. The dream life doesn't seem to have a different framework or to involve a different approach. So it's just a sort of slightly less concentrated and conscious version of the same thing as during the day."[7]

As an alternative to the ideas of both Chomsky and Koestler in this matter, I wish to amplify my suggestions about relaxation during sleep. Though, as I have argued, it is wrong to think that the dreamer relaxes the conscious rules of logic, it is certainly the case that being asleep and having a dream provides the person as a whole with an essential means of escaping from the tension and mental as well as physical exertion that pervades normal consciousness. The bombardment of external stimuli that register as conscious sensations and perceptions is then quieted or at least muffled to a large extent. Within the cocoon of sleep-induced repose the dreamer drifts into a quasi-oblivion that facilitates the restitution of energies that are greatly exercised—sometimes overly exercised—during the hours of wakefulness.

The fact that the oblivion is not complete—and if it were, there would be no dream at all—signifies that openness of brain and mind to which I referred. At the same time the condition of rest and relaxation enables a healthy organism to spring into action with renewed vigor after a few hours. Chomsky's assertion about his creative labors while asleep being identical to his mentality while awake may be taken as a truthful statement of what he remembers immediately after he opens his eyes and regains consciousness. But that memory need not be an accurate representation of what he experienced while asleep. It may very well result from the recuperative power of sleeping that allows him to return to the work he was doing before. Having been reinvigorated, he resumes his efforts now so rapidly that what seems like a memory of his dreaming state really belongs to the initial moments of awakening.

Something in the dream may be instrumental in this fashion, but since the components of a dream are generally so unstable, and often so transient, their usefulness is normally very limited. The crucial part for the doing of the relevant task, and its creativity, is what happens when the sleeper regains consciousness and *reconstitutes* the contents of his dream. The act of transformation is thus what matters most. In Chomsky's case, he experienced an apparent continuity in the ideas and problem solving that he ascribes to the thinking process while he slept. I am suggesting that his interpretation gives the experience of dreaming more credit than it deserves.

As a continuation of what I have been saying, consider how dreams are regularly portrayed in works of art. In literature their quasi-visual reality is distorted by the mere fact that they are inevitably presented in the language we use throughout conscious discourse. In *Finnegans Wake* James Joyce offered an extensive experiment to the contrary, but it is neither characteristic of most literary productions nor wholly successful as a portrait of the sleeping mind. In surrealist paintings and the related animation in many movies, their deviation from any sleeper's awareness is due to the magical transformations these productions effect in serving the aesthetic perspectives that largely belong to those art forms.

The extremely manneristic images concocted by Salvador Dalí and deployed by Alfred Hitchcock in *Vertigo* visualize dreams in a way that is perfectly valid for the narrative meanings that are present in that film. The same could be said about movies like *The Wizard of Oz*. To that degree their special effects succeed as cinematic transformations. But in none of those films are such images literally true to what dreams are like. The imaginative renditions of Dalí and his fellow artists may be creative accomplishments that somehow reflect their creator's own experience. But they do not represent a generic source of creativity in what they show us. They cannot be adduced as evidence to support the notion that by its very nature creativity is always and already available in our fanciful slumbers. It is true that in ordinary parlance people often do identify creating with dreaming—one film studio calls itself

Dreamworks with that meaning implied. Nevertheless, this metaphoric locution, arresting as it is, cannot be taken at face value.

Having said this much, we may now perceive what sense can be found in Russell's assertion that he gives orders to his unconscious and that after weeks or months it solves some difficult problem for him. Perhaps the explanation lies in a remark that Russell makes in a preliminary statement about his creative experience. He says: "If I have to write upon some rather difficult topic the best plan is to think about it with very great intensity—the greatest intensity of which I am capable—for a few hours or days, and at the end of that time give orders, so to speak, that the work is to proceed underground."[8]

Under these circumstances, one might infer that the cognitive blockage Russell encountered issued not only from the problem he was trying to solve but also from the "very great intensity" of his striving to attain a solution. If it was indeed the greatest intensity of which he was capable, and if it lasted for hours or days, the strain and total fatigue that his mind/body was undergoing could itself have put his intellectual powers at a disadvantage. Having turned away from actively working on the original problem, which he did in relegating the subject to the unknown forces that operate "underground," he directed his mental faculties toward other things and thus released himself from the debilitating effects of this intensity that was getting him nowhere.

Russell ends his report by gleefully stating that when he returns to the topic some months later he finds that the work he had ordered has indeed been done. I surmise again that his creativity was caused by his relaxed and rested condition with respect to the question at hand. The creative experience was not engendered in some mystical realm called the unconscious anymore than in some dreamlike offshoot of it.

Further Testimonies

In his book *A Sense of the Mysterious*, Alan Lightman describes his first creative experience as follows:

I felt terribly excited. Something strange was happening in my mind. I was thinking about my research problem, and I was seeing deeply into it. I was seeing it in ways I never had before. The physical sensation was that my head was lifting off my shoulders. I felt weightless. And I had absolutely no sense of myself. It was an experience completely without ego, without any thought about consequences or approval or fame. Furthermore, I had no sense of my body. I didn't know who I was or where I was. I was simply spirit, in a state of pure exhilaration.[9]

Once or twice in my life, I have had an experience of that sort. My creative experiences have rarely been like the ones of Kekulé or Archimedes. Mine have usually been less histrionic than theirs. Troublesome ideas that enter into my thinking often linger for months and years in an unresolved welter of confusion. Without my ordering them to go underground, as in Russell's account, they seem to moulder in a semi-conscious muddle to which I eventually become accustomed and mainly ignore. If and when they ripen into an advance of which I am cognizant, that happens gradually and unobtrusively. Even so, there normally is a time at which I realize that something has reached a further level of development. But at first I am not aware of what could be the cause of this increased percolation in my thinking. It may be occasioned by some wholly unrelated gratification that soothes my self-esteem and reminds me of what I am capable of achieving, thereby giving me emotional encouragement to go on with this aspect of my desired creative life.

After that, it is a matter of pushing a boulder up the mountain, like Sisyphus, groaning step after step until the tension of this arduous labor dissipates. When things go well, it is as if I were Sisyphus running to catch up with the boulder as it descends downhill in a momentum of its own. I feel the vibrancy of that, but hardly ever does any sense of "Eureka!" issue forth.

As examples of the few times that I have had an experience vaguely comparable to Kekulé's or Archimedes', I can attest to a couple that were very meaningful to me. I had been invited to give a public lecture at a college in Oxford. Having just finished *The Harmony of Nature and Spirit,* which had not yet been published, I affixed the same title to the lecture. I envisaged it as a condensation of what I considered to be the most salient features of that book. As is my wont, particularly before an audience that I am not familiar with, I sat on a table and spoke without using any of the notes that I had briefly prepared, while looking all the time into the eyes of those who were present, in the hope of establishing contact with them and gauging how much they were gleaning from what I said. I especially like this method of lecturing because the sheer informality of the interaction sometimes elicits a few ideas that had never come to me before. That happened at Oxford but not in an extraordinary amount. The next day, however, when I traveled to Madrid and gave a different though partly related lecture at the university there, the effect on me was surprising and much more powerful.

In Madrid I followed my usual procedure and peered even more intently at the audience. I was speaking in English and as I talked I kept searching for clues about the ability of my listeners to follow what I was saying to them in my foreign tongue. Despite this effort, or possibly because of the increased acuity of observation that it involved, I found that not just a few new ideas surfaced in me but many, one after another as I went on. As can happen in this kind of improvisatory situation, designed to be as spontaneous as possible, the words poured out of me as if they arose with no premeditation on my part and as if I were merely a vehicle they had chosen in this particular setting.

When I am in that state I frequently hear the lines I am speaking with a sense of being a member of the audience myself. I feel a wonderment about where all this is coming from, who or what is really making these utterances. My mind functions with much greater rapidity than ordinarily—at an exceptional pace for me—and I sometimes stumble verbally because the words have difficulty keeping up with my delivery. Possibly I may then be talking too fast, but the experience is so exhilarating at the time that I seem to have little control over the flow of language gushing on by itself, apparently as it wishes.

When I was a student at Harvard, one of my mentors—Henry David Aiken—told me that during his class lectures he was totally oblivious of his surroundings, or even the words he uttered. It was all, he said, "as if I were Jacob wrestling with the angel." Similarly, Leonard Bernstein remarked to me once that while he was conducting an orchestra he was so greatly immersed in the music that he had no recognition of anything else—in particular, the position of his body, his facial gestures, or the expressive sounds that came out of his mouth. I pointed out that in a videotape of him as he conducted the last movement of Mahler's Ninth Symphony, with perspiration and possibly tears streaming down his face, he moans at one point "*Momma!*" He did not deny the accuracy of my observation but assured me that he knew nothing about what I was describing. His plaintive expression had interested me because it occurred simultaneously with a tormented phrase in Mahler's music whose meaning Bernstein interpreted better and more creatively than in any other performance of that movement I had ever heard.

The creative experience of mine to which I have alluded has happened to me not infrequently, but the lecture in Madrid stands out because of the multitude of ideas that engulfed me then. In Madrid as well as on the lesser occasion at Oxford, the new ideas were mostly extensions of what I had written in the finished though as yet unpublished book. But also there were quite a few that convinced me that I had failed to carry out one or another important line of reasoning in that text. The experience as a whole affected me so much that after a day or two with friends in Madrid I traveled alone to a seaside resort on the west coast of Spain where I thought I might write out the thoughts elicited by the lectures while also enjoying the proximity to the ocean. It was a place I will always cherish, called Punta Umbría. The town was almost entirely deserted that early in the season, and its solitude sustained me for the next two or three weeks as I started new writing that I hadn't known was in me. By the time I returned to America, my book *Feeling and Imagination: The Vibrant Flux of Our Existence* was progressing apace.

As I remarked, this extraordinary event has not been representative of my more pedestrian creative life. That consists of components of a different sort. I believe this applies to other people as well, and perhaps to everyone. The following chapters will try to throw some light upon characteristics of creativity that exceed the merely personal or experiential. I turn first to an analysis of the creative process itself, which is more definitive of the nature of creativity than any isolated experience or event—however exciting its impact—that may be identified with it.

3

The Creative Process

Thus far I have been focusing on very dramatic, even melodramatic, events that sometimes occur in creative experience. This characteristic is evident in Archimedes' exclamatory utterance, and in the fact that he ran naked through the streets in his impassioned haste to proclaim his success. Though not irrelevant to the nature of creativity, that kind of explosive outburst need not accompany other authentic instances of creativity. The Eureka effect is just the tip of a creative iceberg. Or better yet, it is a mountain peak on which some intrepid climber puts up his nation's flag as explicit proof of what he has accomplished. The achievement itself appears in the prolonged and often arduous process that has already occurred and may then go on to even higher peaks for which it also strives.

Even if creativity is spontaneous in its enthusiastic manifestation of whatever pervades the immediacy in our personal experience, creative success does not exist apart from the temporality in which we live. On the contrary, creativity both engenders it and depends upon it. When I earlier discussed Bertrand Russell's claim that the unconscious solves problems at his command, I raised doubts about that as a creative mechanism. Here I want to call attention to his saying that the solutions arose some weeks or months after he ordered that the job be done. The mere passage of time is a factor within any creative process, as it is in the growth of plants.

In *The Harmony of Nature and Spirit* I delineated the vegetative element in our species as a fundamental source of human desire and well-being. Once we accept and even revel in the fact that our creativity operates through principles of time-dependent vitality that are comparable to those in trees and shrubs and "lower organisms," as we call them, we facilitate the attainment of what we value. Much more is needed, of course, but nothing would flourish in any such quest without the continuity of organic processes that develop over a period of time and finally reach some optimal condition of satisfaction. Though creativity is not the same as happiness, for instance, this much is true of both.

On Russell's model, creativity arises from a rational act of problem solving, a person of intellect like himself giving instructions to the unconscious to take over the job. Russell never explains how this communication could occur. What in this quasi-cognitive exchange enables the unconscious to comprehend the task it is being told to accomplish? Presumably it is not rational in itself, any more than a stone or thunderstorm is. The image of Russell ordaining a task for it to do is reminiscent of Xerxes commanding the Hellespont to let his troops pass safely over its waters. In dealing with recalcitrant nature we all would like to have such verbal powers, but no one does.

In the view I have been outlining and will elucidate in further chapters, reason plays a different role entirely. It arises out of our vegetative being as the rose issues from the soil in which it is implanted, and its blossoms from the stalks that hold them up in the world aboveground. The mere existence of rationality is a great achievement of human nature. It certainly participates in the quest for creativity. But it can function creatively only as a tool or submissive agency within nonrational processes that manage to benefit from it.

Creative Reason and Learning

Reason plays many roles in life: most obviously in the reaching of valid conclusions, the making of practical decisions, and the fabrication of formal structures as in logic or mathematics. Most philosophers, especially those who belong to one or another school of Rationalism, have devoted themselves to the furthering of such advances of the mind. Thinkers of that sort often show massive and highly commendable talent in the pursuits I have named; and being devoted to their work, they naturally idealize the importance of rationality itself. To understand how reason contributes to creativity, however, one has to see each in relation to the human capacity to learn. In part at least, this entails cognitive aptitude while also illustrating the extent to which both that and the ability to learn are rooted in our temporality as well as a gamut of developmental feelings that are not themselves rational. Nothing is learned instantaneously or in an emotional vacuum.

Even learning how to ride a bicycle takes time. Some people need very little preparation before jumping on and keeping their balance. In a flash they seem to learn what is required to ride securely. But facility in doing so, which takes others much effort, comes swiftly to the rapid learners because they have already acquired through similar activities the knack or know-how needed to stay on a bike without falling off or crashing. It is through our learning capacity that creativity occurs and continues within some durational period that is integral to it.

As a result of the harmonious adjustment between learning and creativity, the vegetative in our being can burgeon through motives that instigate the constant search for new and greater goals. When innovation exists in its proper context, the outcome in art or science or practical life embodies capabilities that come into existence because they are requisite for the desired creative process. This too can be illustrated by the example of learning how to ride a bike. Mastery in doing it involves various things—attaining an idea of how to distribute your weight, knowing where to put your feet and how to turn the handlebars without falling forward, as well as habituation to this type of locomotion, so different from walking. All that takes time in which you must become increasingly aware of your changing posture from moment to moment. Success or failure is contingent upon the individual's physical strength, sensory alertness (visual, for example), degree of self-confidence or courage, and comprehensive faith in oneself as both a mental and material entity engaged in this activity. Those who have been well equipped through prior experience and learning need less time, but the general pattern is alike, though different in everyone. Something similar is true of the creative process as a whole.

Creativity is not the same as imagination or the acquisition of knowledge. The creative process is a way of *using* them. Through imagination we conceive of possibilities that may or may not be actualized. Those possibilities may often be commonplace and routine without altering very much in our life, or even our strength of mind. Likewise, much of the knowledge we collect is extraneous to the growth of creativity. When

Dr. Watson tells Sherlock Holmes the distance between the earth and the moon, Holmes replies that he will instantly exclude that bit of information from his memory. It can't help him in his work as a detective, he says, and it may easily become part of the detritus of mere factuality that may someday blunt his productive acuity. At the same time, nothing can be creative without having emanated from a store of knowledge and imagination, each of which provides a foundation for any innovative thrusts that can go beyond them both.

As a faculty that is distinct from imagination and knowledge, learning may illuminate more of the creative process than these do. But what is involved in our capacity to learn? How does one learn to be creative in one field or another? And how can we learn to have a life that is itself creative? Does learning of any special sort make it possible to *live* creatively?

Before the days of "progressive education," which mainly emerged from the writings of John Dewey, learning was rarely considered to be the cultivating of creativity. Young students in particular were expected to learn by rote. They were treated as malleable recipients of amassed data dealing with accumulated discoveries and methodologies, and, above all, the established values embodied in their older and wiser instructors. In the course of the twentieth century that belief about the nature of education was widely contested. In primary schools nowadays, and frequently at higher levels of learning, one or another mode of creativity serves as the principal tool for supremacy in most and possibly all subjects. The principle is that students who are creative will garner for themselves the means of developing skills and techniques that can enable them to learn whatever they wish.

I think this is a healthy development in the field of education. In the context of Dewey's moral and aesthetic philosophy,
his emphasis upon the bond between learning and creativity,
and their joint operation through a passage of time, derives
from his theories about the continuum of means and ends.
That—to which I will be returning hereafter—underlies
Dewey's basic idea that ethics as well as the evolution of
human values as a whole is an agency by which our species
learns how to adapt creatively to its environment. One may
nevertheless ask how the creativity essential for learning to
function at its best arises in the first place. Must creativity itself
be learned as a prior acquisition, and if so, can it be taught by
another person? Is creativity at all teachable? Some things are
not.

For instance, you cannot teach anyone to have absolute
pitch any more than you can teach color-blind people how to
see the colors that most of us perceive just by opening our
eyes. No amount of creativity or learning would further
develop the having of such experience. You can, however, help
individuals be creative in accepting their actual limitations in
this regard. They can be helped to learn how to cope with their
situation. At this point, the problem becomes the same as with
learning in every other area. Ultimately the question is: How
does one teach anyone anything? After answering that, we
may be able to understand the role creativity plays in employing learning and all that goes with it.

I suggest that creative learning, which includes the learning
of how to be creative, depends upon one's facility in learning
by and for oneself. To do that, one must get from a teacher, or
similar authority figure, the *ability to learn* that this person has
and then imparts to us in whatever manner. He or she may do

so unawares, just in being a model whose talents we emulate in some fashion. The teacher teaches by reinforcing the pupil's desire to appropriate the teacher's own capacity to learn. Having been suitably inspired and encouraged, the pupil develops the instruments needed to teach him- or herself. The creativity of this results from the inherent novelty, uniqueness, and authentic individuality of the pupil as well as the teacher. The creative teacher devises imaginative ways of eliciting a pupil's creative response. Pupils who are creative have learned how to learn accordingly and in keeping with their own aptitude and interests.

Education that is not creative is static and generic, a form of indoctrination that descends mechanically upon everyone subjected to it, initially the teacher but finally the pupils whose differences of mentality and potential growth are systematically thwarted or neglected. In contrast, effective learning is basically creative; and the creativity we revere may itself be thought of as an extension and application of the learning process.

Teachers learn how to teach by teaching themselves how to learn, partly from the mere contact with students or other beneficiaries of their expertise. In one place Orson Welles expresses his admiration for the French phrase *assister à* (to be present at) in relation to the aesthetic experience of a theatrical audience. He interprets the phrase as emphasizing how greatly the audience reaction contributes to, *assists*, the quality of what is happening on stage. This creative role exists, to one degree or another, simply by being present and reacting to what is presented to us.

In a similar fashion, creative teaching issues out of the teacher's ability to learn from the moment-by-moment experience of teaching others to teach themselves. He or she learns not only how to reach the minds and personalities of the educational recipients, but also how to evoke new ideas in oneself through an interpersonal ricochet with the diverse and often unpredictable responses of those who are attending to what is being communicated to them. By inference we can say the same about most, or virtually all, of life in society, insofar as it is indeed creative.

The Creative Process in Shakespeare and Mozart

This line of thought also reinforces what I was saying previously about time as connected to creativity. Learning to be creative, and certainly learning how to live creatively, takes time and inevitably reveals the causal momentum of time. Though discovery and inventiveness can occur spontaneously and seemingly out of nowhere, creativity is normally a progressive, even evolutionary, culmination of much that has been going on through the days and weeks and years of our life. In youth this can often happen with remarkable speed. But though everything appears to become slower with age, older people can often realize, and appreciate, how much lived duration the mind requires to produce a truly valid outcome for some personal situation or vital problem. In maturity one also learns the virtue of extending in time, not pushing too fast, an enterprise that one hopes will be creative. What occurs without significant preparation is often half-baked and unfinished.

Shakespeare partly meant this when his weary but world-experienced Hamlet says near the end: "The readiness is all." It takes perseverance through a temporal span to become capable of dealing with life's vicissitudes, and so attain an all-important readiness. The same applies especially to the creative work of an author or other artist. In my own case, I frequently resist the excitement of a bright idea that has suddenly dawned in me. Instead of snaring it on the wing and expressing it in a fervor of composition, I keep returning to it a little at a time over sessions of incipient writing. What I end up with, after ten or fifteen or twenty drafts, is frequently something I could never have foreseen.

In relation to the creativity of Shakespeare's mind, or rather a cinematic representation of it, consider the scenes in the film *Shakespeare in Love* that portray his hectic life as he rushes through London, burdened with a contracted project he feels he cannot fulfill. It is an early version of what will later become *Romeo and Juliet*. While hastily walking through the streets concentrating upon the difficulties of his literary task and oblivious to the noise about him, he passes an evangelical cleric on a platform who is haranguing a small crowd he has gathered. In his ferocious diatribe the preacher shrieks his venom upon two opposing factions that he condemns. "A curse on both their houses!" he shouts. Shakespeare hurries by, his head down as he ruminates on his personal problems, and apparently hearing nothing the preacher has said. We in the audience, however, recognize the line as something in what will eventually become Mercutio's final speech in *Romeo and Juliet*.

I mention this witty sequence because it truthfully shows how an artist collects material from his surroundings as they haphazardly impinge upon him, unexpectedly and without his perceiving them overtly. In the movie, Shakespeare's ears have picked up the preacher's words, although he has not listened to them or in any way thought of putting them in his writing. But once they have been lodged within the sensorium of his creative memory, they become available for aesthetic employment. The imagination of a Shakespeare is filled with such meager bric-a-brac, which it stores automatically. If something like the line that Mercutio will utter pops up, it appears in the right place in the play because of the author's regular acceptance of everything he has encountered as possible fodder for some inventive use he may want to bestow upon it within his art. He is, in effect, a pack rat of creative possibilities made available to him by his sheer retention of vivid fragments amassed throughout the immediate flow of his personal life.

As an alternate example I will mention something here that I discussed in another setting in my book *Cinematic Myth-making*. In *Amadeus*, Milos Forman's film about Mozart, there is a scene in which the composer's mother-in-law viciously berates him. The anguished, haglike sounds she utters are shocking and unpleasant. Throughout her tirade Mozart sits silently, looking at her face in a kind of passive trance. But the camera has other things in mind. While the ugly creature carries on incessantly, she is morphed into the Queen of the Night singing her second aria in *The Magic Flute*, with its tormented assault upon the guiltless Sorastro. Instead of suffering under his mother-in-law's hideous attack, as we naively thought, Mozart was seeing past it, transforming it into a coloratura expression of what the evil woman in his opera might sing as a fictional character. For Mozart as for Shakespeare, his creative talent arises from his being open to such transformations, assimilating for artistic use rich and fertile material that in others would never get beyond the level of ordinary details in a familial situation.

Being astute about this phenomenon, creative people like Mozart and Shakespeare have learned how to profit from gratuities of this sort that the world throws at them from time to time and without any assurance that their artistic ventures will always, or ever, be able to benefit from such serendipities. But to the creative process that does not matter. The ripeness and the readiness are what counts.

Michelangelo's *The Slave* and Our Craving for Creativity

In musing over these ideas, I often see in my mind's eye the famous statue by Michelangelo called *The Slave*. Generally considered unfinished, it shows a human form half buried in the rough, unpolished marble that surrounds it. I think of it as more than just work abandoned in an early stage of creation. I perceive it as a sculptural statement about the permanent and always incomplete striving of human nature, seeking to emerge from the limitations of matter even while its restraints are present within some art or other flowering of the spirit that aspires to transcend them. This applies supremely to the process of creativity as a whole.

Being dependent upon the duration of time and the ongoing acts of learning, imaginative ideas that mysteriously issue forth in us are indicative of creativity not only because they seem wondrous in their unknown origin, but more essentially because they stem from forces within ourselves that are often crude or rudimentary, and always partly hidden. The machinery of creation shows itself only slightly and is never perfect in its operation. As even the most creative people will attest, there isn't any one "act of creation" (the title of Koestler's book). The relevant process is usually more of an endless enslavement to inevitable difficulties rather than a single or all-resolving Eureka-like termination. Perhaps that is why so many theorists have associated it with dreams. Those are not completions of anything, and they frequently contain a sense of desperate search for some evanescent meaning beyond themselves.

The Intuitiveness of Creative People

Because dreams predominantly arise out of the vegetative in a way that is different from conscious experience, they elude the kind of learning that occurs within our waking life. This alone is further reason to doubt theories that ascribe creativity to a dream someone has had. Similarly we should be suspicious of views that identify creativity with what is called "intuition." That term has a variety of meanings that I do not need to go into here. Instead I want to remark that the intuitive powers creative people may be said to possess do not signify an ability on their part to circumvent the time-related dimensions of creativity. On the contrary, the productive learning on which creativity relies can happen so rapidly that we fail to recognize its presence. There is no reason to believe that those who are creative avail themselves of a special and profoundly mystical faculty that less fortunate or less talented persons do not have.

The remarkable rapidity that creative insight sometimes displays, together with the emotion of delight that success unleashes, does bespeak an intellectual refinement and penetration of thought that most people lack. One might even describe it as a congenital gift that others can never match. For example, idiot savants in mathematics are able to reach astounding and instantaneous solutions to extremely difficult problems in multiplication or addition that are posed to them. We have no idea of why they can do so. But such persons should not be taken as paradigmatic of those whom we consider creative, or imaginative, or even intuitive. They have brains and minds of a different sort.

The intuitiveness of creative men and women is sometimes adduced to their ability to imagine and to do inventive things without the recourse to trial and error that even very intelligent people require. To use a visual metaphor, they can detect clearly and directly something others have to squint at in order to see what is right there before their eyes. But though the sensations and perceptions of us all are usually intertwined with various interpretations and classifications, they too appear in consciousness with a minimum of deliberation or tentative surmise. We just open our eyes and there's an image of some object, an image that is so stable and convincing that without any noticeable reflection we just accept it as our reality.

To some epistemologists that alone is evidence of the creativity in virtually everyone. They may be right, and I will argue for that possibility later on, but even if they are not, the lack of similarity between commonplace awareness and the high-speed mentality of those who are truly creative suggests something else. Though creative individuals are indeed like those for whom learning occurs through time as a variable prerequisite, the former have acquired the capacity to accelerate this part of the process to a degree that most human beings cannot understand or approximate.

Regardless of how we define intuition in people who either are or are not said to be creative, the relevant feelings and ideas sprout in each of them as if by magic. The conclusions that come forth are eruptions out of the animal and vegetative faculties that the rational part of us cannot fathom, and need not. For these manifestations to have creative utility, we must formulate them in accordance with the technical devices of some art or practice. If they are musical ideas, they have to be fitted and transformed into recognizable sonic patterns. If they are thoughts or literary possibilities, they reverberate as the words and phrases, and often prefabricated sentences, that convey their meaningfulness. Living with the linguistic materials that occupy his or her mentality, an imaginative author turns them over in the constant reshaping that comprises the creativity of one's writing style. Without the transformational techniques for doing this, ideas of every kind are too often insubstantial, inactive, and of little value.

Education consists in harnessing the ability to apply these techniques that we will have learned from others but must now revive within ourselves, while also employing additional notions that arise in us freely on their own. Either they come or they don't come, as we may say about experience itself and its serendipitous occurrence. Once we have learned how to make ourselves receptive to creative life enhancement and available for its reawakening, we can then enjoy whatever contributes to suitable advances in this procedure. They alone will make us feel more confident about further achievements of which we may be capable.

Further Thoughts about Dreaming and Daydreaming

Since neither dreaming nor daydreaming has much place in what I have just described, I feel reinforced in my assertion that these components in our life are not major determinants of human creativity. At the same time, both dreaming and daydreaming do contain creative elements of their own. In being abstractions from selective bits of conscious experience, they have a peculiar though unquestionable aesthetic quality. Like other types of representation, they transform the fluidity of daily experience into contrived vignettes that may be hard to comprehend because they are so different from events in normal wakefulness but that follow each other with an unrelenting boldness that convinces the viewer that it must all make sense. The dreamer sees him- or herself in one place and then some other, in one guise and then suddenly a different one, usually without any noticeable transition between them. He or she senses nevertheless a pervasive continuity as being indeed awake. The dreamer does not reflect on his or her condition, however, and the mobility of dreaming is so fast that the images just skirt along, confusedly though still appearing to have some quasi reality in them. Sometimes this is pleasant, and sometimes not.

If we think of dreams in this fashion, as creative vehicles without there being an explicit creator of which we are aware, we may categorize them as usually very primitive works of abstract and expressionistic art, mainly visual, occasionally vocal as well. Not in their content or ability to *induce* creativity, but rather in their overall character, they are the forerunners of motion pictures. Because it is plausible to assume that men and women have had dreams since the beginnings of the species, we can say that throughout all history people have wanted to realize this potency within themselves by turning it into an art form that is somewhat dreamlike but also more grandiose and inclusive as a combination of the other art forms humankind has produced. The invention of photography, and then silent movies, served as a prelude to films as they now exist insofar as each is an apotheosis of the presentations that we all create in our heads while we are asleep.

Without the movies, Michelangelo's slave would still be twisting hopelessly in his effort to free himself from his mindless immersion in the stone. Cinema, and the visual media kindred to it, have now given him a greater opportunity to cope with that ancestral state.

Renoir's Methodology Contra Platonic and Romantic Ideology

As a testament to the fact that the type of process I have been describing matters more in creativity than either dreams or any mystical and romanticized event, I relish Jean Renoir's account of how he made the films for which he is renowned: "You discover the content of a film as you're shooting it. You obviously start with guiding principles that are as firm as possible, but when the subject is worthwhile, each step is a discovery, and this discovery brings others, and so a subject."[1] Renoir does not tell us much about these "guiding principles." Where do *they* come from? Are they always the outcome of some momentous experience without which the creative process could not originate? Even if this were true, however, Renoir clearly means that the creativity of his filmmaking is mainly fabricated by the ongoing process itself. Amplifying the statement I have quoted, he says that movies have become so important in the history of civilization because "the film medium carries technical obstacles that make it a slow means of expression (you can't shoot a film quickly), and this battle with technical obstacles forces you—more than in any other medium—to discover and to rediscover. You benefit from forced pauses that a writer would be obliged to impose on himself. The halts, the delays, are very good for the quality of a film."[2]

What we can derive from this, as from the example of Michelangelo's slave, is an explanation of creativity that runs absolutely contrary to the one that Plato enunciated. As we will see more thoroughly in chapter 5, Plato thought that all works of art worthy of the name begin with a vision of the formal abstractions—what he called the Eidos, the Forms— that reveal the underlying being of reality. With particular forms in mind, he says, an artist represents or even duplicates them as best he can within the limitations of his art. According to Plato, their perfection as what they are, whatever that might be, is a literal and essential prerequisite for attaining both truthfulness and beauty.

The trouble with Plato's theory is that, beautiful as *it* may be, it is not truthful itself. Artists do not proceed by copying an a priori model that guides them at every step. Whatever has inspired them at the beginning becomes submerged in the creative process. Aesthetic validity occurs in relation to possibilities—as embodied in an artist's imagination—that issue out of the act of production rather than being caused by some image of prior perfection.

In romanticism as it developed throughout the nineteenth century, the rationalistic bases of Plato's doctrine were superseded by the belief that creativity arises not from any contemplation of the Forms, or other abstract ideas, but rather from some previous feeling. Creative artists were thought to have the quasi-magical ability to reproduce in their works the actual sentiments of real men and women who did or might exist in the world. Yet that too, persuasive as it might seem, cannot elucidate the creative process. The Romantic approach implies that the feelings or emotions are preestablished nuggets that can be inserted into a work of art, for example, and that creativity entails the making of this insertion with accuracy and concomitant beauty in view of what real people are like.

That way of thinking misconstrues both creativity and the nature of feeling. Try as we might, we can never be wholly certain about what we feel at some moment in which we are having an affective response. Only our following or concomitant behavior can disclose what we *really* felt. A creative artist may be able to depict, and even mimic, this situation. But his or her creativity must show itself in the aesthetic transformations effected by and throughout a particular medium. These transformations are not produced by mere reliance upon unprocessed feelings as they existed before the work itself. Since we discover what we actually felt through the subsequent acts that reveal our individual affect as well as its motivation, the Romantic perspective is pointed in the wrong direction.

Theories that give greatest importance to the unadorned experience of creativity, or to a glittering outlook that is either Platonistic or Romantic, can rightly claim one significant virtue. They captivate us with their imaginative depiction of the sheer wonderment of human creativity. To this extent, the theories are creative in themselves, and that is fine. But a more precise conception would have to make insightful reference to the routine and pragmatic, frequently laborious, aspects of creativity. Whether or not Mozart took dictation from God, he put in many hours of work each day in order to compose the music that supported his family. He accepted commissions of almost every type, even writing music for garden parties at which the guests idly walked about and talked to each other while scarcely taking any notice of the marvelous sounds that had been created for their musical enjoyment.

Mozart's lifelong concern about the money he would receive was not just an external motive. It was for him, as for many creative people, a part of the creative process: it stimulated the phagocytes (as a doctor in George Bernard Shaw's play *The Doctor's Dilemma* says about his invigorating medicine) and mobilized the imagination even before its fruits could begin to appear. The earthy soil of everyday life matters, however crude it may be, and however little we like to think of its sustaining role in our existence.

As another example from my own experience, I can cite the evolution of my book *Three Philosophical Filmmakers*. It began because I was asked to give a talk to a group toward which I felt a sense of obligation. I thought that some of my off-the-cuff ideas about the movies of Hitchcock might be of interest. Afterwards I wrote out my notes in a short essay, which expanded into many drafts of what could eventually be a lengthy chapter. I later gave a similar talk to the same group about Orson Welles, and that also developed into a possible and growing chapter. I wondered whether there might be a little book in the making, but the parts still seemed too insubstantial even when put together.

Having always loved the work of Jean Renoir, and already written about his masterpiece *The Rules of the Game*, I did some research to find whether there were any theoretical writings of his that would fit into the general design of the two other segments. To my surprise, I discovered his book from which I have quoted here. It was exactly what I needed, and I contrived to write a new chapter on Renoir that would serve as a companion piece with those on Hitchcock and Welles. I nevertheless felt that something was still wanting, and I added a brief introduction and then a long comparison of the three filmmakers at the end to unify the disparate pieces.

I present this process of mine, familiar as it is to almost all authors, as a personal example of how the mind works, whatever its level of creativity may be. At no time, or in any of its many details, did I know beforehand what would emerge as the contents of that book. One might say my whole life went into it, but that only reinforces my suggestion that whatever is creative in the finished product issues primarily from the act of working toward it over a period of time and in many imperfect but continuous efforts. As the French proverb tells us: *L'appétit vient en mangeant* (The appetite comes from the eating). Something of the sort applies to everything else I have written, including the book you are now reading.

A Problem in Epistemology

If we approach creativity as the process I have been portraying in this chapter, we may find that some of the problems in epistemology and linguistics become a little easier to resolve. In this place, I mention briefly an answer to a query in the philosophy of language as Stanley Cavell poses it. He entitles an essay of his, as well as the book to which it belongs, "Must We

Mean What We Say?" The issue Cavell addresses is the relationship between meaning something and verbal discourse that may or may not be an expression of our intention.

As I see this circumstance, the problem occurs because language is capable of existing in alienation from the human communication for which it is designed. What we say (or gesture or depict in a painting or a chart or even a mathematical formula) can have a meaning only because the form of life by which people convey sentiments and ideas is meaningful to others who can actively respond to it with some degree of comprehension. All meaning in what one says or feels or thinks reflects an individual's reactions to relevant stimuli produced through one's vegetative and animal faculties as well as one's intellect.

In the creative process these responses are honed to a point where they cooperate massively, or at least with great efficacy. Within this organic totality the separation between meaning and saying may often be intentional, as a type of lying or deception for instance, but that does not constitute a philosophical quandary about the nature of language. In being creative, people mean what they say because they have learned how to use verbal, and other, types of communication to articulate what they really do mean. For them there is no problem. If one exists, it does so only for those who cannot communicate successfully and with a sufficient amount of authentic creativity. The creative process is linked to acts that are communicative through what we do and make as well as what we say. As we shall see further in this book, different modes of creativity will entail meaningful communications that are different from each other, but not because of any ineluctible conflict between what we mean and what we say.

4

Three Myths of Artistic Creativity

Several unwarranted assumptions about the creative process in general, and artistic creativity in particular, have permeated our common descriptive language. I discuss them here as mythic artifacts because the views they purvey are shibboleths that many people take for granted and even consider obviously true. In the theories of the major thinkers I will be discussing, these views have wide ramifications that seem to me untenable. Using convenient labels that I introduce as a way of studying the principal ideas, I call them myths of regression, communication, and revealed individuality, respectively.

The Myth of Regression

As the terminology for the first type suggests, it is found both in essays of Freud such as "The Relation of the Poet [for which the term *Creative Writer* is sometimes substituted] to Day-Dreaming" and also other remarks of his about childlike wish fulfillment in art.[1] Speaking as a psychologist and not as an art critic or analyst of its formal techniques, Freud portrays what the artist is and does by referring to mechanisms that are regressive in individual development as a whole. They originate presumably in children's play, in the fantasies of daydream-ing, and in the unique constructions that "the unconscious" displays in people's dreams each night. Freud sees them all not only as the means of simulating fulfillments that we wish to experience in our conscious existence but also as residual duplications of characteristic stages of individual development that children undergo. Throughout his general theory, Freud wavered about the question of whether such regression is necessarily neurotic. In much of his later work, he shows his ambivalence by speaking of ordinary adulthood as "normal or neurotic," with the implication that normal and neurotic forms of behavior are very much alike.

Freud's conception of children's play derives from nine-teenth-century theories, most notably those of Konrad Lange. According to Lange, creative art is a mature form of childhood play, both being make-believe that involves illusions, flights from reality, and what he called "conscious self-deception." In this view, the artist escapes from the hazards of everyday life by creating "a more satisfying ideal" of his own. Even music or architecture is thought to be based on "illusions of feeling."[2]

This approach supported Art for Art's Sake theories that treated the aesthetic as comprising a different world from ordinary life. Comparable views were also present in Platonis-tic dualism, in the writings of Hegelians who contrasted the concrete Becoming of things with the more ultimate reality of Being, and, as we shall see, in the philosophy of intuition-ists like Henri Bergson who believed that artistic creativity relies upon nonrational modes of discourse. In general, creative people were envisaged as children—marvelous, inspired, spontaneous, and often very productive children—who excel without having recourse to the merely prudential necessities of social responsibility or even practical concern about themselves as functioning human beings. Characters in many of the plays of Shaw and the novels of Thomas Mann are often depicted in that fashion.

Freud's use of this conception differs from those of others in emphasizing that children's play is an attempt to create a realm of one's own by using things in the world that the child finds available and very gratifying. Freud believed that what children want most of all is to grow up and live the way that adults do but they cannot. Their playing is therefore not irrational. It is a serious and largely innate effort on their part. When they become adults, Freud maintains, the connection with reality changes and their playing is permeated with fantasies present in day- or night dreams motivated by unsatisfied wishes.

According to Freud, this is especially true of people who are pervasively unhappy. "Happy people never make phantasies," he says.[3] Imagination itself he deems just a special type of fantasizing: "Imaginative creation, like day-dreaming, is a continuation of and substitute for the play of childhood. . . . Some actual experience which made a strong impression on the [creative artist] had stirred up a memory of an earlier experience, generally belonging to childhood, which then arouses a wish that finds a fulfillment in the work in question, and in which elements of the recent event and the old memory should be discernible."[4]

To the extent that the creative artist lives in fantasy of this sort, he resembles the neurotic. But Freud does not claim that the two are identical in every way. He recognizes that artists are often resourceful, and not pathological, insofar as they may derive considerable benefits from their fantasies, which are more interesting and more elaborate than anything a *mere* neurotic can generate. Also there is a social demand for what the artist does which can enable him to succeed in worldly and material ways that everyone craves. According to Freud, this results from the fact that artists express for many people the fantasies they too experience but repress or are simply incapable of transforming into enjoyable productions. Artists have an inherent knack, an unfathomable knack, Freud tells us, for disguising fantasies—their own as well as those of other people—thereby causing these fantasies to be pleasant and palatable, while somehow enabling the others to satisfy relevant needs as a result. Moreover, this is said to happen without the audience realizing what is being done.

For Freud it follows that someone who is creative begins with a sense of failure in the usual desires that we all have for the good things of life and that most individuals can fulfill better than the artist. In their basic unhappiness, artists have fantasies of wish fulfillment that they manage to incorporate in artifacts for which they may subsequently be rewarded, since the recipients of their work treat it as expressive of what they too experience.

How the artist is able of do this, Freud does not pretend to know. He calls the transformational process, the actual means by which the artist employs techniques he employs for his aesthetic goals, "mysterious," and about that Freud says very little. In his final summation, he remarks that when the artist uses his fantasies creatively he "opens out to others the way back to comfort and consolation of their own unconscious sources of pleasure, and so reaps their gratitude and admiration." The artist has then "won—through his phantasy—what before he could only win in phantasy: honor, power, riches, fame, and the love of women."[5] This is what the artist sought all along but could not attain directly. As a creative but regressive person, he or she is a consummate and even triumphant neurotic.

Critique of Freud

I consider Freud's theory a myth of creativity because it is a panoramic view that is not based on much, if any, empirical or statistical data submitted with it. Instead, it presupposes generalizations about repression, wish fulfillment, and a vague conception of the artistic process that we are expected to accept on faith. At the same time, Freud's argument can be formulated in a syllogism worth studying and, I believe, subject to criticism in each of its assertions. His reasoning runs as follows:

1. Creativity, and the imagination that occurs in it, resembles daydreaming inasmuch as all three are continuations of, and substitutions for, childhood play.
2. The play of children is determined by their wishes.
3. Therefore, imaginative creation fundamentally expresses the wishes of the artist, and in itself art is a form of wish fulfillment.

This syllogism is valid, but the conclusion is unacceptable since its premises are both false. For one thing, as I will argue, the concept of childhood play needs to be totally reformulated. Even the slightest observation reveals that it is of three sorts — games, undisciplined outbursts or enactments, and behavior that is contrived, or at least fully conscious.

Games that children play, such as hopscotch or even peek-a-boo, have rules that systematically impose their indigenous parameters. These rules are like the rules that define adult games: if you insist on having four strikes in baseball, you are no longer playing that game. But arts are different from this. Many of them do have some kind of rules, but theirs never *define* what does or does not eventuate as an artwork within a particular medium. Artistic rules are much more fluid than the rules of a game, and sometimes are even optional. Above all, artists who are highly creative freely bend or break whatever rules might have seemed indispensable as the basis of a fad or stylistic fashion in some art form.

With respect to undisciplined activity in childhood play, that too has been misconstrued by Freud. Any such expressiveness consists in screaming, roaring, running back and forth, scribbling idly on a blackboard or piece of paper, and so forth. Here there are no rules and often little control over the originating motivation, which is the free venting of one's feelings and momentary inclinations. Yet creativity in art, or anything else, is much more than just a venting of feelings. A person who is creative is consciously, and to a variable degree self-consciously, critical of what he or she simultaneously imagines and produces.

In that respect, art may be seen as resembling the third kind of childhood play that I have mentioned—its reliance upon responses that are not especially spontaneous but rather deliberative and premeditated. These responses occur when the child is wholly aware of what he or she is doing, and may even have thought about how to proceed, without being constrained by rules of virtually any type. To say this much, however, is already to cite an example of authentic art, and possibly creativity. It is "children's art" and need not be relegated to the lesser category of mere childhood play.

In the twentieth century the artwork of children, and for that matter chimpanzees and homespun amateur men and women, began to be appreciated as more than just playfulness. The individual productions were treated as belonging to a special and wholly reputable art form. Nowadays that is taken for granted. The fact that the artists are children or natives that some people consider primitive or merely members of another species is no longer assumed to lessen their aesthetic potentiality. In fact the word *play* may not be used any longer in reference to this mode of creativity. In any event, the terminology has become a minor consideration.

If we now apply our analysis to the first two kinds of childhood play—games and purposeless venting—Freud's interpretation in terms of wish fulfillment seems very suspect, to say the least. Even the venting is not in itself a fulfilling of any wish. It may be related to a primal drive, like the flexing of muscles, through which the child manifests and expresses energies that are either routine or joyfully accepted, scarcely noticed or vividly welcome. In art—as in the vibrant cluster of colors on a canvas or the loud and jubilant outburst of sounds in music—something comparable often happens. But neither in games and the act of venting nor in their aesthetic counterparts does all this signify wish fulfillment as a basic, or even concomitant, feature.

In the case of play as an explicitly critical occurrence, the situation is somewhat different. There one does often find a propensity toward wish fulfillment. Children draw food when they are hungry, portray people they hate as dead or wounded, and often indicate what they may crave in some moment of their lives. Evidence of this sort might lend support to Freud's theory if it were not for the fact that he is making claims about the origin of art in its entirety. *Some* works of art, like *some* examples of childhood play, are indeed expressions of fantasies related to wish fulfillment, but certainly not all.

As a clear example of wish fulfillment, Freud cites what he calls "less pretentious" novels in which the hero is a wholesome and worthy person who finally manages to marry the girl he wants and then lives happily ever after with her. This form of art, which we would not consider paradigmatic of good art, and possibly of little aesthetic value, does involve wish fulfillment. So do many fairy tales that are cherished by adults as well as children. They are often artistic and also worthy of being deemed creative. They are not representative, however, of what we may call "more pretentious" works of art.

The entire tradition of realistic novels, going back to Cervantes' *Don Quijote* or even tales in the Hellenistic period that issued into literary masterpieces of modern times, repudiated the fantasizing romances that Freud's argument relies upon. And when you think of abstract art such as nonfigurative painting, music of all sorts, architecture, rug weaving, and the culinary arts, it seems obvious that they cannot be invariably explained in terms of wish fulfillment. In one place, Freud too admits this difficulty but thinks he can resolve it. He says: "Many imaginative productions have traveled far from the original naïve daydreams, but I cannot suppress the surmise that even the most extreme variations could be brought into relationship with this model by an uninterrupted series of transitions."[6] What then is that series of transitions? Isn't Freud being hopelessly reductive in assuming that there must be a single model of any kind for all of art?

I believe that he is, and that his being so underlines the mythic character of his perspective. Although some kind of wish fulfillment can creep into any aesthetic production— even the most realistic novels of Flaubert, Zola, or Proust have their escapist elements—this is not sufficient to treat art in general as based on, or significantly bound to, wish fulfill-ment. The uninterrupted series of transitions to which Freud alludes has never been documented as present in any art form. I venture the opinion that it never will be.

One might say that Freud's principal error comes from an ambiguity in the term *wish fulfillment*. It can mean either that an activity or pursuit is undertaken as a way of getting some-thing one wants, or else as itself embodying a partial substitute for what one wants. The former is harmless; the latter, as well as the former, is what Freud intends. The former does no harm because it blandly links art or creativity to most, at least a great deal, of life without telling us very much about the nature of these modes of existence. All of what we do and say and think may be related to some amelioration of drive tension that we would like to mitigate. Similarly various types of personal re-sponse can be used as psychological data for understanding the creativity of whoever succeeds aesthetically. But that applies equally to someone's gait, or handwriting, or choice of clothing, or taste in food and sexual bonding, as well as in the works of art that he or she produces and others enjoy. In short, the limited connection between art and daydreaming or fantasizing is unable to perform the ambitious job that Freud assigns it.

Since all art may be seen as springing from the lived experience of its creator, artworks can sometimes express that origin in subtle and devious ways. But *how* the individual artist will in fact use his experience in what he paints or composes or writes creatively cannot be predicted through Freud's simplistic theorizing. If we knew enough about the psychodynamics of Shakespeare's life, we could perhaps infer that in devising the plot of *Hamlet* he was creatively working at emotional problems he had as a child. Yet even then we could scarcely say how much of this suggests that he was fantasizing in his writings or fulfilling some elusive wish. Working at a problem in art is like working at a problem in other areas of our life. It involves trying out different possibilities and imaginatively reconstructing actual facticities, while also deploying technical know-how in the making of one or another contrivance for eliciting affective as well as cognitive responses in an audience. Little, if any, of this amounts to the having of daydreams or the rest that Freud describes.

To his credit, Freud overtly confesses that he has not explained how it is that an artist can create something that is both pleasurable to others while at the same time psychologically rewarding for himself. He calls that the "innermost secret" of the artist and leaves the matter there. In his book on the interpretation of dreams, Freud does try to go further, but in his aesthetics he fails to provide any analyses that might help to penetrate whatever innermost secrets that may be present in the disparate nature of artistic creativity.

Creativity as Playfulness

The myth of regression that Freud's thinking embodies also appears in an interesting deviation that Carl Gustav Jung offers as a correction to it. Before discussing that, however, I want to make some further remarks about the idea that artistic and all other kinds of creativity duplicate childhood play. Instead of viewing the latter as an early level of individual development to which later creativity regresses, or reenacts within the settings of adulthood, I have been arguing that childhood play, like childhood art, is itself just a special case of both play and art that occurs prominently in our species and is apparent at every developmental stage. This being the case, play and playfulness must be understood as essential elements in creativity as a whole.

For example, consider the mind and professional attitude of the physicist Richard P. Feynman. He is often quoted as having remarked, "What I cannot create I cannot understand." In saying that, he was succinctly summing up his characteristic procedure in handling scientific problems that many of his "serious" colleagues in the field dealt with laboriously without regard to their own involvement and often with a traditional disclaimer that any such "subjectivity" has an appropriate place in science. Unlike them, Feynman presupposed that the solutions he sought could be found only if he himself was adequately creative in his search for them. That meant starting afresh more than others usually do and creating a model or diagram that seemed right to him intuitively as something that might lead to practical, useful conclusions. Approached in this way, the doing of physics was an enjoyable divertissement to Feynman, and he ascribed his capacity to have fun in playing with trivial experiments as the beginning of the creative achievements for which he became famous.

In one of Feynman's books, aptly entitled *"Surely You're Joking, Mr. Feynman!": Adventures of a Curious Character*, he describes a period of self-doubt about his professional abilities that ended when he allowed himself to engage in pointless probing and idle fooling with problems that no one else thought worthy of attention. On one occasion, he noticed that while the angle of rotation of a rotating plate is very small, the medallion emblazoned on it rotated at a wobbling angle that was twice as fast as for the plate itself. Though he was convinced that this was of no consequence at all, he worked out equations of the wobbles. He found himself thinking of the movement of electrons and "before I knew it (it was a very short time) I was 'playing' —working really, with the same old problem that I loved so much . . . my thesis-type problems, all those old-fashioned, wonderful things." He concludes by telling us that what he was doing "was effortless. It was easy to play with these things. . . . I almost tried to resist it! There was no importance to what I was doing, but ultimately there was. The diagrams and the whole business that I got the Nobel Prize for came from that piddling around with the wobbling plate."[7]

The crucial role in creativity ascribed to play and playfulness I interpret as resulting from the fact that imagination in itself is a playing with possibilities that exceed actualities with which we are familiar. Having possibilities, without which there would be no imagination, is itself a sport of nature, a wondrous mode of mental (and spiritual) entertainment. It arises mysteriously out of the situations that make up our reality. At the outset it is almost a nothing, an unreality that may sometimes become real if we choose to instantiate the possible. Shakespeare conveyed what I am feebly struggling to say in Prospero's speech about the characters and ephemeral players in the spectacle he has created as a diversion for Ferdinand and Miranda: "These our actors, / As I foretold you, were all spirits, and / Are melted into air, into thin air."[8] To which we might add the exhortation of the Prologue of *Henry V*: "On your imaginary forces work." Without them there can be no creativity, either in the audience or the artist or the work itself.

Jung's Rebuttal of Freud

Since playfulness exists in both children and grown-ups, one might dismiss the regression type of myth as unneeded and thoroughly corrupted by its faulty reductivism. Jung's version of the psychoanalytic theory of creativity offers itself as a remedy to the deficiencies in the Freudian approach. Jung applauds Freud's emphasis upon psychogenetic factors that can make a creative person neurotic. But he claims that Freud fails to reveal the artist's "innermost secret" because he confuses the maker of art with art itself. "The personal idiosyncrasies that creep into a work of art are not essential," Jung says. "In fact, the more we have to cope with these peculiarities, the less is it a question of art. What is essential in a work of art is that it should rise far above the realm of personal life and speak from the spirit and heart of the poet as man to the spirit and heart of mankind." Jung thereby separates the psychology of the artist himself from what he is in being creative: "In his capacity as artist he is neither auto-erotic, nor hetero-erotic, nor erotic in any sense. He is objective and impersonal—even inhuman—for as an artist, he is his work and not a human being."[9]

Paradoxical as this statement may be, one might think that Jung is finally repudiating the regression myth of creativity. But that is not the case. In fact, his explanation of what he means by the spirit and heart of mankind entails an

augmented regressiveness of its own. Without invoking childhood play and commonplace wish fulfillment as the source of
artistic creativity, his account of the artist *as* artist, rather than
as some deviously successful neurotic, harkens back to even
more inscrutable origins in the past. In denying that the artist
is an ordinary man, Jung exalts him into the condition of being
man "in a higher sense." "He is 'collective man'—one who
carries and shapes the unconscious, psychic life of mankind."[10]
In that capacity, the creative person is thought to revert to the
unconscious of the entire human race from its start to the present. Art is thus a molding of primordial sentiments that have
been "buried and dormant in man's unconscious since the
dawn of culture."[11]

Jung uses this idea as an explanation of the artist's creativity: "The secret of artistic creation and the effectiveness of art
is to be found in a return to the state of *participation mystique*—
to that level of experience at which it is man who lives, and not
the individual, and at which the weal or woe of the single human being does not count, but only human existence."[12] Given
his theory of archetypes and their mythic role in cognitive as
well as instinctive responses throughout civilization and its
forerunners, Jung would probably welcome the idea that what
he is proposing is itself a myth that recognizes a primordial
basis of creativity. Whether his mythmaking is acceptable as a
whole or in part is a different matter. I find no reason to think
it is acceptable either way.

The Myth of Communication

The second myth of artistic creativity that I will examine
presents it as a rare and special ability to communicate with
other people. Especially in art (though something equivalent

is often extended to scientific work), a person's creativity would therefore involve the ability to transfer his or her thoughts and feelings to an appropriate audience. The vehicle for this is the artwork itself, which must somehow embody a creative artist's experience. What the artist has personally undergone is presumably rendered into a material object open to public surveillance and capable of instilling identical feelings in many others.

This particular myth overlaps with "expression theories" of various kinds. For our purposes, those of Leo Tolstoy in his book *What Is Art?* will suffice as an introduction. After dismissing all attempts to define art in terms of beauty or pleasure, Tolstoy argues that by its very nature artistic creation is a communicative phenomenon, which he characterizes as follows: "To evoke in oneself a feeling one has once experienced and having evoked it in oneself then by means of movements, lines, colors, sounds, or forms expressed in words, so to transmit that feeling that others experience the same feeling— this is the activity of art. . . . Art is a human activity consisting in this, that one man consciously by means of certain external signs, hands on to others feelings he has lived through, and that others are affected by these feelings and also experience them."[13]

As a paradigmatic example, Tolstoy depicts the experience of a young boy who has been greatly frightened by encountering a wolf in the forest where he was walking. The boy turns and runs home still quivering with the fear he felt. There he narrates to his parents the details of his adventure. They are horrified by what he tells them, and they react with tenderness and concern for their child's welfare.

As Tolstoy points out, all the elements of what he defines as art are present in that example: the conscious conveyance of feelings that the teller of the event has himself experienced; the words, and his delivery of them, serving as the means of this communication; the duplicating of his feelings in their acute effect upon those who have heard his narration and will react to it. The boy has been more or less constructing a short story that could have been fictional, though in this case it is not. According to Tolstoy, the artistic creativity in the boy's account is evident in the emotional infectiousness that he is able to evoke through his deliberate attempt to convey his experience to his parents.

In formulating this theory of emotional expressiveness, Tolstoy also distinguishes questions about what is essentially artistic from those that explore what is truly valuable in art. His underlying view of creativity pertains to both. The values he sees as separating good or great art from what is superficial and inferior are those that unite people indiscriminately and as a community. In keeping with his Christian outlook at this stage of his life, Tolstoy relies upon ethical and religious ideas about the brotherhood of man and the love of humanity. At its pinnacle of aesthetic excellence, he maintains, art and therefore creativity must be instrumental in the cultivation of compassionate and loving attitudes that will be awakened in an audience as a reflection of what the artist himself has already felt.

Deficiencies in Tolstoy's Views

With respect to each of the criteria that Tolstoy establishes, his theory has been widely criticized. Much of creative art is undoubtedly a form of communication, but not all of it is. Decorative arts, such as the painting of nonexpressive patterns on kitchenware, and in general all useful and purely abstract arts are often devoid of either the purpose or explicit value of overt communication. Moreover, in eliminating the search for beauty as definitive of art, Tolstoy neglects an important component in many artworks, including those that may also seek to communicate something an artist has experienced. In itself beauty is a frequent property of objects that are simply pleasing to one or another of the senses.

Even when it is only present in the materials or formal structure of an artwork, beauty exists as a gratuitous quality that refers to nothing past or present. It is what it is, a serendipity of color or sound or tactile sensation projected on its own or through its harmonious combination, and possible interaction, with other aesthetic qualities—as in opera. What we experience as beautiful is usually something that delights our sensorium, or else our intellect, when it relishes an elegant bit of reasoning or mathematical proof. For this, there need not be a predominant interest in communication as such, whether through feelings or ideas.

During the years in which Tolstoy wrote *What Is Art?*, his literary efforts were all geared to enunciating a message of humanitarian love and dedicated Christianity. Communicating this perspective, and also the feelings he had himself experienced as a motive for writing about it, was foremost in his mind. Indeed I am willing to think that his theory of communication as the key to artistic creativity may very well have resulted from his religious beliefs at that time. In accordance with these convictions, he denounced as virtually worthless his earlier novels *Anna Karenina* and *War and Peace*, as well as many other great masterpieces of Western literature and even music.

To illustrate what is real art and authentic artistic creativity, Tolstoy cites short stories of his final years such as "God

Sees The Truth, but Waits." Devotees of Tolstoy's writings, and almost everyone else, have all been astounded by his faulty judgment in this regard. For one thing, the rejected master-pieces also express, and invoke in many of their readers, the kind of love and compassionate feeling toward suffering hu-manity that Tolstoy makes central in his aesthetic philosophy. But in any event, their profound insights about human nature, their social realism and narrative power, cannot be accommo-dated by the rigid constraints of his subsequent theory.

I have elsewhere called Tolstoy an "anti-Romantic Roman-tic," and that term is suitable here as well.[14] In the course of nineteenth-century romanticism, feeling was intentionally glorified as a corrective to the emphasis upon rationality that had dominated European thought in the seventeenth and eighteenth centuries. It was generally erotic feelings that were deified as either the fulfillment of interpersonal cravings or else a prologue to honorific marriage. Tolstoy attacked this conception in works such as *The Kreutzer Sonata*, and he blamed the impassioned music, literature, and painting of his era for promoting and disseminating such deceptive ideas. He was convinced that they could only cause people to welcome feelings that are vile and immoral as well as harmful to the persons who are beguiled by them.

To this degree, Tolstoy's thinking resembled Freud's in relation to prevalent attitudes about love and sex. At the same time, Tolstoy was himself a Romantic insofar as he conceived of creative art as not only the communication of the artist's feelings (whatever they might be) but also as an embodiment of them that would instill humanitarian feelings in the audience. Tolstoy's description of the nature of art, and the ethical and religious import of the subject matter he required in it, was an extension of the mystifying Romantic myth that he himself attacked without realizing his inconsistency.

Problematics of Communication Theories

Like some other expressionist accounts of art, Tolstoy's can scarcely comprehend the empirical facts about creative production. Most artists are not driven by any obvious desire to communicate feelings they have had and now seek to incorporate in their works. Much of Mozart's most cheerful music—designed to be played at a festive occasion—was composed when he suffered from illness and even grief. He needed the money for his family and steeled himself to acquire it through whatever commission he might receive. Like the vast majority of creative people, he entered into his artistic labors with a dedication to the techniques that were required by the composition at hand together with a fascinated interest in developing one or another musical idea that his imagination provided.

Even in works that were not written to enliven a social event—his symphonies and concerti, for instance—it was the sensory character of motifs and melodic possibilities that Mozart sought to express in his music. For him, as for Beethoven and the more Romantic composers of later decades, the musical expressiveness was usually not preceded by emotions or comparable feelings that elicited them and were now being consciously transferred through them. And when these affective components did make their appearance in the music, they were always highly transformed sonically and often unrecognizable.

This is not to say that musicians or other creative artists are cold-blooded craftsmen who try to hide or mask their private emotionality. Creating is not only exhilarating and life-enhancing in itself but also a source of joyful and powerful feelings that awaken an artist's developing inventiveness and motivate his or her most technical innovations. What is actually created, however, can only express an aesthetically reconstituted version of affective experience that the artist considers pertinent and worthy of being incorporated in the production.

Whether or not the funeral march in Beethoven's Third Symphony was originally designed as a memorial to the recently deceased Napoleon Bonaparte, it expresses sadness in a way that only music can. Regardless of how sad Beethoven may or may not have been when he sat down to write his "tribute to a great man," he was not conveying his own sadness but rather creating a musical portrayal of what many other people had also felt in some moment of their lives. One could say that he was identifying with them through his work, or that in this special context he was making a statement of support and approval for their sentiments. Yet that too is not the same as claiming that Beethoven's feelings of sadness or whatever were being objectified and explicitly duplicated in the notes he wrote for this composition.

However programmatic or abstract a work of music (or of any of the other artistic media) may be, the feelings it portrays are not replicas of the artist's. They are manifestations of his or her sensitivity and imagination, albeit in relation sometimes to what he and others may have felt. When these manifestations are fertile or inspired, we may possibly infer facts about the emotionality of the creative individual who has used his work to express the relevant feelings. In that vein, we might say not only that Beethoven's slow movement is sad but also that it is an expression of sadness. Some writers have even claimed that it expresses the *essence* of sadness. Yet that would not sustain the communication myth of artistic creativity. The music is instead an artifact that renders in engaging sound an *interpretation* of feelings that anyone might have had. The actual experience of the artist is usually incidental to this achievement, as much as we may adulate him or her for this way of using it.

In its totality, Tolstoy's theory is suspect most of all in its requirement that the audience must undergo the *same* emotion, or other feeling, that the artist experienced and intentionally expressed through the created work of art. The suggestion that creativity belongs to a process that involves other people and their interests in life is unquestionably correct. So too is the emphasis upon the affective, over and above the cognitive, elements in the aesthetic reaction of the audience. But the assertion that people who are fully responsive to the Eroica Symphony's Funeral March must relive the feelings Beethoven had while writing it is simply erroneous. Even the most intuitive and astute listeners cannot be sure what Beethoven did feel at the time. And if they could be sure, this information might have little impact on them as listeners. Far from expressing sadness or the sorrow of losing a great man, their own feelings may be the quite different ones that result from focused pleasure and accomplished recognition of the artfulness in this music, as well as gratitude for the beauties these harmonies are graciously yielding and anticipation about what will follow in later segments of the symphony.

In his allegiance to the myth of communication as the unique goal in creativity, Tolstoy precludes my kind of criticism by affirming—as we saw that Freud also did—the superiority of art that is "less pretentious," less sophisticated and cerebral than what I have chosen as examples. Criticism such as mine would not have dismayed Tolstoy. He would have replied that, in terms of popular appeal, the art he commends comes close to vindicating the communication theory he advocates. Not just folk tales and sentimental songs, but also the words and accompaniment of recent rock music do succeed to some extent in meeting the demands of Tolstoy's theory. Nevertheless, his saying that the kind of art he favors has the highest aesthetic value, and is definitive of what all artistic creativity should be, suffices by itself to make us discard the myth that he proclaims.

The Myth of Revealed Individuality

What I am calling the myth of individuality that art reveals is more challenging and more persuasive than the other two we have discussed. It is best illustrated by Bergson's views about the creation of art. As he describes it, all art has a mission to overcome the distance between nature and our experience of it: "Could reality come into direct contact with sense and consciousness, could we enter into immediate communion with things and with ourselves, probably art would be useless, or rather we should all be artists, for then our soul would continually vibrate in perfect accord with nature."[15] From this, Bergson infers that the creativity in art enables us to perceive the individuality of things and animate beings, which we are normally not able to do. For reasons of survival and practical accommodation, we scarcely see the actualities in our life, he says: "In most cases, we confine ourselves to reading the labels affixed to them."[16] Creative art thus exists as a partial remedy of that condition.

In taking this stance, Bergson presupposes a dualism that develops and constantly recurs throughout his philosophy.

It is a radical modification of the dualism that Descartes established, which then became a foundation of Western philosophy. Bergson's version is an original reorientation since, instead of the separation between mind and matter, it delineates how human experience consists of different, even opposing, components of dynamism and rigidity, of vitality and mechanization, of intuition and intelligence, of spiritual strivings and those that are overtly materialist and pragmatic. Bergson's last book, whose contents I have already touched upon, sums up his dualism magnificently. As its title indicates, it depicts the contrast between "the two sources of morality and religion." The values that humankind has routinely cherished Bergson sees as deriving from the first of these sources. The practical adjustments that are inescapable in this category must nevertheless be subjected, he claims, to the second source, which transcends it, as mind transcends the body and selfless love transcends the pervasive selfishness of creatures in nature.

Given this bifurcation within daily life as it routinely exists, even when it is sustained by intelligence or rationality, Bergson focuses upon the individuality that everything has in itself as an objective entity that we can know through intuition alone. He refers to a "veil" by which nature encloses itself. It raises the veil only a bit at the corners, thereby allowing some access to its ultimate reality. Creative art, Bergson asserts, is our human attempt to penetrate more thoroughly: "Art is certainly a more direct vision of reality . . . a deep-seated reality that is veiled from us, often in our own interests, by the necessities of life."[17]

In this way, according to Bergson, "Art always aims at what is *individual*. What the artist fixes on his canvas is something he has seen at a certain spot, on a certain day, at a certain hour, with a colouring that will never be seen again."[18] Creative art is consequently "a return to pure nature."[19]

"The Veil" in Bergson and in Proust

The Bergsonian concept of "the veil" reverberates throughout Marcel Proust's speculations about the "image" that prevents a lover (and presumably other persons as well) from understanding and properly appreciating the qualities of someone who has elicited an affective response and erotic attachment. Proust claims that people are always impeded by their material involvement in nature and its imperious demands, which hamper our attempts to reach beyond one or another falsifying image. The only remedy he admits is creativity in art.

When that occurs, as explained in the last volume of Proust's *À la recherche du temps perdu*, the narrator/artist discerns the individual and basic realities that had systematically deluded him as a lover, or at least a participant in behavior geared to love and other interpersonal values. Having attained this final level of awareness, the protagonist in Proust overcomes the fallacies that filled his previous life. He no longer seeks to love anyone. To use the term that Sartre employs, he recognizes that love, and also sex, is a "futility."

Bergson's philosophy is more comprehensive, but it too differentiates between two kinds of imagination—one that creates the deceptive veil and the other that is designed to reveal the lived realities hidden by it. I consider this approach to creativity totally mythological because it is based upon a conception of reality that is nonempirical and, under the circumstances of human experience, nonverifiable. Moreover, the Bergsonian approach is not true to the nature of imagination as a whole. That province of the mind is not explicable in terms of the nonrational content of what Bergson calls intuition.

Describing artistic creation as the revelation of reality, which entails showing forth the individuality of what is real, Bergson assumes there is some separate and more ultimate reality lurking behind the veil that hides it from us. Useful for practical purposes as intelligence or rationality surely is, Bergson believes that they can only be implements of the veiled condition. To say this, however, is to misconstrue the nature of both imagination and any intuition properly understood. Imagination is not a process of stripping away the labels or the generalizations with which we live. It is instead an innate capacity by which the mind exceeds the limits of whatever we experience as an actuality. Though imagination is itself a reality, it is a device for envisaging possibilities that are not real, entities and events that may someday come into being but as yet are still *non*existent.

Imagination is the workshop of all make-believe and as such it includes the realm that art inhabits and out of which it generates every form of artistic creativity. When imagination operates at its peak, it can culminate in what we call aesthetic truth. This in turn may be revelatory, as Bergson also says, but only because artistic creativity employs the same raw actuality that his idea of intuition sought to transcend. At its best, imagination digests yet does not minimize the familiar world of labels and habitual generalizations. The individuality of everything is a part of that world. Through our creativity we vividly detect and then amplify the fact of individuality, but only with the help of intelligence and common reason.

To the extent that aesthetic truthfulness occurs within creative arts, it is compatible with everything that pertains to the
material and pragmatic dimensions of the world as we experience it daily. In that respect, enlightenment through art leaves
everything as it was, which is the message of Buddhist satori
as well as Ludwig Wittgenstein's conception of linguistic analysis. Bergsonian intuition is not needed for awareness of individuality in what is real, and so his mythological notion of art
as the only means of attaining that kind of perception is mis-
directed.

In a subsequent chapter, I will continue my critique of
Bergson's philosophy. Here it interested me primarily as the
articulation of a beguiling myth that we have to discard—like
the two other myths I discussed.

5

Aesthetic Creativity

The Artist's Creativity

As a continuation of my discussion of creative experience in previous chapters, I now address the general nature of aesthetic creativity that will lead into more specific aspects of creativity in the rest of the book. In this chapter I largely resort to historical analysis that eventuates in coordinate speculations of my own. The main problem here is whether, as I believe, we can properly consider the aesthetic to be paradigmatic of all creativity. If so, since creativity must be approached in relation to some relevant process, we would then need to determine how it may occur not only in the fine arts but also in aesthetic components that belong to science, technology, mathematics, and the vast variety of practical pursuits. These interwoven types of experience differ pluralistically within themselves. This, too, will have to be explained.

We should not assume that what is creative in the art of poetry, for instance, is the same as what is creative in music or painting or any other subdivision in this part of the spectrum. Moreover, the conglomerate of what we call fine art is not identical in its creativity with the creative elements of cooking, or child rearing, or legislating, or all the other useful arts in which people engage. And, finally, what we call an art form may be understood as a combination of three different factors: the artist's effort, the audience's imaginative response, and the material entity—the object or performance—that mediates between them and is sometimes called the "aesthetic object." Each of these contains creative dimensions of its own.

In view of the need for ever finer distinctions, one may wonder where to start. But possibly it does not matter, and so I arbitrarily begin with the artist's creativity. That is what catches the fancy of many art lovers and readily unites with their admiration toward the person who initiates their communal love of any art. We all stand in awe of a man or woman who reconstructs and thereby transforms the world through aesthetic inventiveness deployed as an expression of whatever matters most to that person. We are impressed by the fact that someone who looks like us, and more or less negotiates a similar path of life in merely existing as we do, is able to confront so effectively the problems within the search for meaning that we ourselves also face daily.

Artists simultaneously inhabit a second, overlapping realm of being that the rest of us can appreciate and possibly cultivate only secondhand. Their condition emanates from the special creativity, which in our adulation we call "God-given," that is available to such chosen individuals through innate aptitudes that most other people do not have. Everyone wishes to be creative as artists are just in being themselves. And yet, as T. S. Eliot puts it, between the essence and the descent falls the shadow. Knowing our own inadequacies, we both extol and envy their access to the plenitude of aesthetic meaningfulness that we can apprehend only through their efforts.

In his dialogue *Ion*, Plato puts the following words into the mouth of Socrates: "And as the Corybant revellers when they dance are not in their right mind, so the lyric poets are not in their right mind when they are composing their beautiful strains: but when falling under the power of music and metre they are inspired and possessed. . . . For the poet is a light and winged and holy thing, and there is no invention in him until he has been inspired and is out of his senses, and the mind is no longer in him: when he has not attained to this state, he is powerless and is unable to utter his oracles."[1]

This characterization emphasizes how greatly an artist may be swept along by some creative impulse. In the act of inspired composition he or she may feel like a different person, or like the same person but immersed as Alice was in a wonderland that transfigures the ordinary experiences that people have when they are in their "right mind." At the same time, there is something radically misleading in Socrates' depiction. Most artists feel no need to make oracular statements or undergo a form of Corybantian ecstasy. Being creative need not mean undergoing madness, even the madness that Plato metaphorically calls divine or, at least, an offshoot of divinity. On the contrary, the artist is more likely to feel the earthly joy of expressing hidden and at times private aspects of his or her sheer humanity.

It is true that creative individuals are favored in being talented, but neither they nor anyone else may be able to explain what this signifies. Though the ideas for their work seem to come out of nowhere, suddenly and without much evidence of their provenance, the same applies to life in general. We can localize a pain in a particular part of the body that quivers at our touch, yet the sensation itself just comes

upon us. We can describe its history and medical implications—
which themselves are often obscure—without our knowing
about its causation much more than what Hume referred to as
a "constant conjunction." Likewise, the painter staring at a
blank canvas and then feeling the gestation of lines and colors
that stir within him may have little awareness of whence this
creative process originates.

Some theorists are content to say only that the act of
creation manifests a momentary "inspiration," which energizes
the artist's desire to paint, for instance. Still that scarcely
clarifies the situation. Breathing in a substance that comes
from without, which is what terms like *inspiration* or *being
inspired* mean literally, is different from what happens in the
doing of creative work. That depends instead upon a kind of
breathing out, an expiration that bestows upon the environment something new and welcome and usually less ephemeral
than the air one exhales.

One might even claim that aesthetic inspiration is an
igniting of combustible matter that has been simmering, or
even smoldering, in the creative person until something turns
it into active kindling. How this can happen we do not really
know, since creativity acts in ways that are always somewhat
mysterious to us. All the same, neither the artist nor anyone
else who tries to understand his mode of being creative need
invoke a mystical or deified agency over and above the
potential for productive growth that inheres in human nature
itself.

Ancient and Medieval Perspectives

Throughout the ancient and medieval world, the concept of
creativity that Plato voices in *Ion* was variably accepted by

many theorists. But even in Plato there occurred another view that was more fundamental in his thinking, and possibly contrary to these ideas about the nature of inspiration. Like most Greeks of his period, Plato believed that artistic creation was an example of *techné*, which is to say, a skill or undertaking designed for making objects not found in nature. Through techné humankind exceeded the instinctive and unconscious elements of our being. Socrates assumes this view in *The Republic* when he argues against Thrasymachus that there is an art of governing that forces the ruler to seek the welfare of his subjects.

Later in *The Republic*, as well as in other dialogues and the *Apology*, Socrates denigrates the working artists he knows because they are generally ignorant, insufficiently aware, of the underlying character of their professional activities.

They have little knowledge, he says, of what is implied in their pursuit of creativity, specifically its capacity to transcend the limitations of material nature. In the twentieth century, George Santayana reverts to a comparable view when he offers the following insight into aesthetic creation: "The emergence of arts out of instincts is the token and exact measure of nature's success and of mortal happiness."[2]

Plato does not attempt to reconcile his two conceptions of artistic creativity. But in the *Timaeus*, one of his later dialogues, he talks about God as the Grand Artificer who uses techné in his making of the universe, and thereby serves as an icon of artistry that propels all other creations. The *Timaeus* depicts the primal origin of everything in an image of God molding formless matter while under the spell of his vision of the eternal Forms. They are the ultimate source of his endeavors, and the world he creates is both good and beautiful because the highest Forms inspire him to act in accordance with their unique ideality. In later centuries this notion became the basis of theorization by Neoplatonists like Plotinus and some of the early Christian philosophers. They saw it as a harmonization of belief in art as techné with a portrayal of mystical afflatus that might resemble, or even induce, a special type of madness to which human artists are sometimes liable.

The concept of techné had the great virtue of treating the different arts and crafts alike as practical behavior. In the medieval period, as in much of the ancient world, artists were envisaged as craftsmen one might hire to provide a useful service for which they were especially competent. A painter would not be asked to do the job of a carpenter, and neither would pretend to be carried away by a metaphysical intuition that elicited their particular mode of creativity. On the other hand, the doctrine had no place for the phenomenon of beauty that might issue from the mind of an artist but not necessarily from that of a craftsman, since the latter would be mainly oriented toward some utilitarian outcome.

Moreover, this view scarcely recognized the presence in the artist's work of a personal and possibly profound expressiveness that might never appear in an object produced by craft alone. In the Middle Ages the idea of techné was supported by the church as a way of thwarting the pretentiousness of artists who might willfully seek to promote religious beliefs that were not orthodox. As a result, we don't even know the names of many medieval artists who, working alongside the craftsmen, did their job in comparable anonymity. Though some of them must surely have seen themselves as servants of the Lord, they were discouraged from thinking that what they created could arise from a special access to divinity on their part.

The artists worked in teams—on the cathedrals, for instance—and did not believe they were hired to display their individual being through their creativity. The church ordained the style as well as the content of what was to be expressed, and the artist was required to submit to ecclesiastical authorities in almost every detail. He was expected to be an instrument, a tool and mere technician, that conveyed the vision of those who spoke for the authorized dogmas. The following rule enunciated at the Second Council of Nicaea held for almost five hundred years: "The substance of religious scenes is not left to the initiative of the artists; it derives from the principles laid down by the Catholic Church and religious tradition. . . . His art alone belongs to the painter, its organization and arrangement belong to the clergy."[3]

Not only did the techné approach neglect the important role of beauty in art, but also it defined beauty as a moral or even intellectual property in the world, distinct from anything artists might create. Moral deeds and the metaphysical context from which they arose were to be seen as literally, not just metaphorically, beautiful. In principle, at least, all reality was thought to manifest aesthetic perfection by conforming to the orderliness of God's original design. It therefore was not the artist's talent that created the beautiful. A similar notion of beauty had characterized much of Greek philosophy that pervaded the medieval conception. In being a purposive imitation consciously realized, creativity in art, as in craft, was just an approximation of what had already been created as a model. Using natural materials to which form was already given by the prior plan—a divinely inspired blueprint—both art and craft could only duplicate whatever was established by the celestial exemplar.

The second of Plato's theories to which I referred not only amplified the idea of techné but also redirected it in ways that moved in other significant directions. This development is quite evident in *The Republic*. Toward the end of that book Plato diminishes the value of artistic creativity by depicting it as just the producing of a copy of a copy of reality. In this conception, a vision of the Forms is needed to show forth the essential being of anything; a material object in the world is a copy of some relevant Form; and an artist's representation is merely a copy of that copy. But earlier in *The Republic*, Socrates compares, as I have mentioned, the workings of an accomplished artist to what the Grand Artificer does in molding raw matter into the physical objects we see about us in ordinary experience. In the *Phaedrus* he describes authentic human art as different from what an imitative craftsman does, insofar as the former issues from the divine spark that emulates the creativeness depicted in the *Timaeus*.

Apart from revisions that Plotinus and others in the third century developed, this aspect of Plato's thinking became a prominent approach to aesthetic creativity only in the later Renaissance. Michelangelo refused to be called *scultore* because he thought it identified him as a craftsman, and even the keeper of a craftshop. He insisted on his name of Buonarroti as more indicative of his personal vision and native talent. In trying to show the godliness of creative art, others treated it as pursuing the same mission as theological studies, not mimicking divine creation but teaching the truth about it. Sir Philip Sidney explicitly states as much in his defense of poetry (1595), claiming that this art form is moral and philosophical like theology.

As time went on, the medieval view became outmoded and what remained was the belief that artists search for beauty and goodness but without any single religious faith that might underlie their efforts. In the nineteenth century, remnants of Neoplatonic thinking of the third century and the Renaissance survived in a greatly emancipated form, as in theorization about "Art for Art's Sake." Our modern ideas about aesthetic creativity cannot be understood without some awareness of what that movement entailed.

Art for Art's Sake

Taken in its totality, the propounding of the Art for Art's Sake perspective represented a major attempt in European/ American culture to assert an independent and autonomous justification for aesthetic creativity without its having to be didactic or uplifting. The useful functions of art had been strenuously maintained by most thinkers in the seventeenth and eighteenth centuries. Art for Art's Sake theorists opposed them.

The principles of the Art for Art's Sake were fourfold:

1. The artist is different from other people in having a predominance of sensory intuition and enhanced inventive imagination that are definitive of human creativity.

2. An artist is a specialist in the techniques of his own art, and insofar as someone is a philosopher, scientist, moralist, politician, or the like, that person is not an artist.

3. Great art is not created exclusively by people of high moral character.

4. Artistic creation in itself is the supreme goal of life.

The first of these theses was predicated upon a phenomenological distinction that German Idealist philosophers often made. On the one hand, they tended to think of (fine) art as a pursuit of beauty, which was a showing forth in sensation of metaphysical truths that transcend the everyday world while also explaining its nature as a whole. On the other hand, they realized that survival of our species, and of ourselves as well, depends upon practical reason with which we are all endowed. While men of action in politics or business or the common pursuits of purposive existence devote themselves to practical reason, artists were considered more directly attuned to the gratifications afforded by the sensuous dimensions in our experience.

Without being bestial sybarites given to the base enjoyment of their bodily faculties, artists were believed to intuit the ideality of beauty and goodness that results from a highly refined cultivation of the senses. To a musician this would happen through sonic constructions; to a poet through metaphoric and suggestive uses of language; to a painter through the visual splendor of lines and colors. Whatever the art form might be, its special difference from the standard character of ordinary life was thought to yield the possibility of an aesthetic perspective that human beings could attain through sense-related intuition they also have.

In defining the creative artist in this manner, Art for Art's Sake theory adhered to an even more extensive distinction between mediate and immediate experience. As Kant and many other philosophers maintained, what is given to us as a primary source of consciousness is simply the flux of sensory data as they impinge upon the organism. These are the components of our experience that even a skeptic must deem indubitable, a certainty without which we could not attain knowledge of any sort. This immediate experience, this slender layer of being that is undergone solely in its immediacy, was taken as epistemologically, though not temporally, prior to any reasoning that can, and does, tell us what our actual world is like. That would result from mediate experience, categorization and intelligence, memory and expectation, that links past, present, and future instances of sensory immediacy into a conceptual construct capable of yielding reliable truths about our human condition as well as the world in which it exists. While the artist lives on both planes, like the rest of us, his or her aesthetic creativity was viewed as deriving from superior access to the immediate aspects of life rather than those that are mediate.

This formulation of the two types of experience has been attacked by a great many philosophers in the last two hundred years, and there is no need for me to rehearse their arguments. At present I am more interested in the implications of any such belief in Art for Art's Sake doctrine. They entail that artists need no longer think of themselves as artisans or practitioners of a craft, and that nothing requires them to further through their artwork any type of intellectual or moral or utilitarian ends. By the middle of the nineteenth century the very meaning of the word *artist* had changed. It now referred to an "imaginative creator," a person whose exceptional appreciation of sensate possibilities made it unnecessary for this individual to portray general nature as it exists, or delineate through discursive reason the character of ideal goodness.

This meant in turn that the accomplished aesthetic creativity of authentic artists entitled them to articulate and express their individual intuition of beauty whether or not it is true to life. They had only to make something that was congruent with their own vision, selective though it may be and even idiosyncratic. In this vein James Whistler asserted: "To say to the painter that Nature is to be taken as she is, is to say to the player, that he may sit on the piano."[4]

Among Romantic artists, the new approach encouraged a venting of passions through one's art that had been frowned on by society in the past. But realists also took it as justification for the stylistic detachment they tended to cultivate. They believed that the artist had only to step back from reality, select from the plenitude of stimuli with which it bombards us at every moment, and then transmit coolly and with emotional withdrawal the contents of his or her sensuous experience. Gustave Flaubert insisted that "passion does not make poetry and the more personal you are the weaker you will be."[5] Visiting an insane asylum on one occasion, he remarked about how beautiful it was as a display of human suffering.

In his preface to *The Portrait of Dorian Gray*, Oscar Wilde declared that "the artist is the creator of beautiful things. To reveal art and conceal the artist is art's aim."[6] In the writings of Émile Zola, Ivan Turgenev, and Henry James, the novelist presents himself as an impartial spectator communicating to the reader through narrational bits of experience that were mainly observational. Their heightened sensitivity as *reporters* of reality, they thought, alone defined their creative capacity.

James Joyce sums up the general viewpoint of this movement in his autobiographical novel *A Portrait of the Artist as a Young Man*:

The personality of the artist, at first a cry or a cadence or a mood and then a fluid and lambent narrative, finally refines itself out of existence, impersonalizes itself, so to speak. The aesthetic image in the dramatic form is life purified in and reprojected from the human imagination. The mystery of aesthetic like that of material creation is accomplished. The artist, like the God of the creation, remains within or behind or beyond or above his handiwork, invisible, refined out of existence, indifferent, paring his fingernails."[7]

Further Principles of Art for Art's Sake

Wholly coherent with the reliance upon sensory intuition in the first principle of Art for Art's Sake is the emphasis on technicality in the second one. Being a skilled technician, an artist was conceived as someone who specializes in the formalistic devices that belong to his or her chosen art. Unlike a philosopher or scientist or moralist or propagandist for some cause, the artist was seen as an expert in the particular styles and techniques of some medium. A person is a poet if he or she knows how to use inventively the linguistic contrivances of meter and possibly rhyme; a composer of music if the elements are sonic rhythm, harmony, or melody; a painter if the visual effect of suggestive lines and interesting colors is dominant and compelling in the work; and so on with the other arts.

Beyond the fact that aesthetic creativity requires appreciation of sensory beauty, it was thought to depend upon the mastery of faculties, such as sight and hearing, that pertain to the formal structure of one's art. Creative ability would thereby evince whatever artistic proficiency was requisite, and the degree of aesthetic creativity could be determined by the artist's subordination of all other aims and purposes to those of consummate talent and the related perfection that might eventuate. Roger Fry and Clive Bell were famous proponents of this position.

These ideas about the nature of aesthetic creativity were explicitly intended to liberate art from its subservience to doctrines of morality or received ideology. John Ruskin had upheld the earlier position by asserting that painters were similar to preachers. He thought they were both uniquely qualified to comment about infinity. Goethe and Baudelaire rejected those ideas on the grounds that an artist who creates with a moral or edifying aim is sure to be inferior because the attempt inevitably precludes originality. Art for Art's Sake theorists extended their attack by seeking to protect the artist from all extraneous impositions—including those that derive from ecclesiastic or aristocratic patronage as well as censorship by public opinion that might not approve of what an artist creates freely and without external control.

The two remaining principles of Art for Art's Sake deal less with aesthetic creativity as such than with its place in society. Eighteenth-century artists had been expected to enlighten the audience, glorify the struggles of the virtuous, reveal the final defeat of evil, and illustrate a kind of poetic justice that descends upon those who deserve to be punished. Art for Art's Sake held that in any such endeavor the so-called artist ceased to be a genuine example of one, but rather became a moralist or would-be edifying philosopher instead. Advocates of the traditional teachings often claimed that aesthetic value of any kind, and beauty above all, was proportionate to the ethical and spiritual capabilities of the artist. Plato had talked about Homer from that point of view, and Ruskin argued that beauty can be created *only* by persons who have a reverential and affirmative attitude toward life.

In rejecting this conception, Wilde maintained that art and morality were not only independent of each other by definition but also incompatible in a creative individual even at different moments. He insisted that artists do not have ethical sympathies. And in reference to great artists of the past, Whistler stated: "No reformers were these great men—no improvers of the ways of others! Their productions alone were their occupation."[8]

Testing Ruskin's assertions about a positive correlation between moral nobility in life and aesthetic excellence in an artist's creative efforts, other critics pointed out that Virgil's tenderness and Pope's severity in their writing were not the expression of a benevolent disposition but were instead indicative of these poets' training in formalistic conventions and literary techniques. Since this showed itself in their work, undue interest in the artist's autobiographical existence could thus be dismissed as inappropriate. Even his famous painting that came to be called "Whistler's Mother," Whistler polemically entitled "Arrangement in Grey and Black." The identity of the sitter was of no importance, he said. In Walter Pater's literary criticism toward the end of the nineteenth century, analysis was likewise directed largely toward formal aspects of some work of art.

The last of the four principles that I have mentioned rounds out the argument. It alleges that since aesthetic creativity is superior to practical action or cognitive reflection, one must infer that the former is the highest goal of all human enterprise. This means that art is not just moral in itself but also *more* moral than anything else. Since the artist is the creator of beautiful things, any possible conflict between art and morality disappears once we recognize the goodness of beauty. In other words, aesthetic value alone determines what may clearly count as moral value. The critic A. C. Bradley recognized Art for Art's Sake as an ethical and quasi-religious movement, and on those grounds he condemned it. Bradley agreed that art is *an* end worth pursuing as the expression of creativity, but, he said, it is ridiculous to think that art is the whole or supreme end of life.

Bradley was doubtless referring to the fine arts. If so, we may readily accept his culminating judgment. Nevertheless, one can affirm, as I did in the last volume of *Meaning in Life*, that art is the harmony of nature and spirit. In making that suggestion, I supported the idea that one might indeed proclaim that art is the supreme goal of human life, provided we consider art in its broadest reference rather than limiting it to any of its subdivisions, such as those we arbitrarily designate as being "fine." This ambiguity in the terminology of art and the aesthetic may be unavoidable, but its recurrent presence should not pose too great a difficulty.

Going beyond Art for Art's Sake Theories

To free ourselves from the shortcomings of Art for Art's Sake dogma, we do well to return briefly to the prior mistakes built into the history of Western thought, beginning with those in Plato. His conception of techné is manifest in his approach to the nature of representation, of imitation, and of imagination in general. As I have said, Plato thought that however creative an artist may be he inevitably remains thrice removed from reality since he can only make a representation of a representation. Accordingly, what a painter paints is recognizable as a particular object, a bed, let us say, only because it embodies the abstract Form that shows forth the bed's determinate being. Its physical existence in the real world being itself a copy or representation of its Form, the painter's portrayal is quite remote from ultimate reality since it can only be an imitation that represents this object's representation. As a result, creative imagination that goes into an artistic process can be nothing more than a derivative and essentially minor act of image making.

In formulating this metaphysical hierarchy, however, Plato ignored the fact that imitation and representation are not the same. As someone who portrays a bed, the artist might be said to have made a representation of it. But his depiction need not be an imitation. Though it is a copy, it may not be a literal copy. The physical object, the bed, can be seen as the embodiment of whatever Form that enables it to be recognized as what it is. To that extent it would be an instantiation of the relevant Form. But it is not necessarily an *imitation* of that Form, and neither does a painting of it have to be seen as something that copies or duplicates the object. A painter's portrayal can be considered an instance of its own Form *as a portrayal*. In being a mode of transformation, it is far from being simply duplicative, and so its representation of reality cannot be reduced to whatever representation may have occurred in the real-world object's relation to a Form.

This kind of critique underlies Plotinus's radical changes in the Platonic doctrine. It is especially telling, I believe, because it shows us how to repudiate the notion that imagination is just a matter of image making. Aesthetic creativity can show itself in the making of images, but this showing belongs to an activity that functions as much more than just imitating something or even representing it in an image.

Imagination that contributes to creativity depends on our ability to envisage what is possible, or even impossible, regardless of anything that exists. The artistic process that then occurs presents to its receptive audience an experience of the novelty and suggestiveness in the materials, the design, and the expressive capacity of a work through which its creator has expended his or her inventiveness and revealed his or her personal view of reality. The beauty, or other aesthetic value, that arises from this achievement cannot be explained exclusively in terms of the being or the quality of any represented object. Plato's thinking about techné totally distorts this aspect of aesthetic creativity.

Aristotle's doctrine is not basically different from Plato's, but it introduces some alterations that took on great importance in later centuries. While accepting the idea that art is a craft-like and fundamentally imitative phenomenon, Aristotle emphasizes its additional ability to purvey general truths that elude literal and therefore limited presentations. That is the burden of his assertion in the *Poetics* about tragedy being more philosophical than history since the characters in tragedy need not be imitations of an actual person but are instead manifestations of how some type of individual might possibly behave under circumstances creatively chosen by the play-wright. That way of reasoning fed into eighteenth-century views about the didactic role of art—the outlook that Art for Art's Sake theorists found pernicious. This much of the Aristotelean approach they considered invalid because it ignored the formal and technical originality in works of art, and thus made the creative process appear more rationalistic than it is.

In the twentieth century the relationship between art and craft was examined by several philosophers who do not align themselves with Art for Art's Sake ideas but share its dissatisfaction with techné theory. Since I am not writing a history of aesthetics, I will address only a few of their ideas about artistic creativity. In the writings of R. G. Collingwood, for instance, there is a distinction between arts and crafts that is very much worth exploring as a classic statement of this point of view. Collingwood contrasts the two categories in relation to differences between means and ends, planning and executing, use of raw materials and concern about a final product.

In general, Collingwood examines diverging attitudes about form in relation to matter. He suggests that crafts are only the employment of means that are distinct from the ends for which the means are needed. Cutting iron as a way of ultimately making a horseshoe would illustrate this difference. But Collingwood also says that even when something similar happens *within* an art, it does not explain the nature of art itself. Though using a dictionary of rhymes or attaining a rhythm by pounding on the floor might be comparable to writing poetry, that art form defines itself in terms of the thinking and its musical expression that the poet employs as ends that pertain to his creative process rather than as a means to anything. The ends comprise a final outcome that one cannot fully contemplate in advance, whereas in a craft one foresees throughout what will serve as adequate means.

Collingwood concludes that in crafts as opposed to arts the form is imposed upon raw materials as a contrivance for changing them into something one desires. He claims that in art the form and matter are so intricately interwoven that they cannot be viably separated in this fashion.[9]

Challenging as Collingwood's argument is, it fails to recognize how dynamic is the relationship between arts and crafts when each exists within a creative context. The household objects made by Picasso through the craft of ceramic jug making, or his craftlike creating of other utensils, resulted from a procedure that is similar to—or at least an extension of—what he did when applying a paint brush to a blank canvas. In these activities the bond between means and ends is not identical, of course. The goal of jug making is to mold a container with a spout that can hold a fluid, while the goal of a painting is the creation of lines and colors that are arresting in themselves though possibly expressing a gamut of feelings and ideas. The latter goal can be modified as the act of production progresses; the former is more circumscribed by some serviceable function that must be accommodated. That is a difference of degree, but not as extreme as assumed by either Collingwood or the techné tradition he wished to supplant.

Moreover, the arts themselves are not all alike in this respect. The art of architecture begins with planning, as in a craft, but culminates with the executing of blueprints that inventively carries out their designs. Such creativity differs from creativity in poetry or music or most other fine arts since these progress more freely in each case, or in a somewhat tentative and probing fashion, until they reach a terminal yet not completely predictable stage of accomplishment. But even in architecture or a craft like carpentry, the plans are often altered in accordance with what happens in enacting the initial intention. This, in fact, is characteristic of all aesthetic creativity. It is something that applies equally to crafts as well as arts.

Contra Both Platonism and Romanticism

Other theorists in the nineteenth and twentieth centuries have sought to undermine the Platonic notion of techné by denying that artistic production is inherently "rational." The denial was reinforced by the Romantic perspective in aesthetics, which thought of the artist as someone who gives vent to his feelings and thereby expresses himself or his unconscious inclinations as thoroughly as a human being can. The approach is inimical to Plato's theory of art as the purposive and mainly cognitive imposition of form upon recalcitrant matter. Plato's critics emphasize the instinctual side of life as more relevant to creativity in aesthetic as well as other pursuits.

The trouble with the Romantic view is its tendency to overlook the degree of rational control and deliberative idealization that is especially prevalent in art. The bird who instinctively builds a nest is not an artist, though it may often do a better job than someone who is. Neither is a child being creatively artistic when he or she stamps in fury or splashes colors blindly. Aesthetic creativity cannot occur until the agent is capable of reflective criticism of the activity in question. It follows that being aesthetically creative entails an inclusive rationality of its own. This means that thinking about the product, throughout the ongoing process of creating it, is pervasively necessary, together with thought in some degree about its presumed completion and likely consequences. When Ruskin denigrated Impressionist painting by saying it is not art but only the result of throwing a can of paint upon the canvas, he was wrong about the aesthetic effect the Impressionists were able to achieve. But he was right about the nature of artistic creativity. Jackson Pollock was creative not because he dripped paint on a canvas but because he devised a way of doing so that imaginatively displayed the chaotic feelings of himself and many others.

In addition to its own type of rationality, aesthetic creation also relies upon feelings and emotions without which reason cannot be an expression of the human spirit. These issue from, and then contribute to, the values that make life worth living for members of our species, specifically the individual artist and whatever audience that can respond creatively to the work of art he or she offers it. The rationality of the artistic process is largely geared to the satisfaction and dissatisfaction that the artist undergoes while being immersed in, or just experimenting with, creative possibilities that are pervasively meaningful. Eventually a decision will be made that there is nothing more to be done. Before that happens, a painter, looking at a color, might say: "No, that doesn't *feel* right." What he or she "feels" is a conscious and evaluative reaction to the color in relation to the painting as a whole, together with a sense of disapproval in this case. Thinking about this and judging it is an act of reasoning.

If we consider rationality in this fashion, we realize how different it is from anything Plato said. Far from fabricating an a priori portrayal of abstractions like the Platonic Forms that serve as ideal models, it involves a dynamic interaction between cognitive and affective dispositions grounded in the artist's experience of the world, which the work registers and transforms without actually copying it in any respect. Each decision and relevant satisfaction or dissatisfaction leads to further exploration, with no precise and definitive idea of where the process will terminate.

The aesthetic activity ends not because of any pre-determined ultimacy that has been miraculously attained but rather because the artist becomes sated, and possibly exhausted, with this particular project, and senses that further alteration may ruin what he has done. He may also feel motivated, for whatever reason, to put his energies into something else that now clamors for attention. Various artists work from a preliminary plan, but in working *from* a plan, an outline or sketch, the artist is always revising it moment by moment. According to Dewey, consecutive revision of this kind can properly be seen as a form of intelligence. Dewey's conception encapsulates his thought about the ends-means continuum, and of values that evolve and are explicable only as part of the biological and social questing that progressively permeates our experience. That sustains our ability to create consummatory goodness through art despite the imperfections in everything we do. Talking about the futility of defining creativity in terms of abstract reason or a prefixed plan of any sort, as contrasted with the pragmatic intelligence of doing and making, Dewey says: "The production of a work of genuine art probably demands more intelligence than does most of the so-called thinking that goes on among those who pride themselves on being 'intellectuals.'"[10]

A theory of aesthetic creativity such as this helps us to free ourselves of both the Platonistic and the Romantic theories. The second of these concentrates on the fact that art is personal and self-expressive; the first underlines its being purposive rather than irrational. By reinterpreting these notions as I have suggested, we clarify how it is that art becomes creative through reasoning that is neither tightly programmed in advance nor random and erratic, but intelligent instead. In seeking to articulate and make explicit some vague idea that may seem to come out of the blue, a creative artist knows that the less effusive and also less regimented his effort becomes, the more it is likely to succeed. Enlightened self-criticism is crucial in that as in other practical situations.

The Platonic philosophy is itself an exquisite work of art predicated upon an imaginative vision about a priori reason. But aesthetic creativity does not require such suppositions. On the contrary, it depends upon the act of *working and living with* the materials at hand, as well as the informed ability to use them in a meaningful search for any possible satisfactions they may evoke, both during and after the acts of imaginative production.

Creativity in Fine and Servile Art

In his approach to questions about aesthetic creativity, George Santayana begins with a Platonistic, or rather Neoplatonistic, belief in art as a form of craft. Santayana is nevertheless more flexible than Plato with regard to the nature of techné. The distinction between "fine art" and "servile art" that Santayana proffers does not limit creativity to either at the expense of the other, nor does it deny that they interweave in fruitful ways. Though both servile art and fine art are infused with elements of craft, Santayana says, the relation is more pronounced in the former than the latter.

Santayana sees servile art as a predominantly instrumental means to some further end. We do not manufacture hammers and saws as delightful objets d'art, he says, or because we think their shape or function is especially aesthetic. Machines can usually produce such utensils better than laborers using some primitive mode of manufacture. On the other hand, fine art is presumed to have a more elevated goal. Servile art prepares brute, and usually refractory, material; fine art employs any suitable matter that will contribute toward ends thought to be ideal harbingers of what human beings value. Unlike servile types of techné, fine art exists for its own sake, and often only for its own sake. It is not necessarily instrumental to anything else. In Santayana's view, the aesthetic creativity that goes into the making of fine art differs to that extent from the creativity that an ordinary workman might hope to attain in turning out a useful tool on his lathe.

To me it seems that even this moderate view is too extreme in separating fine art from the sort that is called servile. For one thing, the ideality that fine art is devoted toward, according to Santayana, needs much clarification in itself. The concept encloses a panoply of ethical and religious interests that remain unspecified and are probably derivative from one or another conventional preference. If we can agree that pursuing a goal "for its own sake" applies to anything that is enjoyable or satisfying, we may well repudiate the traditional belief that certain ideals—in particular, beauty and elevated moral goodness—uniquely characterize fine art. Any enjoyable product would do just as well. But then we can readily conclude that craftlike activities may also be creative in themselves. Though useful in serving some other purpose, as they normally do, this need not prevent them from being thoroughly acceptable as ends of their own sort, and to that extent capable of being valued for what they are in themselves and apart from their utility.

Furthermore, the arts to which the term *fine* is usually attached are not necessarily, or on all occasions, exclusively enjoyable. There are many other reasons why men and women dedicate their lives to creative work in fine arts like painting, music, sculpture, literature, and such. The artists may be hoping to achieve fame and recognition of their latent talents, pursuing financial benefits they cannot find elsewhere, or wishing to display, purge, and even express fully their private feelings, or seeking to support a humanitarian cause, or just hoping to become admired by others. Few of these causal factors that motivate aesthetic creativity are entirely and invariably enjoyable. The routes they prescribe are often not very gratifying. For neurotic artists they can be a trial and tribulation.

Consequently, we may say that both of the types of art in Santayana's distinction—the "fine" and the "servile"—are frequently instrumental as well as sometimes being forms of creative behavior that people enact in their pursuit of one or another consummation. The artful cutting, polishing, or cleaning of otherwise untreated marble, or any other stone, is as aesthetic as carving a profile out of it. We value great sculptors more than great stonecutters because the creativity in the stonecutter's profession exists only as a preliminary to the achievements of sculpture that we prize. But those achievements are themselves valued as the conveyors of imaginative and desired goods that cause the particular art form to exist at all. Objects that may be called servile—chairs that are comfortable but not very pleasing in shape or coloration, shoes that cushion a foot properly but are not handsome in outward design—can manifest creativity in their production that differs greatly from the making of fine arts that serve no comparable function. Chairs or shoes are different from paintings or poems, of course, but that has no bearing on our attempt to explain the nature of aesthetic creativity.

Some Aesthetic Applications

The distinctions proclaimed by Art for Art's Sake theory, as well as the more recent analyses of art as contrasted with craft, usually emanate from related distinctions that are also untenable. If the artist is defined as a person with a pre-dominance of sensuous intuition or imaginative versatility, this is easily taken to suggest a difference from others who are more reflective or more interested in factual truth. But, as writers like Coleridge insisted, imagination is not the same as unbridled and unrealistic "fancy" (fantasizing). To think or act imaginatively, one must be able to apply the possible world of our invention to the ordinary one in which we live day after day. Authentic imagination provides an originality of insights for examining and restructuring our assumptions about the actual world. In being *merely* inventive, fantasizing is incapable of criticizing or controlling its mental output. Far from resembling what is artistic or creative, it is limited at best to virtuosity alone. It can freely invent but not properly contemplate anything with clarity or insight.

Imagination begins when an individual can conceive of more than one frame of reference at a time, and when he or she is able to use either in accordance with a novel apprehension of different possibilities that may elucidate given circumstances. This entails the self-criticism that is a part of intelligence and excludes either insubstantial fantasy or bare sensory intuition. Very young children and many adults are deficient in that respect. Aesthetic creativity, whether in an art or craft, or some intermediary combination of them, depends on intelligence commingled with imagination, the two being then interwoven harmoniously. By itself imagination is not necessarily creative. It degenerates into *mere* fantasy when it is unrelated to some making or doing that develops constructively in a new and fertile direction. The term "creative imagination" refers to that possible achievement.[11]

Seeing the artist as a kind of craftsman who draws upon forces of rational intelligence in conjunction with imagination means we cannot distinguish him or her from moralists, or philosophers, or even prophets, in any sharp and definitive manner. While their pursuits are not the same, they all work at them in practical ways that frequently overlap. Artists need not be political activists. Insights about the nature of things or a relish for the beauties of well-wrought forms can be sufficient for a great many talented people. But a poet or novelist who scans the world from a philosophical or even politically engaged perspective does not thereby relinquish the right to be considered a creative artist. For all its narrative and realistic power, Dostoyevsky's *The Brothers Karamazov* is rightly deemed propaganda about the love for humanity. The aesthetic creativity that nevertheless imbues that work operates in the deepest dimensions of human thought as well as in the more formal and technical aspects of its novelistic medium.

Therefore we cannot infer that great writers, painters, composers, and the rest either should or should not attempt to express in their works moral or ideational or religious attitudes that matter to them. Whichever option they choose, their doing so can enrich their special creativity. On the other hand, they do not have to experience any of the ardent passions and proclivities that Romantic theorists found indispensable. As often happens when theory becomes a heated battleground for opposing beliefs, conflicts about artists being original thinkers or else not thinkers at all are likely to be unhelpful.

The critic F. O. Matthiessen lamented the fact that Henry James never finished two of his last novels (*The Ivory Tower* and *The Sense of the Past*) because James in his closing years threw himself into unremitting activism during World War I. Matthiessen said that almost anyone could have done the war work that James did in that period of his life but that no one else could have finished those final novels as only he might have. This may be true, and surely the absence of endings for these works is unfortunate. But would James have been the creative writer that he sought to be if he had not had the moral sensibility that made him feel a need to counter the miseries of that war with all his strength? It is hard to know how to answer this question since creativity, in the case of James as well as everyone else, may or may not presuppose such motives of morality. A priori, we must remain open to both alternatives.

The same holds for the idea that artistic creativity is the end of life, the highest and most noble goal of our existence as human beings. That outlook, not unrelated to Nietzsche's, is credible, I believe, if by "artistic" we also include all the many different modes of aesthetic creativity that people cherish. As I have been suggesting throughout, this involves a broadening of the concept of art across the spectrum of discernible affect and cognition. How that attempt can possibly be useful in understanding the nature of creativity in science, technology, or mathematics, and in practical decision making as well as ethics and religion, is what we must yet determine. As a step in this direction, I offer in the following chapters some remarks about creative elements such as expression, metaphor, myth, humor, and the coalescence of the prosaic and the absurd.

In conclusion to this chapter, I must point out that most of my discussion has dealt with creativity in the artist and the corresponding creativity in an audience that reacts to his or her production. In an excellent essay entitled "The Act of Creation," Monroe C. Beardsley suggests that the nature of artistic creativity in art is most evident in the manner in which a work of art can be creative *in itself*, by containing original and inventive configurations within its own aesthetic texture: "The important creativity is in the operation of the work itself.... The powers [the artist] works with are, in the end, not his own but those of nature. And the miracle he makes is a miracle that celebrates the creative potentialities inherent in nature itself.... Artistic creation is nothing more than the production of a self-creative object."[12]

The suggestiveness of that insight should always remain with us throughout these explorations. It stands in sharp contrast to Schopenhauer's metaphysics of music as unique among the arts in bypassing the phenomenal world and directly expressing what Kant called the "thing-in-itself." For Schopenhauer that is the Will, or life force, that secretively maneuvers and determines everything that exists. Schopenhauer believed that through its aesthetic abstractness music, only music and apart from any practical use of it, expresses the all-pervading being of the Will.

But Schopenhauer's doctrine bypasses the obvious fact that music is constructed out of sounds, rhythms, variations, and embellishments of what appears within the empirical world. A metaphysical account such as his is egregious to what every music lover recognizes as the beauty and the sonic temporality of both abstract and applied music. Aesthetic creation in that art consists of the imaginative and partly *self-created* organization of selected sounds that have been drawn from, and sometimes represent, the auditory nature in which we all live. Music does differ from other arts, such as architecture, sculpture, and abstract painting, whose creativity does not occur through a comparable preoccupation with time as it passes. But like them, music belongs to the world of concrete human experience and not to any metaphysical realm of being.

Music relies upon a sense of lived duration, beginning with the regularity—and occasionally irregularity—of our body's heartbeats and including the massive momentum and sweeping emotionality of all-engulfing movement, as in some of the symphonies of Mahler or Sibelius. The nonmusical arts resort to other aspects of our existence—the acuity of visual perception, for instance, without which we could not be the creatures that we are. Each art employs and reflects one or another aspect of nature as we live in it, and aesthetic creativity is always a presentation of the magnificence that nature unwittingly bestows upon us through the work some creative artist has wrought for the purpose of consummating that universal resource.

6

Creativity in Expression, Metaphor, Myth

Expression in Art Revisited

I begin this chapter with an account that leads into a gamut of creative modalities. After the devastation Vienna had suffered during World War II, Beethoven's *Fidelio* was chosen to celebrate the reopening of its opera house. *Fidelio* is a work about the triumph of marital love and female heroism over the cruelty of official tyranny. When the singers came out for their curtain calls at the end, a middle-aged woman forced her way onto the stage and wildly pummeled the man who enacted the role of Pizarro, the odious villain in the piece. It was obvious that this character represented to her the evil that had been visited upon the Viennese people, and possibly herself, throughout the Nazi hegemony. One may believe that it was not the hapless singer on whom the woman was venting her fury but rather Pizarro as Beethoven portrayed him in the opera. Though he is a fictional entity, he embodies traits that characterized the murderous rulers who had only recently been evicted. A question that aestheticians ask is: What exactly constitutes the nature of this embodiment?

We may reply that Pizarro expresses the hatefulness of people who use their power to harm others willfully and for corrupt purposes of their own. We might also say that Beethoven's work arouses the anger and indignation that members of most audiences are likely to feel toward such individuals. Despite its being melodramatic fiction rather than explicit history, we experience *Fidelio* as true to the reality to which millions of innocent men, women, and children have been subjected in the modern world. These joint properties— expression or expressiveness, on the one hand, and truthfulness, on the other—are often present in art, and serve as ideal possibilities for many of them. But the nature of this expressiveness and whatever kind of truthfulness a nonfactual makebelieve can have requires further analysis. After examining how various philosophical thinkers have approached this problem, I will suggest that a rarely understood but important type of creativity is enclosed within its resolution.

I discard in advance an answer that I once invoked to elucidate a case history similar to the one with which I began this chapter. Citing the passage in Cervantes' *Don Quijote* where the protagonist pulls out his sword and attacks the moor in a puppet show who is abusing a fair young maid, I said that this signifies that, for whatever reason, Don Quijote is unable to appreciate the nature of a work of art. That explanation, however, is not appropriate for the furious woman at the opera. Violent and egregious as her actions may have been, she waited until the performance ended before making her demonstration against the kind of inhumanity that Pizarro exemplifies. She was not trying to alter the plot, as Don Quijote was in his mad and ludicrous behavior. She was responding, with a modicum of rationality, to what Beethoven had conveyed through the expressiveness embodied in the character of Pizarro.

We have already examined the analysis of expression in art that occurs in Tolstoy's *What Is Art?* I rejected that approach not because it entailed an expression theory of art but rather because the type of communication that Tolstoy described was faulty. He defined both the nature of art and its variable aesthetic excellence in terms of feelings the artist experienced himself and then infused into the work of art with the result that an audience subsequently undergoes them as well.

In John Dewey's book *Art as Experience*, one finds a highly attenuated and more satisfying version of the theory of expression. As a crucial element of his conception of creativity in art, Dewey remarks: "The artist embodies in himself the attitude of the perceiver while he works."[1] Dewey amplifies this by pointing out that the audience's aesthetic perception "involves activities that are comparable to those of the creator. But receptivity is not passivity. It, too, is a process consisting of a series of responsive acts that accumulate toward objective fulfillment. Otherwise there is not perception but recognition. The difference between the two is immense. Recognition is perception arrested before it has a chance to develop freely."[2] This leads into Dewey's nuanced statement about the Tolstoyan version of any possible communication theory: "I can but think that much of what Tolstoi says about immediate contagion as a test of artistic quality is false. . . . Those who are [nevertheless] moved feel, as Tolstoi says, that what the work expresses is as if it were something one had oneself been longing to express. Meantime, the artist works to create an audience to which he does communicate."[3]

Dewey clearly believes that the audience a successful artist reaches, and in that sense creates, is one that creatively responds to the creative object, which thereby serves as the essential link to the creativity of the artist. Many other critics of Tolstoy have pointed out that artists normally work under conditions that are quite different from the romanticized stereotype Tolstoy describes. In agreeing with them, I have wanted to emphasize that the artist's feelings are almost always muted and completely altered by whatever creative process he or she employs in making the artistic object.

My previous remarks warrant further amplification in this place. Though Beethoven's volatile feelings of anger, disgust, and frustrated tenderness surely play an expressive part in much of the music he wrote, his artistic creativity is more than just a premeditated transmittal to other people of what he may have felt at any moment of his life. Instead it is a transformation of his feelings, and his ideas, within the formal and material structure that individually pervades one or another musical composition. The actual moods and affective responses of Beethoven are not "handed on" to some imagined audience but rather reconstructed, as opposed to being purveyed through an attempt to copy what he himself experienced.

To say that *Fidelio* expresses Beethoven's political sentiments, his ardent beliefs about freedom and brotherhood, his outraged feelings about the abuse of power by cruel and callous officials, is also correct. It is likewise appropriate to hear his Pastoral Symphony as an expression of the joyfulness and, in his case, mystical sense of oneness with nature that he may have experienced on some day in the spring. But these sensations or emotions, and even the birdcalls and the thunderstorm in that symphony, which he renders in his own fashion, are not affective entities or events that he packages in a sonic equivalent designed to elicit the same feelings in his listeners. The programmed effects are instead raw data that his art creatively draws upon for an expressiveness that uses them like blips of electricity that energize the brain. The outcome in both instances will never be identical.

In Beethoven's more abstract music, the feelings are so greatly modified that we cannot precisely associate them with something else that either we or the composer may have lived through. Can anyone give a name or detailed paraphrase for what is expressed in the unmatchable music of his last quartets? They are often said to be very "spiritual," but that is only an admission of defeat. There is no use of language that can equal or truly comprehend their supreme expressiveness. Certainly they do not function in the manner that Tolstoy's kind of theory imagines.

How then should we explain the creativity in artistic expression? Theorists who criticize the Tolstoyan model usually accept the idea that art can express human feelings, but they then deny that there need be any particular reference to psychological events that occur in the artist's experience. They insist that happy or sad or even troubled as the music may be in itself, there is nothing further, nothing beyond it, that the art form can truly express. In his lectures on the poetics of music, Stravinsky asserts that music cannot express anything but itself. If it does express something, he says, it merely expresses its own musical being.

In other places, Stravinsky modifies this idea a bit, and in his musical notation he freely inserts the traditional instructions about passages that are to be played with expression, *espressivo*. But whatever Stravinsky or some other composer tells the instrumentalists about feelings they should introduce at any point, they all know that the nuances of affect and personal involvement the players supply can only be their own conception of what the composer intended. In that sense the feelings that an audience directly responds to originate in the *performing* of the music. Far from communicating what the composer has felt, his written score is the projection of interpretative, cognitive possibilities that will finally create the expressiveness in one or another performance.

Even if we know nothing about the programmatic context of the slow music in Beethoven's Third Symphony, to revert to that, it is entirely appropriate to say that it is sad. There is no illusion or anthropomorphism in describing it as such. The terminology is metaphoric, of course, since the somber pace and absence of ebullience or rapid movement do not exist in the music as they do in people who are feeling grief. If we go on to say that Beethoven's dirge is not only sad but also an expression of sadness, that only means that, over and above the sounds we hear and the formal patterns to which they belong, this score suggests or noniconically refers to the *state* of being sad that bereaved people might undergo in the advent of a hero's death, and in many comparable circumstances. Here too the extended meaningfulness in that is metaphoric.

Beethoven's creativity consists in harmoniously interweaving the two types of metaphor—the one that enables us to assert that this music is sad and the other that conveys the sense that it is an expression of sadness in general. Without such creative transformations, works of art would not have the expressiveness for which they have always been highly valued. Schooled and sensitive audiences are those that know how to appreciate this aspect of the artistic process. In responding to the creativity of the composer as they do, listeners become creative themselves. They are not just submissive receptors of what the artist is communicating to them.

In the Tolstoyan account, art enlivens an audience by allowing it to share feelings of the artist in a manner to which only his intimate associates otherwise could have had access. Even if that were true, it ignores what the members of the audience bring to the relationship. They have to be aware of what the music is, as whatever kind of music it may be and as a special type of creation that employs its ingredient materials and form. But also they must be capable of making a creative leap that is requisite for apprehending the creativity of whatever expressiveness there is in this aesthetic object. Insofar as everything metaphoric is creative, as I will argue in this chapter, that fact alone reveals the creativity in perceiving sadness or other feelings in a work of art. To see, or hear, or read it as an expression of relevant affect, one must acquire in oneself a supplemental mode of creativity whose reactions are appropriate to what is being creatively presented.

Expression as Different from Representation

Thus far I have been using the terms *expression* and *expressiveness* as if they were virtually interchangeable. It will therefore be helpful to consider a philosophy of art in which the two are sharply separated. In *The Sense of Beauty*, the book on aesthetics that Santayana wrote toward the beginning of his career, he distinguishes between the form and materials of a work of art and its ability to use them as a means of saying or depicting something about the world. The latter he calls the expressiveness of art, and under that heading he lists representation and expression as different components.

In its representational capacity the aesthetic object, as Santayana conceives of it, is a conjunction of formal and material properties that refers beyond itself to realities that either exist or possibly could do so apart from the artwork. In contrast, Santayana thinks of expression as involving another kind of meaning. It entails a reflexivity in the overall expressiveness that "objectifies" the referential thrust by merging or incorporating its content with the form and matter that belong to an aesthetic object in itself. Instead of being merely representational, and so distinct in principle from whatever it refers to, the artwork attains its expressive meaning, he says, by displaying how its referential capacity not only emanates out of the formal and material properties but also fuses with them. Santayana calls this an act of "objectification" and a type of expressiveness that is different from representation alone.

In providing this analysis, Santayana understands that imagination is needed for the objectification to occur, and throughout his masterful writings as a philosophical critic of literature and the arts, he gives innumerable illustrations of what his theory implies. But he scarcely tells us how it is possible for imagination to merge what is present in our perception of the aesthetic object with something outside to which the work refers. We can accept the idea that imagination is needed for any representation to occur at all, but Santayana does not explain how imagination may possibly amalgamate the generative form and materials with something that is being expressed. He does remark that the expressiveness of art is inherently pleasurable, the aesthetic as a whole being positively hedonic by definition, and he also affirms that through expression proper we experience a relevant pleasure afforded by the forms and materials of the artwork. In my opinion, that does not solve the problem. It simply compounds the obscurity of Santayana's concept of objectification.

Consequently, I do not see how the expression of sadness, in the Beethoven movement to which I alluded, is clarified by Santayana's theory. The sadness reaches us through the sonic forms and materials in this music, and therefore one might say, though dubiously, that they embody it. Still, we need to know what it might mean to assert that the expression of sadness, or of the pleasure people get in listening to this presentation, can result from some kind of fusion with what we hear.

As a possible response to such questioning, I suggest that the situation Santayana has in mind can be explained more simply as referential content being relevant to the artwork's form and matter while also being creative in its imaginative and transformational use of them. To make sense of that condensed statement, however, I need to insert at this point some elementary analysis in aesthetics. As I have said, most philosophers of art divide their subject matter into three categories—the creative process, the work of art, and an audience's experience of the work of art. The first deals with issues about the artist's involvement, the second explores the nature of what he or she has brought into being, and the third probes the effect of any such production upon appropriate audiences and their reaction to it. I have been arguing that creativity pertains to all three of these categories, not only the artistic process as many others assume, and therefore that a solution of the expression problem must demonstrate how their different modes of creativity are systematically and harmoniously united to each other.

If that perspective is acceptable, we can now suggest not only that an artist is a person who creatively produces something that others enjoy and commend, but also that the artistic process through which this happens includes the artist's awareness of what he or she will even consider as a creative work of art. This, in turn, can lead us to envisage a creative audience as one that has an experience that is largely based on the creativity of whatever product the artist has made available to the audience. The concept of relevance that I mentioned earlier as a substitute for Santayana's notion of objectification presupposes that creative bond as native to art. The occurrence of expression that is more than just perception of the beauty or pleasurability in the form and materials depends upon this interwoven kind of creativity within the three categories.

Expression without Representation

Expression can be so important in art that it often exists without any overt representation. Even the sadness in the Beethoven funeral march, or the joyfulness in the village band motif that prepares us for the Ode to Joy in the Ninth Symphony, is not representational in the explicit manner that the birdcalls are in his Sixth Symphony. The latter work, being programmatic, is rightly designated as "pastoral." The two former examples are not programmatic at all. We speak of the sequence in the Third Symphony as a funeral march because its expression of sadness is reminiscent of how people feel when they march at a funeral, not because it is portraying that event. Similarly, the bit of happy music, and the orchestration that conveys its cheerfulness in the Ninth Symphony, calls to mind something a village band might play without depicting or otherwise representing anything more about it.

Since so much of nonrepresentational painting and sculpture of the last hundred years expresses feelings and visual ideas through pure or partial abstraction, we have many examples of those arts from which to choose. I am especially fond of a statement that Piet Mondrian made about the referential meaning in some of his most famous works: "Impressed by the vastness of nature, I was trying to express its expansion, rest, and unity. At the same time, I was fully aware that the visible expansion of nature is at the same time its limitation; vertical and horizontal lines are the expression of two opposing forces; these exist everywhere and dominate everything; their reciprocal action constitutes 'life.'"[4]

It would be a mistake, I believe, to interpret this manifesto as an afterthought on Mondrian's part. I take it to reflect an aspect of his ongoing creativity that entered into his experience as a painter and that can be understood only through an act of related, but not identical, creativity that one must have in order to respond correctly to it. The aesthetic quality of Mondrian's art is not explicable solely in terms of the beauty of the color, the alluring pattern of the lines and figures, or anything that could be represented by them. In addition, one has to know how to see what is expressed *through* the abstract design. That is a creative feat that art lovers have acquired in modern times to a greater degree than ever before.

Those that do acquire it may then occasionally see the expressive artwork as itself being representational at times. This is a complicated idea, but I can elucidate it by relating an experience of my own. When I was in a plane to Amsterdam once, I noticed, as it was descending to make a landing, that the landscape below looked just like an enormous Mondrian abstraction. The terrain was criss-crossed in more or less straight lines that were horizontal, vertical, and often parallel. I assumed they were canals and ditches that the Dutch had dug this close to the North Sea. They existed as something in the real world, etched in nature for wholly practical purposes. They obviously were not a representation or expression of other realities, and I have no reason to believe that Mondrian had ever seen them from the air as I did. But since I was familiar with his paintings, I could imagine how in their being as works of art they too might be taken as represented or expressed by a comparable pattern on the ground. Incidentally, when I pointed out the scene below to a stranger who was sitting next to me, he didn't seem to know what I was talking about. But after I repeated the word *Mondrian*, he looked again and said: "Oh yes, Piet Mondrian."

The idiosyncratic effect to which I referred is parodied by Oscar Wilde in his wonderfully comic essay about nature's imitation of art. Having been coaxed into watching what was described to him as a glorious evening sky, Wilde's spokesman laments: "It was simply a very second-rate Turner, a Turner of a bad period, with all the painter's worst faults exaggerated and over-emphasized."[5]

Art as Based on Expression

Within the category of expressiveness, it is sheer expression that identifies an object as a work of art. Representation alone has no such capacity. A photographic snapshot of a house represents that building as something that might have and once did exist in the world. The photograph may also represent an individual house at the corner of some street, and we may even have lived in that house or known it very well. In itself, none of this lends an aesthetic aura to the picture, though such information can be pertinent to its artistic quality. If, however, the house as portrayed can creatively express a sense of Southern stateliness or Victorian opulence or Colonial simplicity, the photograph in itself becomes an aesthetic artifact. Uninspired as the paintings of Edward Hopper may seem to be, their merit as art largely derives from the expression of loneliness and sometimes soulless desperation that they emit through their expressive presentation of the brute actualities they portray.

If we ask whose loneliness or desperation is being shown in Hopper's paintings, we have to admit that we do not know. They could be what the artist felt himself, or possibly the people (none of whom are on view) who live in the gloomy houses on the abandoned streets, or more obviously the men who are lunging at each other with arms that are too long in the prizefight pictures. But this vagueness of representational content does not deter from whatever it is that the works express. The greatness of Edvard Munch's series entitled *The Scream* is not diminished by the anguished woman having only the caricature of a face and, except for the suggestion of a bridge that she is on, the background having no identifiable location. In each case the creativity of the artist consists in his use of the right forms and materials that can cause an observer who is responsively creative in looking at paintings to appreciate the expressive impact of these works.

As a more startling example of what I mean, we need only consider some of the middle and late achievements of Picasso. They offer themselves as portraits of women, most often, whose features are so displaced and contorted as to have little resemblance to what any person looks like. If Picasso had been trying to represent the facial beauty or ugliness of real human beings, he could not have put their eyes on the same side of the nose or drawn the outlines of their cheeks in the sharp angles that cubists favored at the time. But in these paintings Picasso was not interested in representing the appearance of anyone's face. He was instead making abstractions based on only minimal amounts of representation, enough to suggest a generic portrayal whose scarcity of recognizable details enables an artist to bestow upon these fictional females the lines and forms and colorations that express feelings one might have toward them or toward the world at large. The creativity of these paintings stems from the primacy of their inspired expressivity. The aesthetic excellence issues from the creative power with which ordinary representation of some object has been transformed for the sake of increasing a personal and more assertive expression that mattered to the artist.

Creative Metaphor

As another approach to the same idea, we can say that all art is capable of being metaphoric in one respect or other. Creative expression in paintings renders them into visual metaphors on a par with the sonic metaphors that exist in music or the linguistic metaphors in poetry and other forms of literature. In fact the live metaphors in ordinary language as a whole change the prosaic character of purely representational discourse into a rich and expansive art form through which almost everyone can communicate. The fact that much of it is vulgar or plebeian is immaterial. A good illustration of that is the street slang and nongrammatical talk of uneducated but definitely talented people. Though we may think of them as inchoate poets of colloquial speech, they successfully manage, at their best, to use expressive metaphors that stodgy academic language cannot equal.

In all its modalities, metaphor is a creative form of expressive transformation that exceeds representational communication by providing what it is incapable of articulating adequately in itself. For some logicians and analytic philosophers that is a demerit of metaphor, not an advantage. The entire program of logical positivism in the first half of the twentieth century, and in more recent versions, stems from the belief that ordinary language is irremediably corrupted by metaphors that keep it from yielding a precise and literal representation of reality. In supplanting metaphoric language with the artificial but more accurate terminology of symbolic logic, these philosophers thought they might satisfy the needs of science more or less as mathematics does. Aesthetically barren though the outcome might be, this would happen because the expressive character of vague and quasi-poetic language will have been totally expunged.

The fallacy in this perspective underlies the assumption that science itself is in principle nonmetaphoric. I will return to that issue in chapter 9. Here I want to note that if the positivist program reached fruition, it would have lost any relevance to the life of men and women like ourselves. By shrinking our experience of the world in a rigorous but reductive manner, not only expressive discourse but also the aesthetic itself becomes invalid. Animate beings whose communication was thereby limited to representation alone would be akin to mechanical robots. Yet even though our existence depends upon materiality similar to what exists in these creatures of artificial intelligence, I see no justification for denying the importance of the aesthetic in organisms of the sort that we are. Like the nonaesthetic, the transformational aesthetic use of our live metaphors also arises out of matter, but in a way that does not apply to purely robotic devices.

In speaking just now of live metaphors, I meant to contrast them with the dead or overused metaphors that fill our daily speech. When the nurse in *South Pacific* says and sings that she is going to "wash that man right outa my hair," her washing metaphor is alive and kicking (a live metaphor itself). If, however, she had spoken of kicking the man out of her house, that utterance is so commonplace and familiar that we might not recognize it as a live metaphor. When we refer to the leg of a table or to a person's good heart—to choose two of the innumerable other dead or dying metaphors, the latter phrase being itself one that is half alive and half dead—our utterance has lost much of the expressive and creative import that it may have once had. Experts who chart the taxonomy of metaphoric verbal communication are archeologists of the linguistic talents that people have acquired but often lost throughout the ages, in all languages, and in the sciences as well as the arts.

Everyone who meaningfully uses a graphic phrase or gesture of any kind resembles to some extent the artist whose mode of creativity is laden with lively metaphorical expressiveness. In everyday experience we may not give thought to this imaginative gift we bestow upon one another, but its availability is virtually universal in our species, and in other species as well despite their not having what we might call a language. In Molière's play *Le Bourgeois Gentilhomme* the social-climbing protagonist studies French grammar and is astonished to learn that it is what he has been talking all along without realizing that he did so. We who laugh at his discovery may be surprised to think that just by casually speaking our native tongue we exemplify, in part, the creativity of poets and other artists. Yet we do.

Creativity in Mythmaking

A parallel situation may exist among scientists who staunchly wish to escape from mythological explanations of the world, instead of which they try to understand it in its pristine reality uncorrupted by ideas they consider false because they are fictional. They must nevertheless confront the fact that their own professional theories are also shot through with mythic as well as metaphoric formulations. By its very nature, our language, in all its uses, manifests and usually relies upon such phenomena. Myth and metaphor belong to a special category of imagination that directly provides creative possibilities entertained by their wide-ranging outlook. The fundamental structure of that aptitude therefore requires a type of analysis uniquely appropriate to myth as well as metaphor.

Since each of them is often linguistic, philosophers have traditionally believed they belong to various tropes within habitual language. In Aristotle's *Poetics* he defines metaphor as the transferring of a word's meaning from its "proper sense" to another, as "either from genus to species, or from species to genus, or from species to species, or by analogy."[6] In recent years some thinkers have rejected the idea that metaphor must be treated merely as a form of language. Instead, they suggest that it is a primary mode of thought and only secondarily linguistic.[7] Myth differs from metaphor insofar as it is inherently linguistic, although more than that as well.

Myth invokes a narrative that generally expresses a large-scale view of the world and a cluster of basic problems or dilemmas experienced by a great many human beings, perhaps even all of them. The universal appeal of myths, and their pervasiveness throughout the history of virtually every society of homo sapiens, results from two of their ingredients. First, myths delve into feelings and attitudes about our mere existence in a way that other devices can hardly approximate. Second, their use of narrational forms of presentation makes them largely inventive. Myths are fictions of a typically probing sort that philosophy itself usually seeks to avoid as inimical to its adherence to unsullied rationality.

The myths in Plato's dialogues do play a part in establishing the persuasiveness of his comprehensive metaphysics. But it is obvious, especially to modern readers, that Plato includes those fanciful depictions—for instance, his story in *The Republic* about the soul choosing its path in life before it is born—as a sop to the irrationality of unbridled imagination, which may help laymen appreciate the much greater grandeur of the adventurous reasoning in his philosophy. We easily tolerate this maneuver because we recognize that a segment of imagination, which I call "the imaginary," yields meaningful references to *impossibilities* as well as possibilities of different kinds.[8]

All fictionality entails the imaginative as such, but mythmaking does so supremely. In beguiling us with its magnified type of make-believe, it precludes any fear or anxiety that we might have in reading about unborn souls, or all-powerful gods who somehow resemble human beings, or heroes as well as divinities whose great fallibility does not prevent them from enjoying an enviable existence that we ourselves cannot attain.

Just in being fictional, the narratives in every mythology employ metaphorical language beyond any literal communication. Since metaphor permeates so much of our discourse and social life, practical or routine as well as artistic and often elevated, mythic tales resort to quasi-historical accounts that seem quite fabulous in their telling. They are indeed fables that excite and delight their audience by an imaginative ability to depart from pragmatic language that is useful for biological survival and well-being. As a result, the creativity in myth-making inherently shares a common goal with linguistic creativity that is metaphoric. We cannot understand either without keeping in mind the connection between them.

Mythos and Logos

Specialists in mythology often make a distinction between mythos and logos. As Karen Armstrong says in a recent book, logos offers a rational view of the world, as in science or history, rather than the storytelling and unverifiable expressions of faith that mythos provides and that have flourished in earlier centuries of human civilization as well as in the life of people everywhere. Armstrong describes mythos as "rooted in the experience of death and the fear of extinction"; as "usually inseparable from ritual"; as "about the unknown; it is about that for which initially we have no words"; as about "the correct spiritual or psychological posture for right action, in this world or the next"; and as attuned to "another plane that exists alongside our own world." This other plane serves as a "counterpart in the divine realm, which is richer, stronger, and more enduring than our own."[9]

As opposed to mythos thus conceived, logos is thought to incorporate the views and attitudes that have developed in modern times as mainly congruent with the principles as well as methodology of science and its employment of inductive and deductive logic, of empirical observation, and of the verifiable knowledge that is thereby attained. Like many others, Armstrong laments the decline of mythos in our age, which she ascribes to the mounting attacks of the logos that has systematically condemned it.

There are significant difficulties in this argument as it is enunciated by Armstrong, Joseph Campbell, Mircea Eliade, and other equally eminent mythologists. In relying upon the distinction between mythos and logos, they are mistaken in crucial details and normally ignore the extent to which the two overlap. From her characterization of myth as discourse concerned with an unknown for which we have no words in our ordinary language, Armstrong infers that this unknown is the "divine" realm, richer and stronger than the one we inhabit while also being supportive of our lesser condition. That description is true of religious myths, as in the Gospels or the five books of Moses, but inaccurate with respect to hero myths as well as the myths that imaginatively glorify the universal pursuit of ideals—one of which is heightened imagination and unmatchable creativity. Though sometimes without having articulate conceptualization, many people cherish and order their lives in accordance with myths of the nonreligious sort. In the myth of Don Juan or Tristan and Iseult or Orpheus and Eurydice, not to mention various others, traditional religion may play a part but very often it is only a meager one.

Those myths are not about living a life of "transcendence," as Armstrong calls it, meaning something that propels us into a mystical world beyond our own. When Tristan and Iseult eventually die because the love potion they drank was both magical and fatal, they are indeed raised into a superior level of being in some versions of the myth, but usually they are not. What matters more in this myth is the fact that their adulterous sexuality was not sanctioned by society although it remained throughout a fulfillment of their natural desires as a man and a woman. This conflict between social and personal ideals lies at the heart of the mythic tale and explains why people have been profoundly moved by it.

Likewise, in Mozart's opera, when Don Juan gets dragged down to hell at the end, an event exceeding any possible punishment that could be meted out to him on earth, it mainly signifies the enormity of his moral turpitude. Transcendence is not part of the story. In the case of Orpheus, the hero travels to Hades not as a means of eluding the imperfections of this world, but instead to bring back to earth the wife he loved but failed to appreciate sufficiently when she lived with him.

These examples, each a counterinstance to the standard interpretation of myth as transcendence, are especially note-worthy because they are still meaningful and operative in our contemporary world. Though they originated in eras that preceded our current age of scientific logos, they endure for us, and even achieve new aesthetic transformations because of technology that never existed before. Film, which is scarcely more than a hundred years old, is a principal means of disseminating, and so preserving, both classical and modern myths. Though the heroic quest into some unknown region, or dimension, of the cosmos frequently occurs in science fiction movies, it is normally attired in mythic garb that manifests the actual or possible achievements of logos. In the fashion of all the great myths, science and technology—whose astounding wonders never cease—are thereby glorified. Some kind of transcendence may also belong to these modern mythologies, but most frequently it appears as a hazy and futuristic goal for logos to attain sooner or later. Even in the cosmological myths that still intrigue us, the idea of a traditional deity who is outside time and space has lost much of its appeal.

In claiming that modern Western culture has mainly repudiated mythology in toto, Armstrong cites the repugnance that eighteenth-century scientists like Isaac Newton felt toward mystical dogmas within the Christian faith, which they sought to defend on only rational grounds. She interprets this attempt as an incursion of logos upon the domain of mythos even in a religious context. On the other hand, she ends her account with laudatory statements about literature and the other arts that may have little or no dependence on religion but are nevertheless able to equal its mythic view of the human situation. Without their being liturgical or set apart from life, she says, they too can reveal how "it must be experienced as part of a process of personal transformation."[10] As her conclusion, Armstrong asserts: "If professional religious leaders cannot instruct us in mythical lore, our artists and creative writers can perhaps step into this priestly role and bring fresh insight to our lost and damaged world."[11]

I think there is more to be said, not only about the differences between logos and mythos but also about their interrelation. In the advanced state of our contemporary sophistication, we recognize the importance of this; and yet we tend to forget that the creativity of the two poles has always resulted from the strength of their underlying bond. When

Bishop Gregory of Nyssa argued in the fourth century that Trinitarian beliefs reflect the human search for oneness with God and cannot be established by any form of reasoning, he nonetheless assumed that the quest was itself grounded in the reality that logos presupposes. Though contemporary scientists are often adherents to an alternate and contrasting faith in their methodology, they too may be engaged in a mythic and even quasi-religious search for "the knowledge of everything," which is to say, objective reality as a whole.

In the humanistic myths of love, particularly the ones I have mentioned, though religious faith may only have lesser importance, it too plays a role in their mythic outlook. It provides an ontological framework, which logos also seeks and most people crave, that yields a type of mythological grounding, minimal and basically secular as it may be. The greatest literary version of the Tristan myth, written by Gottfried von Strasbourg in the fourteenth century, is completely naturalistic and sometimes scornful of references to either a miraculous love potion or a divinity of any orthodox sort, but sometimes it too employs religious terms that suggest the holiness of true love in its struggle with invidious attitudes that finally destroy it.

While the split between logos and mythos has greatly widened in our times, even as tentative a plea for their reconciliation as the one that Armstrong makes is somewhat misleading. Among the art forms to which she turns for the needed harmonization, she fails to recognize not only the vast achievement of film in combining the two poles, but also its offspring in the media arts that have issued from the computer's use of the moving image. Through their enormous ability to be both realistic and magical beyond the parameters of reason alone, these aesthetic creations effect a transformation of the ordinary world that empowers our burgeoning imagination to make our existence in it worth living. Through their own form of storytelling, their creative narratives graphically enrich whatever conceptions of reality we might have independently.

In science fiction movies the mythic sense imbues the portrayal of material factuality as a whole. The entranced spectators are left with a feeling that the apparently meaningless universe assiduously studied by science, and recombined by technology, may contain a hidden but essential meaningfulness that belongs to the grandeur of logos as well as mythos.

Cinematic mythmaking is a harmonizing endeavor that augments all attempts to surmount the frequent disharmony between reason and imagination, quasi-scientific investigation and mythology, and the cognitive and affective dimensions of our being. Film and its related art forms are inventions that most extensively promise a creative culmination of earlier efforts to overcome these divisions.[12] By their very nature, cinema and its electronic progeny resemble and possibly constitute a universal faith in which billions of people throughout the world may participate as co-religionists in the future that lies ahead. By means of these unique expressions of the aesthetic and the useful, we jointly cultivate our deepest feelings and furthest searchings, both artistic and scientific. Our salvation lies in that ongoing creativity.

7

The Prosaic and the Absurd in Their Creative Context

Prosaic Elements in Creativity

As I have remarked, Nietzsche thought that life itself can possibly be made into a creative work of art. But does this mean that mechanical and even boring parts of it will somehow become creative like the more aesthetic moments we may aspire toward? A suggestion of this kind seems to me wildly fanciful, and a latter-day reflection of nineteenth-century romanticism at its worst. For one thing, it misconstrues the repetitious necessities of daily life and the less than ideal intervals that exist in even the most successful works of art. It precludes a true acceptance of what these prosaic realities are, and how they function in aesthetic as well as nonaesthetic productions.

Mozart's compositions often include passages and techniques that are mainly transitional to the bright and beautiful developments that follow on their own. Moreover, his creative mind was so quick, and so eager to get beyond almost any musical idea it may have entertained, that not infrequently he shifts suddenly to something different that often shapes the total content of his works. At the same time, he realized the value of having those layers of sonic mortar, which are also verbal in the arias, that make their needed contribution to the harmonic patterns he constructs. In the hands of a master, in life and in art, even the pedestrian and uninspired can play a part in the creativity of the whole.

Maria Callas complained that her Verdi arias were accompanied by commonplace music that was all ta ta dumpt, ta ta dumpt, ta ta dumpt. She didn't realize that it was Verdi's way of unobtrusively supporting and highlighting the magnificent and highly expressive sounds that he had written to be sung by a prima donna like Callas, who could deliver them as only she might. Callas's remark is a little like a ballerina lamenting that in her greatest dances her male partner often has little to do but keep her from falling or wandering beyond her appointed spot while she twirls her bravura steps. To slightly modify the famous line of John Milton: They also serve aesthetically who only stand and wait as components in the artistic gestalt.

In one of his remarks on the nature of creativity, William James opined that habit is the greatest enemy of it. He was assuming that what is habitual is necessarily contrary to the spontaneity and originality that is essential for someone to be creative. In his usual predilection for whatever is vivid and life-enhancing, however, James thereby minimized the occasions on which habits can often be intrinsically creative. Repudiating them all as he does, he ignores the ones that routinely enable creative persons to be creative. That is what Thomas Edison was referring to when he said that genius consists in affixing the seat of the pants to the seat of the chair, and when he and many others affirmed that creative achievement results from 99 percent perspiration and only 1 percent inspiration.

Creative habits such as organizing one's tools in the same way each time, in preparation for the coming occasions when they will be put to productive use, are related to the persistence and determination that Edison extolled. The same is true of the repeated tropes of behavior that many creative persons habitually resort to when they wish to do their best: the baseball pitcher who finds encouragement by touching the tip of his cap before he throws the ball across the plate; or the orchestra conductor who invariably kisses the cuff links that a mentor, deceased many years earlier, gave him when he was a tutee of his; or the author whose writing can occur only if he satisfies a habit of drinking tea or coffee, or whatever, even though he knows such former stimulants no longer have any effect on him. We may call these acts superstitious, but they persist because they have a role in some individual's creative activity.

With these emendations, the Nietzschean dictum is somewhat cleansed of its abstract aeriness. And, once we appreciate the essential utility of the minor components of some outstanding achievement, we can get a more accurate conception of the creativity that may emerge from them. As Nancy C. Andreasen argues in her book *The Creating Brain*, though such "ordinary creativity" differs from "extraordinary creativity," it equally exemplifies the creative.[1] To show this, it will be helpful to return to the panoramic notion of bisociation that Koestler elaborates in *The Act of Creation* and his other writings.

Koestler considers bisociation a principle that underlies all the aspects of creativity that he studies. Having defined creativity as the "bisociation of unrelated matrices," he argues that creative acts yoke together different and contrasting perspectives, concepts, theories, feelings, or attitudes that we usually keep apart, even sharply distinct from each other. In his resourceful investigation, Koestler finds the most obvious examples of such bisociation in humor. That seems like a valid starting point, particularly in relation to the type of humor—possibly the most imaginative type—that resides in the hilarity of what seems utterly absurd.

The Absurd as Creative

As a form of humor, the absurd is a noteworthy, though extreme, variety of comedy. When the absurd is creative, we laugh at its theatrical or literary presentations because they reflect some of our deepest but most unsettling feelings about the world. They address and help us to cope with the bizarre and unfathomable nature of our existence. By juxtaposing the absurd and the prosaic, I suggest, we can penetrate to a recurrent characteristic in creativity as we all experience it. The analysis of this intersection of different matrixes can equally elucidate the creativity in drama as well as comedy.

"The Myth of Sisyphus," the essay by Albert Camus to which I referred earlier, provides intriguing insights into the dialectical relation between the prosaic and the absurd. Camus focuses mainly on tragedy as a heroic transcendence of the suffering in life. But his reflections also end with an image of happiness that Sisyphus might experience as the culmination of his task of pushing a rock up a mountain and forever having to renew this hopeless labor each time the boulder rolls down again. Camus depicts Sisyphus at last overcoming his fate through his consciousness of being what he is *because of* the absurdity in what he must do. "The struggle itself toward the heights is enough to fill a man's heart. One must imagine Sisyphus happy."[2]

This is an extravagant conclusion, fraught with a variety of difficulties. What I mainly derive from Camus' interpretation is the contrast between the prosaic character of the effort to which Sisyphus is condemned, on the one hand, and its evident absurdity as well as the absurdity of his attaining happiness under these conditions of hateful and futile servility, on the other. I am not concerned at present about the meaning of whatever authenticity and even freedom he may reach in surmounting the fate that has been imposed upon him. What strikes me more forcefully is his ability to accept the pointless action as that which defines not only his punishment but also his (and our) entire being. In itself his response proffers an absurd, though felicitous, solution that could not have been expected ordinarily. It discloses a vein of dark comedy in Camus' account that turns the tragedy of the myth into a mode of uplifting affirmation. Through its dialectical interaction with the prosaic need to do agonizing work, the absurdity of Sisyphus winning out against the gods provides a major clue to creativity as it functions in comedy and drama of every sort, unlike each other as these may be.

We laugh or smile or inwardly enjoy gestures and linguistic phrases that lead our imagination to explore conflicting and often inconsistent possibilities. The gamut that runs from facile puns to metaphysical wit frequently consists of varied confrontations between the prosaic and the absurd. I choose a few illustrations at random. When Bertrand Russell inherited the title Lord Russell, he learned that there was already a peer named Lord Russell. After their correspondence kept being delivered to the wrong person, they entered a joint notice in the *London Times* that informed any interested parties that "neither of us is the other one." We burst into laughter because the prosaic statement in this case is presented under the guise of a logical tautology for which we were not prepared. The independence of the two linguistic matrixes is thereby absurdly violated.

Compare this with the familiar story of the man who tells a friend that he is worried about a brother of his who thinks he is a chicken. "He must be crazy," the friend exclaims, "and you must take him to a psychiatrist right away." To which the man replies: "I've thought of that but our family needs the eggs." We laugh because the confluence of prosaic and absurd suddenly makes us wonder who is really the crazy one.

As another example of clashing matrixes, consider the joke about a man who orders a bowl of soup in a restaurant but is shocked to find a fly in it. The waiter he calls over carefully examines the bowl and then cheerfully confirms the customer's observation: "Yes, I see him. But how much can he eat?"

These stories are, of course, fictional, predicated upon what I call "the imaginary." But others, however, that are presumably based on actual events and true to life can make us laugh as well. When Zelda Fitzgerald, the wife of the author F. Scott Fitzgerald, voluntarily entered a mental hospital, she was accompanied by her husband on her trip there. They were together when she had her preliminary conversation with a psychiatrist, and they both provided information about the marital torment that each of them had lived through. The psychiatrist brought to the meeting a secretary, who sat quietly and took notes. At the end of the conversation, he turned to her and said: "Well, whom do you think we should hospitalize?" She is reported to have replied (creatively): "All three of you!" As in the chicken joke, we laugh or smile because the ending is amusing and has caught us off guard. We are scarcely deterred by the fact that in this case the punch line is not really absurd and that the account is probably more or less accurate.

In Orson Welles's film *The Trial*, the intrusive inspectors at the beginning ask K about an object in his room. Flustered by their sudden assault upon him, he says: "That's my pornograph." Though designed as such by the filmmaker, it is an unintentioned pun upon the word that denotes the commonplace and nonsexual machine for playing records. It would be absurd to think of it as an instrument of pornography. Yet K's slip of the tongue reveals to us that, submerged in his character, there lurks a feeling that he must be guilty of some immorality or other that the inspectors are trying to ferret out. When the sexual overtones are accentuated by their finding an oval patch in the floor, which they call "ovular," K insists there is no such word. But though he is right to point out the difference between a haphazard shape in his apartment and a woman's reproductive organs, we laugh at this verbal byplay that creatively highlights forbidden sexual overtones we might not otherwise have thought about. In its combination with the absurdity of what K and then the inspectors utter, the prosaic exchange introduces a bit of comedy into the somber situation.

At the opposite extreme there comes to mind something that Freud includes in his book about the psychology of jokes. He mentions a placard he once saw in the Jewish ghetto that advertised an undertaker's sale of coffins. In large letters it reads: "Prices slashed! Never lower! WHY WAIT?" We would not have laughed if someone had suggested that dying soon, perhaps by suicide, would be preferable to undergoing the degradation, the suffering, and then the horrible death that persecuted people rightly fear. Despite its grotesque implications, the advertisement is laughable because a prosaic reduction in price, which normally might be attractive, presents itself by suggesting a hastening of the termination of the very life that would benefit from a bargain of this sort. There is no logical inconsistency in the wording of the placard, but in context it enunciates an absurdity. Its wit consists in the ambivalent feelings that victimized and impoverished people would have when they consider the futility of existing any longer while also economizing, as they must, in order to stay alive.

A similar interaction between the prosaic and the absurd occurs in the well-known story of the two old friends who meet again after many years. One asks the other how he has been. He learns that his friend has been well. When the friend then says, "And you? How have you fared?" he replies: "I've had a good life. But to tell the truth, I'd just as soon never have been born at all." In answer to that, the other man says with a sigh: "Ah yes, but who can be so lucky?" It is sheer absurdity to think that to never have been born is a state of good fortune that few, if any, people can hope to have. Do we even know what this could mean? There is no prior existence in which people can be happy or unhappy, lucky or unlucky.

One might believe that few or no human beings ever become truly happy, and if any do, it can only be because of luck. Pessimists like Sophocles and Arthur Schopenhauer claimed as much, and their assertion is not illogical. It may be true, it may be false, but it is not absurd. When, however, Sophocles or his spokesman then argues that the best a human being can hope for is to never have been born, he is talking nonsense that is neither witty nor especially creative. It is merely an expression of despair. The reference to luck in the joke I have recounted alters all this. It reminds us that luck is a part of our existence. Its presence or absence makes a difference in our experience from moment to moment, and in lesser circumstances as well as those that have great effect upon us. The cleverness of the joke results from its juxtaposition of the two contradictory statements, which results in bafflement that is fundamentally absurd under the prosaic circumstances of commenting about one's trajectory in life. The punch line is creative in being a transformation of luck as a human possibility into a parodistic access to good fortune one might have in some metaphysical realm that precedes our mortal state.

In metaphysics proper, which is an edifying discipline that some technical philosophers have creatively pursued, the conjunction between the prosaic and the absurd often takes on a highly sophisticated form. For instance, Kant begins his critique of pure reason by asking what seems to be a very simple question: How is it possible that the world we normally experience should be as it is? Kant was not looking for a scientific explanation such as the one that biology might provide, or nuclear physics, or cosmic astronomy. Instead he wanted to know whether reason as a purely deductive faculty of human nature can explicate the prosaic actuality of what we call "the world." In deciding that it cannot, Kant concluded that many of the basic doctrines of the Protestant ethics and religion to which he was born are indefensible as usually conceived, and therefore absurd to that extent.

To go on living, Kant said, he had to invoke nonrational faith in the reality of a transcendental condition beyond the one in which we live empirically. Having done that, he could then reconstitute articles of conduct and belief that had great importance in his life and in the religious views he inherited.

A stark element of absurdity permeates this line of thought insofar as Kant is trying to explain the world as *everyone* experiences it, and yet he resorts to what he himself cares about, personally and with no assurance that it matters to people in a different culture or at a different level of civilized development.

From this perspective, Kant's intricate and elaborate construction, exquisite as it is as a conceptual artifact, seems like a playful, even comic, sport within specialized regions of human rationality. At the same time the enterprise can have extensive implications for understanding the humanity that exists in all people. Indeed many persons have felt that the Kantian mode of reasoning fortifies their moral and religious convictions.

In the unfolding of David Hume's skepticism, which Kant sought to rebut, we might find an equivalent mixture of the prosaic and the absurd. Although Hume recommended the destruction of metaphysics, since it yields neither factual truths nor those that entail a logical relation of ideas, his philosophical exploration of questions about causality and perception is not itself empirical or purely logical. His refined analyses bring into doubt the general presuppositions we usually have about our ordinary experience and the world in which it happens. Having taken the argument as far as it can go, however, Hume too reaches an impasse when he wonders what practical use his skeptical conclusions can possibly have. He tells us that in order to join the company of other men and women, to play parlor games with them or whatever, he has to put aside his insightful cogitations as irrelevant to the social interests that mean so much to him.

Extrapolating from Hume's report, we may affirm—as I do in all my thinking—that the interpersonal background of these social interests are not truly irrelevant, or even secondary, in commendable philosophy. We are what we are *because* we live in one group of humanity or another. The games in which Hume engaged are symbolic of the communal activities that comprise a major substratum of our existence at any time. The questioning about causality or perception arises out of our need to have precise knowledge about the joint reality we all share, and therefore it is egregious to think that philosophical inquiry—whatever its conclusions may be—is unrelated to the extensive network of our interactions with other people.

Hume also sensed this absurdity. As he matured, he too realized that philosophy makes its greatest contribution to human welfare by engaging with the practical problems that issue from the prosaic facts of everyday life, to which he was returning when he rejoined the company of his friends. Reason is not nullified then, but rather applied to pressing and impending issues at hand. To think otherwise is to indulge in the institutional absurdity to which all too many philosophers have dedicated their creative efforts.

I make these comments about the bivalence in thinkers like Kant and Hume not to denigrate their achievements but rather to illustrate the nature of their splendid originality as philosophers. If it seems that I am treating them as humorists, it is because I discern in them a bit of profound wit of the sort that the Greeks ascribed to the gods who laugh at the limitless self-delusion of human earthlings. Those gods did not understand, however, that creatures such as we can attain creative powers by studying our absurd condition, specifically *in relation to all that is prosaic in it*. When Shakespeare's Puck says "What fools these mortals be!" he sees the foolishness but fails to understand the godlike achievement of men like the one who created the play in which he is a character.[3] We should also remember that the generic personage in Shakespearean comedy who is called "the Fool" often speaks with good sense and even wisdom. He is the voice of rational judgment who checks, and sometimes chastises, the mindless principals in each narrative. Seen in that light, Puck's offhand comment takes on a further meaning that he himself could not appreciate.[4]

A Contemporary Interpretation of the Absurd

Having begun this discussion of the absurd with the ideas of Camus, I feel it should be supplemented with the complementary views of Thomas Nagel. He depicts the absurdity of life as amounting to a discrepancy between two aspects of human nature. On the one hand, we find it difficult or impossible to ascribe any meaningfulness to the universe as a whole. As Pascal remarked, we are terrified by the enormity of space and its unknowable beginning or ending in time. As a consequence, Nagel says, our meager appearance on this small planet can only seem pointless, completely insignificant in the long run. On the other hand, we expend a great amount of energy on the trivia of our petty existence. They engross us vastly, and we approach them with utmost seriousness. According to Nagel, the absurdity of the human condition devolves from the coalescence of this intense and immediate concern about whatever matters to us with the self-transcending knowledge or belief that our place within the universe, indeed life itself, has hardly any objective importance.[5] If Nagel is right, this interaction between the prosaic and the absurd produces a scarcely divine comedy in which each of us has a minuscule role.

Nagel sees no reason for dismay or despair in reaction to the kind of absurdity that is typical of our predicament. Camus' view about the heroism that might cause a person to emulate the concluding attitude of Sisyphus seems to Nagel far-fetched and unduly Romantic. Instead he recommends irony as a suitable and also positive reaction to the situation he describes. Nevertheless I feel that Nagel, like Camus, has not sufficiently probed the significance of what he delineates. Not only do their accounts recognize the disparity between the jointly absurd and prosaic character of human experience, but also they illustrate the creativity that can emanate from the simultaneous harmonization of these alternate attitudes. That type of creativity underlies comedy and the sense of humor, as well as drama and its affiliate arts—all of which help our species adjust to what might otherwise seem to be a ghastly, horrifying fate.

To say this is not to deny the splendor that Camus ascribes to the final willingness of Sisyphus to accept his sorrowful punishment and its possible suitability. As a different perspective, my suggestion seeks to explain the meaningfulness that results from his newfound resolution. In itself it exists as a special kind of consummation—the sense of rightness, gratuitous fulfillment, even happiness that a creative decision of this sort can evoke in the face of terrible misery. Irony need not come into this any more than heroism might. The concomitant perception of both the urgency of our mundane interests and the unimportance they have sub specie aeternitatis, these two occurring at one and the same time, is a trenchant example of human creativity at work. The prosaic and absurd are thereby united to effect a vision, imaginative and essentially inventive, of what it is to be human.

The Comic and the Humorous

At the same time, I want to emphasize that the absurdist elements in this combination are not necessarily limited to any particular art form. As a source of agonizing anxiety, a sense of life as basically absurd can be expressed in the mirth of comedy as well as in tragedy. Seeing the sorrows of life creatively, and in view of their ultimate absurdity, may not always be enjoyable. It can be only minimally sustaining, especially when we realize that our creativity under the circumstances is itself an absurd—though highly valued—gesture on our part. The genre of tragicomedy in dramatic literature and in opera exploits this realization. In any event, absurdity is only one of the components of comedy and drama, whether creative or noncreative.

Before scanning the details of these modalities, we should note the diversity between what I will call the "comic" and the "humorous." The former is often a type of performance on stage, although it need not actually be performed on one. The mere perception of events or personalities as comic reverberates in our imagination of them as possibly belonging to a theatrical kind of situation, what in television is called a "situation comedy," albeit a comedy that occurs in the midst of life. Our awareness of the comic is thus a seeing of prearranged events that cause us to treat something in the world as comparable to a staged presentation, whether subtly kindred to a performance or as a gross imitation. In the playacting of ordinary life, the phenomenon gives everyone a role to perform, if only as an observer of what others are doing or saying.

As distinct from the comic, the humorous is much less highly structured or derivative from a specific art form. It encompasses all the amusing and often unforeseeable occurrences that season daily events and make them seem agreeable, or at least acceptable. The winning smile of Cary Grant or Maurice Chevalier is humorous without always being comic: it exudes a cheerful invitation to share the goodwill and seductive charm of the persona these actors project in their screen appearances. When Buster Keaton unknowingly stands in the open space around which the façade of a building crashes down, without his being touched, that is comic. But when he looks deadpan with total inexpressiveness at a beautiful woman he loves, that is humorous. Both can be equally creative, and every comedian learns how to employ one or the other in some appropriate moment. At the same time they are separate modes of creativity.

They can also interweave in some artistic situations. I will give two examples. When Alfred Hitchcock makes his celebrated cameo intrusions in his movies, the brief event is humorous, since we know he is the director and not a character in the narrative. All the same, his self-insertion on the fringes of the plot creates a little comic scene of its own. As another illustration, consider the sequence in the classic film *Pygmalion* when Eliza Doolittle undergoes phonetic exercises. In them she is taught to pronounce the letter *h* by sharply enunciating the sound in front of a candle flame whose movement or lack of it indicates whether she is talking correctly. The line she recites over and again is "In Hartford, Hereford, and Hampshire hurricanes hardly happen." It is an artful contrivance that puts her into a comic mode very suitable for that part of the movie. But when her forceful delivery succeeds beyond her expectations and the flame not only moves as it should but also goes out, she giggles in surprise at the unintended miracle she has wrought. Our watching her and empathizing with her innocent delight provides a humorous effect that retroactively envelops the entire comic flow and may well cause us to smile. We might even laugh a little, and warmly, at Eliza's likable reaction. The comic and the humorous can therefore interact reciprocally in a creative manner, and they frequently do so apart from any element of absurdity.

The example from the Shavian movie has further ramifications. The event portrayed is a very common one—a phonetics teacher guiding his pupil through a repetitive exercise. Its routine character is lucently embodied in the way that Higgins, as played by Leslie Howard, flatly intones time after time the weary word *again*. What makes the sequence both humorous and creative, however, is the little giggle of Eliza (Wendy Hiller). It casts a sense of joyfulness over the entire procedure, as the humorous often does, by revealing a typically human way of making the ordinary—which can be so tedious—into something delightful and even uplifting. Humor is a mode of creativity because it transforms whatever it touches into an experience that may be not only ingratiating but also very welcome. The funniness in what you laugh at results from more than just the content of what you are being shown. It also registers your awareness of the fact that imagination working in you in relation to the fictive situation can cause such prosaic realities to be unexpectedly pleasurable. They aren't always. In the subdivision of the comic called black comedy, they are not. Without the humorous, much of life would be unbearable.

Varieties of the Comic and the Humorous

The spectrum that runs throughout the comic or the humorous includes more varieties than there is language enough to demarcate with any clarity. Nevertheless we can start with the nature of funniness, to which I just alluded, because it occurs in both the comic and the humorous. At the end of *Pygmalion* Higgins remarks that, in teaching Eliza, he did what he did "for the fun of it." We in the audience know what he means because we have made ourselves an audience for these dramatic and cinematic occasions, to which we devote hours of our time, in a similar pursuit of fun. Unless we are critics earning a living by being present, we aren't sitting there in compliance to some practical necessity imposed upon us. We are satisfying a craving for the experience of fun that frequently motivates everyone. It derives from our universal desire to be entertained and have a good time. The comic and the humorous are creative means of effecting that levitation of the spirit.

Closely related to the funniness that elicits fun is what we may call "the amusing." It is very prominent in the visual arts. Much of the painting of Joan Miró is sustained by the little squiggles and miniature figurines that he rendered so imaginatively. They have hardly any symbolic value, as far as I can tell, and those who ascribe some special meaning to them are probably missing the aesthetic point. I see them as very winsome entities that give this portion of Miró's work a characteristic aura of sheer amusement, like the games and rides in an amusement park. Occasionally they contribute to a circus kind of clowning that suggests a comic situation, but for the most part they are just humorous. In neither event, however, can they be said to be either prosaic or absurd since they are as unpretentious as the northern lights or a cluster of snowflakes. Having issued from some pen or brush held by a human hand, instead of falling from the sky, they eventuate as inimitable aesthetic artifacts that Miró has created for our enjoyment. The wonderfully inventive mobiles of Alexander Calder, whose work Miró much admired, are amusing creations of the same sort.

In working toward his theory of creativity, Koestler begins with humor because he thinks it is paradigmatic of everything creative. Keeping this in view, he tries to prove that what we find humorous or comic, what we laugh at and consider funny or amusing, fits his bisociation model. Since that entails a vast disparity between different matrixes of meaning and interpretation, Koestler tends to make the absurd definitive of all varieties of humor or comedy. Though his view seems to me like an oversimplification, there is nonetheless an element of bisociation that is pervasive in them all. I have in mind the playfulness I described in chapter 4. What I said about Feynman's fooling around as integral to his serious work and its creative efficacy applies to bisociation in general. The pitiful clown who walks on stilts pretending to be on the verge of falling down awakens our imagination to the difference between two conventional matrixes: normal human loco-motion on the ground and without stilts as contrasted with our common aspiration to be taller, higher, more lofty than other people.

In effect, the clown in my example is playing with these alternatives in an innocent and beguiling spectacle of his contriving. His act is risible because he cannot decide which of the two he should follow. That is characteristic of playfulness, and all creativity depends on it. Jimmy Durante, a comedian of the 1930s and 1940s, regularly brought the house down by intoning in a kind of singsong the endless refrain: "Did you ever have the feeling that you wanted to go, and then you had the feeling that you wanted to stay? I think I'll go; no, I think I'll stay. No, I think I'll go; no, I think I'll stay." And so on. This casual, and repetitive, demonstration of indecisiveness that we've all experienced elicits our sympathy in a situation that doesn't involve anyone's pain or hardship. Nothing bad comes to the singer, and even if the clown does fall to the ground, he springs back to his feet and exits uninjured. And as in the opera *I Pagliacci*, la gente paga (people pay) for the creativity in the playful clownish performance.

That audience response is inherent to comedy. While these entertainments are enacted by performers who are living creatures like ourselves, we go to them with the foreknowledge that what we will see is only make-believe. The wicked characters will be exposed, and sometimes treated severely; but since their condemnation as well as their whippings are just a part of the fun, we—like the actors—take their chastisement as a form of theatrical playfulness that liberates us from the suffering and the evil that real people often undergo. The inhuman cruelty that Malvolio is subjected to in Shakespeare's *Twelfth Night* does not move us as it would in the real world. Even the infuriated tone of his wrenching final words—"I'll be revenged on the whole pack of you!"— does not impair the happy ending that caps the comedic amusement of this play. When Olivia, rejoicing in her coming marriage, recognizes that Malvolio "hath been most notoriously abused," she seems to be assuring us that she will now rectify the harm that has been done and all will be well.[6] Entranced by the creative magic of the theater, we are eager to believe her.

The Creativity of Wittiness

The phenomenon of wit, as different from these other subdivisions, is a special case. It is generally humorous in itself, but it also relates to situations and even narrative plots that are at least partly comic. Though musical compositions can be witty in their playful borrowing from themes and motifs that appear in other sonic fabrications, the wit in music largely depends upon variations within the same work as it develops organically out of them. Verbal wit that is so resplendent in poetry and literature as a whole is more detachable from its source, and therefore more quotable in isolation. It can be a playfulness not only with the meanings of words but also with some minor or extraneous association built into them. For instance, here is a dictionary's examples of puns: "Handel with care" and "Haydn go seek."

Puns are usually evaluated as aesthetic in themselves but very low on the ladder of creativity. They are thought to have little profundity and too much reliance upon arbitrary sound rather than connotation. Yet they can be enjoyable, and their kind of pleasantry may shock us into a recognition that the native tongue we have used since early childhood to communicate our feelings and beliefs is also able to serve as a creative mechanism that reflexively transforms our worn out words into the casual beauty of such wit.

Moreover, the distance between the intellectually meager puns I have just quoted and a truly probing witticism may be less than one imagined. Place next to the Handel and Haydn puns the remark by George Bernard Shaw to the effect that "A critic is a person who leaves no turn unstoned." In its joining of different matrixes—on the one hand, the commendable diligence in trying to uncover buried truths, and on the other, the implied violence in attacking anyone who has a possibly new idea—Shaw's statement reminds us that by themselves words are able to inflict unwarranted wounds upon other people. Punning cannot often attain originality of this kind, but at its best it manifests a creativity that need not be scorned or avoided.

The creativity in wit of any kind is highlighted in an exchange between Oscar Wilde and his friend James Whistler. Having just heard one of Wilde's snappy quips, Whistler exclaimed: "That's very witty, Oscar. I wish I had said it." To which Wilde replied: "You will, James. You will." We laugh because we know that a clever remark repeated by someone else is no longer spontaneous or novel. Like plagiary, the repetition may be indicative of a second-class mind. Without actually saying that, Wilde was also praising his own exceptional creativity as a wit, which Whistler could relish but never equal. Wilde was puffing himself up while acting out the playful perversity—the aggressiveness, somewhat subdued in this case—that lurked within his comic mockery and verbal skill.

Witty remarks are frequently characterized as being "oft' thought but ne'er so well expressed." This dignifies their wittiness by giving it a universal validity, but also neglects its possible breadth and originality. What is overlooked in both cases is the fact that almost everyone can be creative in this life-enhancing way, and some people very much. As a final example, consider Yogi Berra's advice that "if you come to a fork in the road, take it!" We are initially amused by the playful ambiguity in the words *fork* and *take*, each referring to an object we can grip, or else divergent paths from which we must choose. But then there surfaces the sense in which the taking of a fork in the road signifies a willed acceptance of that circumstance as something we could either ignore for whatever reason or else acknowledge and confront as just the reality that it is. In vigorously advocating the latter, Berra would be affirming an attitude toward life comparable to the heroic stance of Sisyphus in Camus' rendition of that myth.

Henri Bergson on Comedy

Discussing Bergson's theory of comedy and humor in *Le Rire (Laughter)*, Koestler claims that this book is one of "the two most significant theoretical works on the subject."[7] The other book he cites is Freud's *Wit and Its Relation to the Unconscious*. Nevertheless Koestler thinks that Bergson's theory is vitiated by the reductivistic dualism that permeates his entire philosophy. Although, in Koestler's estimation, the Bergsonian view of comedy and humor anticipates his own concept of bisociation, he argues that Bergson squeezes the many different forms they take into a single and dogmatic conception arbitrarily imposed: the duality of spirit and matter. According to Koestler, "Bergson's main sources of the comic are inertia, rigidity, repetitiveness encrusted upon the spirit; his prototypes of the risible are the man-automaton, the puppet on strings, jack-in-the-box, the distracted person (embodiment of the inertia of the mind)."[8]

I think this statement is more or less correct, and it does indicate relevant problems in Bergson's philosophy. I have criticized its kind of duality in various places, but here I wish to analyze it only as relevant to the limitations in his theory of laughter. Bergson perceives the link between comedy or humor and creativity, and with his unmatchable perceptiveness and lucidity of style, he depicts the types of each as well as anyone has. But they are nevertheless preselected to accommodate his supervening dichotomy of mind in opposition to matter, and the life of spirit as alienated from the pragmatic necessities that nature imposes. With this type of dualism before us, we can easily appreciate how useful it was for an understanding of the specific comic and humorous examples that Bergson cites. In promoting them as paradigmatic and all-inclusive, however, his theory flounders and needs to be supplemented or put aside.

Within what I have called the humorous, for instance, the Bergsonian perspective tells us little about our charmed amusement, and even laughter, in seeing kittens tumble with each other or bury their little faces in their fluffy fur; or our good-natured sympathy with the innocent and guileless man, the cockeyed optimist, who becomes the target of those who ridicule his purity of heart; or our identification with the Jack Benny type of comedian who is aware of, but unable to master, his moral frailty—his stinginess or prissy demeanor that borders on unmanliness; or our response in general to the sheer humanity of people in a play or movie whose happy endings we eagerly crave from beginning to end. Similar examples abound.

Since the comic is predicated upon situations that have some dramatic integument in their very structure, the conflicting forces of mental versus physical do frequently appear. Yet even then our desire to be entertained invokes a sense of honeyed agreeability to the proceedings that may countervene the sheer unpleasantness of an anxiety-producing plot, as in black comedy. In tragedy, or the tragic elements that belong to tragicomedy, the artfulness and access to creativity are very different. For one thing, the tragic does not usually address itself to our sense of funniness. Horror films or scary novels often do so, but they are far from being tragedies.

Dreams and Comic Absurdity

In thinking about the nature of this difference, I find myself reverting to a statement of Bergson's that Koestler quotes approvingly, perhaps because the line is reminiscent of what Freud might have said about laughter and wit. In it Bergson remarks that "the absurdity of the comic is of the same nature as the dream's."[9] But dreams are not absurd, though to the dreamer they may seem to be once he or she awakes and reviews their contents from the perspective of alert consciousness that belongs to everyday mentality. In themselves dreams have no inherent absurdity, any more than watching movies does. In each case we silently observe what is being projected before us as a captive audience. The circumstances of this captivity are nevertheless diverse. It is one thing to lie down in bed, to close one's eyes, and to succumb to the weirdness of images that appear and disappear until we are eventually restored to vital activity; it is not the same when people decide to watch images that other human beings have projected on a screen made for that purpose.

Of course dreams, like movies, are also present to us as the products of imagination. In fact, dreams are *purely* imaginative in the sense that they show us nothing but visual (and sometimes sonic) possibilities that are mainly *im*possibilities. It is as if we all have a virtual movie house in the mind, entirely dedicated to this faculty of make-believe and, for the hours it is operative each night, largely independent of the other type of imagination that enriches our waking life. These imaginative productions are not identical in either form or content. In dreams they are created instantaneously by the audience itself, which is to say, by each dreamer ensconced in his or her private screening room.

The two kinds of audiences are alike inasmuch as both are cleansed of the normal human habit of making explicit judgments about what is or is not real and meaningful, or, more to the point, what is or is not absurd. In neither the cinematic nor the dreaming situation per se does the concept of absurdity exist as part of what we see before us, or as something that establishes the boundaries within which these modes of seeing occur. We just watch submissively, and, usually in the dreaming state, selflessly, though we may also react emotionally to what we see. That is why Bergson's notion of "the absurdity of dreams" can tell us little or nothing about the nature of the comic in general, even though there are many comedies that include absurd characters or events. And, also, there is the recent genre that is called "comedy of the absurd."

Creativity in Drama

With respect to drama, the idea of absurdity is largely irrelevant. Some of the salient occurrences in dramas may be very extreme and hard to believe: for instance, a traveler getting into a squabble at a crossroad with an old man he does not know but kills, only to learn decades later that he was his father and the woman he himself has since married unawares is his mother. The outlandishness of this contributes to the mythological power of that plot. We accept the bizarreness at face value and recognize its symbolic import, but not because it is deemed absurd, as it would be if we watched the same plot on *Saturday Night Live*.

Verdi relished such "bizarría" and even accentuated it in his operas. In being part of a melodrama or tragedy or opera seria, even the most incredible and astounding stories—the mother in a stupor throwing her own baby into a fire instead of the one that belongs to the enemy she hates—register as terrifying or painful to imagine but not absurd. What matters most is the dramatic and emotional effect they are capable of engendering in an appropriate audience.

The remarks by Jack Lemmon that I quoted earlier in a more limited context were originally given in his attempt to answer a student's question about the difference between tragedy and comedy. Most of Lemmon's account was intended to explain the latter in relation to its dependence upon the varying reactions of the audience. Not having much access to that in the shooting of a film, Lemmon rose to the occasion by imagining, in his famous scene in *Some Like It Hot*, that he was performing on stage to people whose laughter or reserve would have a direct effect on his delivery.

Lemmon began this anecdote about the performance of comedy by saying that drama has to be approached in another way entirely. He said, in my paraphrase: "When you perform tragedy, the lines are just there, as they are on the page. You just read them." In other words, the actors (and the listeners as well) must take the dramatic language as-is, accepting the written script without dealing with it as in a comedy. Whatever the words in tragedy might be, they have to be spoken as unchangeable, straight and up front, though each actor must, of course, perform them from his or her individual point of view.

The creativity of tragedy and its siblings consists in mastering this particular necessity. Through a crucial focusing of our imagination, we involve ourselves in the mental strife, the convulsiveness of psychological and moral distress that the characters endure, but without our engaging actively with any such possibilities. The creativity in real-life compassion leads one to share the sufferings of someone else, whether or not any final solutions are attainable. In tragedy that does not happen, even when the commiserate feelings are magnified to a point where our cathartic experience of them might later issue into efforts to help someone or other. Aristotle had this in mind when he defined tragedy as fear and pity partly assuaged through catharsis.

The reading of tragic or dramatic lines may create a sense of communal oneness between the performer and the listeners, but in comedy—as Lemmon correctly depicted it—the audience is more overtly engaged in the actor's personal delivery as a means of revealing the character's idiosyncrasies. *Assistance*, the French term for what the public contributes to a live performance, is a creative event that is recognized also in Bergson's theory of comedy. He shows how laughter and the variegated funniness of comedy derives from the imposed moral standards of society—above all, the society to which the audience belongs. That affects, and sometimes controls, what is considered to be either comic or humorous.

The flaw in Bergson's theory appears in his concomitant insistence that society's role in the creation of comedy prevents it from putting us in rapport with what is real and natural. Since Bergson believes that art reveals the reality of what exists as an individual entity in nature, he maintains that comedy cannot be categorized as "art." Yet he understands how greatly comedy functions within one or another social context, which it regularly invokes in its attempt to make us laugh. He concludes that "comedy lies midway between art and life. It is not disinterested as genuine art is. By organizing laughter, comedy accepts social life as a natural environment; it even obeys an impulse of social life. And in this respect it turns its back upon art, which is a breaking away from society and a return to pure nature."[10]

Though I am not at all sure what "pure" nature may be, I feel confident that comedy, like drama, humanizes and enriches it throughout the cognitive and affective playfulness that imbues creativity in the comic, the humorous, the dramatic, and in fact everything that can be called art. None of these breaks away from society but rather reveals how thoroughly the aesthetic channels and refashions our human nature as well as nature at large. Bisociation, which elucidates the dialectical concurrence of the prosaic and the absurd—and also other aspects of comedy and drama—is itself an example of the creative playfulness in either language or thought that makes life meaningful to us. The creativity in art thereby systematically transforms the major portion of our existence that is ponderous, and not at all creative, into a satisfying state of being that causes even the most uncreative components to *become* creative in their new dimension. The outcome shows forth aesthetic creation as a typical human value. This may be what Nietzsche had in mind—for instance, when he spoke in *Die Fröhliche Wissenschaft* (*The Gay Science*) about the frolicsome gaiety of a life that is creative.[11]

8

Creativity in Practice

The Creativity of Practical Arts

As sequels to studying the arts of comedy, humor, and tragedy, this chapter and the next one address practical (and theoretical) arts of a different kind. In many areas of life, human pursuits are said to contain an aesthetic element that is not especially visual or auditory. Those two modalities of sense experience are especially evident in arts like painting or music. But in ordinary parlance we readily speak of carpentry or cooking, and sports like boxing or racing or gymnastics, as potentially containing dexterity and grace that qualify them too for inclusion in the illustrious category of creative art. We may believe that the "fine arts" rely largely, or even entirely, on the aesthetic qualities for which we treasure them, but the practical arts, such as the ones I have just mentioned, are not devoid of analogous properties. To a connoisseur of cutlery, the heft of a well-turned knife or fork has a consummatory value comparable to the beauty of a musical passage or pictorial effect. We can therefore hope to find equivalent, though certainly varied, manifestations of creativity in virtually all of the activities in which we engage as either purposeful participants or appreciative recipients.

By extension we may also study professional behavior in a similar fashion. Surgeons or school administrators or magistrates, even lawyers and their assistants, are likely to deny that what they do should be considered uncreative. Built into the concept of a profession, whatever type it may be, is the assumption that it serves humane ideals that are cherished by many people. These valuational goals may or may not be stated in a formal document, such as rules of one's guild or a constitution drawn up by the founding fathers or explicit mandates that define moral and religious paths of life. And even when the individual goals are precise and totally comprehensive, they are rendered inexact and imperfect by the fact that to be of any use they must be applicable in circumstances that are always changing throughout the corrosive course of time.

What's more, the words by which the ends are designated weather and alter from age to age. The meaning of the language is constantly in flux, and the thinking of successive generations inevitably reflects the new empirical and ideational developments that reestablish what counts as relevant for each society. In practical matters, an intelligent and perceptive person must always run the risk of being in a quandary. The role of creativity enters at this point.

Doctor-Assisted Suicide

As an example of how the creative element functions as an essential part of decision making, I turn to a problem in medical ethics that has begun to receive some greatly needed attention. I choose the practice of medicine because it extensively represents a form of life in which people entrust their physical and mental being to a stranger who inspires confidence in his or her professional commitment, and who often deploys tools of the trade that exceed the expertise of almost everyone other than fellow practitioners. The particular problem I wish to address is the question of doctor-assisted suicide. It typifies what all physicians have to confront in view of the enormous power over life and death that they must exercise for better or for worse.

Medicine differs from other practical activities in several respects. For one thing, it is supremely paradigmatic of a *profession*, and therefore distinct not only from the fine arts but also from ordinary nine-to-five jobs or businesses that may provide what clients want but are primarily geared to the acquisition of personal profit. A profession is not the same as a calling, to be a priest or a schoolteacher for instance, or a dedication to a political or military cause, or a deeply felt need to live in accordance with one's sense of personal rectitude, or even a permanent involvement in some affective attachment— as in sex, love, marital oneness, and the conscientious raising of a family that one has partly created. Medical practice overlaps these other modes of living—all of which can also be subsumed within a comparable acceptance of relevant ideals— but to none of which medicine is reducible.

In the issue of doctor-assisted suicide, the controversy springs from an apparent inability to harmonize two alternate conceptions about the nature of the medical profession. The first of these envisages the doctor's role as devotion to the preserving, protecting, and enhancing of someone's life. It is centered around the patient's hope to achieve or maintain health in body and in mind. Both ancient and modern versions of the Hippocratic oath formulate this conception within modified boundaries.

In the classical formulation of the oath, the doctor swears: "I will neither give a deadly drug to anybody who asked for it, nor will I make a suggestion to this effect."[1] In a modern revision often used, the doctor recognizes his or her "awesome responsibility" that results from the power both to save a life and "to take a life."[2] The older oath precludes doctor-assisted suicide, while the modern one sidesteps the issue and thereby leaves open the possibility for a conscientious doctor to participate in it. Each version affirms adherence to the ideal of protecting and improving life as fundamental in a doctor's medical commitment. But they interpret that commitment differently.

Nowadays articulations of this variable principle are usually accompanied by a further consideration. The traditional view focused upon the godlike restoration and continuance of health. It is significant that in the original wording Hippocrates invoked the gods and goddesses who can both cure those who are sick and also bring the dead back to life. The doctor's dedication is thus envisaged as a human approximation of the benignly redemptive capability of these deities. The modern conception supplements that concept, and in some circumstances overrides it, by recognizing that the power that enables a doctor to strengthen a person's quest for good health might be used, legitimately, to cause potential harm that the patient is willing to accept and even requests. Desirable as it may be in dire and hopeless cases, death is in itself an evil and not a good. In suicide it is a harm one inflicts upon oneself.

The disparity between the two perspectives can be illustrated by comparing their ingredient values with those of religious devotees, on the one hand, and people who belong to the legal profession, on the other. If medical practice is specifically and exclusively directed toward alleviating unwelcome pain or discomfort, in other words, salving bodily and mental distress, it resembles the aspect of religion that offers, at a more ultimate level, some path to salvation. That analogy in the Hippocratic oath is basic and intentional, not just perfunctory. If, however, doctors are understood to provide their merciful services in accordance with the demands of their clients, no matter what those demands may be with respect to life and death, the underlying conception of medicine resembles what is normally expected of lawyers.

The legal systems of most Western countries are predicated upon the authorized attempt of lawyers to defend their clients whether or not there is good reason to think they are guilty. A client goes to a lawyer on the assumption that he or she is a person who has been trained as an interpreter of the law and can therefore help one cope with it regardless of the actual facts in any case. We might argue, as Plato did, that a person who has committed a crime should simply declare his guilt in court. Though the criminal may not like being condemned, the moral burden of his guilt would then be removed by whatever punishment ensues, and he or she would be a better person to that extent. Modern jurisprudence does not function in that way. The accused who is innocent until proved guilty may really be guilty. Through accumulated knowledge of the law and its operation, the attorney for the defendant is hired to find contrivances by which a client may avoid being punished under the legal circumstances, some of which are purely technical.

Though giving medical help differs from giving legal aid, the second view puts medicine in the same category insofar as it too is oriented toward any outcome the client may desire. Doctors who assist in another's suicide can then claim that they are not ethically liable for what the patient wanted since they were merely providing services as requested. The doctor can insist that he or she is not an arbiter of virtue or the lack of it. If suicide is evil or sinful, the blame falls on the shoulders of the individual who knowingly and with full rationality chooses what this doctor has been asked to help perform.

Adherents to the second conception can also point out that assisting a patient who wants to die does not mean harming that person in all regards. Extinguishing a human life would not be beneficial in itself, but the concomitant relief of pain or other suffering would be. Moreover, and most important perhaps, the doctor is then acting in conformity to the decision of an autonomous person who has freely willed to die. Respecting the patient's personhood would seem to necessitate this kind of attitude on the part of the practitioner. The moral and humane effect of the doctor's role is thereby secured. Medical involvement has been solicited because it can and, some might say, should provide this help without which the patient's indefeasible freedom of choice would be violated.

Problematics of Both Perspectives

Rational as each of the two perspectives may be, I suggest that their presuppositions about medical ideals are equally short-sighted. The deficiency in each of these approaches results from neglecting the creative component in the actual situations that doctors generally face throughout their professional life. In their own manner, the alternate views shield the practitioner behind a typical barrier of impersonality. It is designed to protect him or her from the danger of becoming too greatly, and too emotionally, enmeshed in the problematics of a person who stands poised at the edge of imminent death.

That may count as a valid reason for enabling doctors to restrain their eagerness to assist. Proud as these professionals may be when they cure a patient and so contribute to a new lease on life, they are also aware of the fragility of anyone's existence as well as the enormous limitations of medical intervention. More than their patients, perhaps, medical practitioners know they are not gods; and somewhere in their consciousness they usually believe that they must not "play God." By defining their mission as either a giver of health as best they can or else as someone trained to gratify another's demands in crucial ways, society allows them to be properly distanced from metaphysical puzzlements about which there can be no credible authority and no escape from the fact that all human beings must finally confront them alone.

In the matter of doctor-assisted suicide, however, a doctor runs an additional risk in relying upon the type of protectiveness I have mentioned. In most cases of medical practice a physician can depend on rules and probabilities pertinent to research or experience in dealing with pathologies. A radiologist who looks at an X-ray knows that his diagnosis cannot be certain, but he makes it in accordance with approved standards that justify the conclusions, whatever they may be. Right or wrong, they are unlikely to be based on moral or philosophical belief, or intuitions about ultimate reality, or supposedly indubitable feelings of any sort. The medical assurance that results, wherever it does occur, is scarcely appropriate when patients tell the doctor that they want to terminate their existence.

If the patient is in good health but despondent, the doctor can evade the issue by recommending a psychiatrist or other mental therapist. But this just ignores the problem at hand, since the patient may then ask that other person to prescribe poisonous chemicals capable of doing the job. Under these conditions, the only regulations that might apply are external ones—the dictates of a medical association, the law courts, the doctor's religious affiliation, or current social attitudes to the degree that they affect one's professional decisions.

At the same time, and over and above these ambiguities, doctors remain free agents who must decide on their own what truly matters and how they wish to interpret any guidelines that are acceptable for the particular situation in question. Being morally involved no less than the patient who comes looking for assistance, a doctor—remote and august as he or she may appear—cannot wholly escape responsibility for his or her course of action. Though physicians are not wondrous wizards or emanations from on high, they are people who make themselves available under the aegis of their honorific profession, and who therewith enter into a sanctioned relationship with a patient who has faith in their credentials. If doctors think they just administer established rules and regulations, they are deluding themselves. They are ineluctibly people who must either choose to invoke those mandates or else to reject, or qualify, them in some fashion.

The alternate approach that I suggest in the name of creativity cannot be standardized, any more than life can be.

In accepting it, one forfeits the superficial defense against claims of malfeasance that might sully the doctor's authorized use of rule-regulated procedures. Instead he or she adheres, more directly and less artificially, to the reality of the actual circumstance. Doctor and patient are to be seen as involved persons facing what has become a problem for them both. Willy-nilly, they jointly have to cope with impinging facts of human existence to the best of their ability and in whatever conditions that generate the ethical as well as medical dilemma. A formulaic code in this area might serve as a convenient though imprecise rule of thumb, but it cannot tell us whether or when or how we can employ it on any specified occasion, or even if the code ought to be followed in view of the current facts.

The traditional approach survived throughout the ages not only because it guarded doctors against unwarranted charges of misusing the power to which they have access through their training and advanced knowledge, but also because it deterred undue preoccupation on their part with moralistic scruples at a moment when decisiveness is essential for urgent medical action. In matters of life and death, as Hamlet puts it a little too melodramatically perhaps, "Conscience doth make cowards of us all." The two types of professional solutions undid the knot by telling doctors that they had only to act for the continuance of life, or else to carry out the wishes of the patient with diligence and the concern of a good bedside manner.

In going beyond these limits, or rather in placing them within a larger context that the reality of this profession entails, we can more plausibly perceive that physicians face moral dilemmas when they make diagnoses of any sort or enact almost all medical procedures. In each instance, the doctor must finally resort to some personal decision about how to behave within the unique setting related to the patient's symptoms and the doctor's capacity to ameliorate them.

Because of the multiple uncertainties that are inherent in medicine, it is frequently called an art rather than a science. As I will suggest in chapter 9, this assumption is misleading about the nature of science. But it does properly highlight the extent to which a doctor is forced by the exigencies of his or her profession to use imagination and to be inventive, much as a painter is when he stands before an easel. The doctor must respond creatively to the complexities that each patient brings into his office, even when the individual cases seem to fit a textbook description imprinted in the minds of medical students. Indeed alertness and flexibility on the part of the practitioner have always been encouraged. As a way of compensating doctors for the awesome difficulty of this creative task, and for the anxiety that always attends it, members of their profession are accorded the highest respect and, in many countries, a very high level of income.

Creativity in Medicine as a Whole

The third outlook—the one I am proposing—tries to awaken the imagination of medical men and women to the creative possibility of being someone who communicates with a patient in a humane, though utterly practical, manner. Neither of the first two conceptions fully accommodates that potentiality. While not becoming a psychological or ethical or religious counselor, a doctor can acknowledge that his or her relation to the client is more than just a matter of avoiding suffering. It is instead an attempt to act in a way that gives meaning to the lives of both doctor and patient, the fact being that the patient is undergoing physical or other hardship and the doctor is dedicated to helping the patient deal with that misfortune. In other words, it is an engagement between two people, and sometimes others, who are willing to respond conscientiously to this interpersonal phenomenon in its most extensive ramifications.

When that happens, those who are involved seek, from their different vantage points, a genuine and possibly efficacious resolution to the patient's problem. The idea of "dying with dignity," which many people care about, signifies a termination of life that is not brutish or haphazard but rather a culmination that is meaningful in itself. To some extent, at least, the person who requests doctor-assisted suicide is looking for this kind of help—aid in dignifying his or her demise, and thus attaining a mode of fulfillment that partly validates the self-imposed abolition of oneself.

The doctor's role in this is to be present, to assist in the sense of the phrase *assister à* that I referred to previously and that literally means participating through *being* present. Medical attendance then serves to show forth both solidarity and commiseration about the patient's predicament. The doctor listens and reacts in one way or another without imposing a definitive judgment while also aiding the patient to reach whatever resolution seems right to that person. The doctor does not delve into hidden regions of personality that may be embedded in the patient's inclination, as a psychiatrist might. Nor does the physician pretend to be a sage fully equipped with words of wisdom that are suitable at this time.

In other words, the practitioner is there as an authoritative, responsible person whose life is devoted to ideals that matter to his or her client, as well as being someone who knows what is doable through medicine and legally permissible. He or she is both sympathetic toward the patient's plight and prepared to act as needed. Not being a machine or unfeeling technician, the doctor's own pursuit of meaning is an essential part of this relationship, if only because it issues from a willingness to perform creatively. At the same time, medical personnel are not obligated to respond in ways that are abhorrent to their own values or sense of right and wrong. Even if society gives doctors the legal sanction to assist in another's suicide, or in euthanasia under controlled conditions, they are always free to refuse any use of procedures that are repugnant to their moral and religious beliefs.

Critics might reply that, in view of the focused attention to medical details that modern practice endlessly requires, doctors cannot also be expected to aspire toward the mode of creativity I have outlined. But this only means that professionals in medicine have not been adequately and consecutively trained to establish, and to be creative in, the kind of relation that most patients desperately long to have. That deficiency is similar to what formerly existed with respect to the uniting of medicine to developments in engineering and electronic technology. Collaboration between these fields has been extremely successful in recent years, and is now taken for granted by almost everyone in medical circles. A similar and equally creative cultivation of the humanistic ways in which physicians and others can approach the difficulties in life-and-death situations would yield a parallel achievement in the profession.

Medicine as a Paradigm of All Morality

Since there is no infallible manual for the kind of troubleshooting we have been discussing, medical practice duplicates in that regard the ambiguous aspects of morality as a whole. Most societies have long since ordained that doctors can rightly be punished when they are guilty of negligence or insufficient concern about a patient's rights. But, one may ask, how much freedom of action should society allow medical personnel? That type of question is always appropriate, but it applies differentially to every walk of life—legal, educational, commercial, intimate (as in friendship, love, or marriage), no less than medical—and the answer is the same for everyone. Doctors, in particular, should be allowed maximum liberty coherent with the rights their clients retain as individuals whose autonomy must not be sacrificed even for what is deemed by others to be their personal welfare.

Greater than ever before, the profession of medicine in the future will have to produce doctors who see it as a moral endeavor, in the broadest sense, as well as being a way of life that demands great skill, knowledge, and hands-on training. Medical ethicists may be helpful, but they alone cannot solve any of the deeply tormenting issues. They should be welcomed as valuable colleagues in the enterprise but not as sole or final arbiters of right and wrong. That generic necessity falls on the shoulders of every doctor or caretaker, and at every moment of his or her career.[3] And something comparable is true of everyone.

Ethical Creativity

Once we think of medical practice in this fashion, we can see *why* it is paradigmatic of, and not just peripheral to, the creativity in morality as a whole. Reflecting on this has led me to detect a major shortcoming in my earlier writings about ethics. In both *The Harmony of Nature and Spirit* and *Explorations in Love and Sex* I contrasted Kant's rationalistic approach with Schopenhauer's insistence that morality is based on feelings of compassion. I sought to profit from each by emphasizing the primacy of rational respect for the autonomous personhood of other human beings while also recognizing that there could be no ethical system at all without the compassionate feelings that exist in creatures like ourselves who live in a natural order that is not governed by reason.

In mapping out anew the details of this state of affairs, I now believe I ignored the all-pervading importance of creativity in it. Formulating their alternate philosophies, Kant and Schopenhauer defined themselves as metaphysicians who used their intellectual acumen to formulate the premises and modes of inference from which one could deduce conclusions about the ideal structure of our personal and social relations. They assumed that their systems of thought would enable men and women of good will to derive valid judgments about the right way to live and behave in the practical and often erratic decision making of daily life. But this presupposes that beyond or beneath or within our experience there resides an ultimate and somehow fixed reality from which one could draw the principles of a good and moral existence. The cognitivist approach in contemporary science, and the philosophy that seeks to model itself on it, retains this rudimentary faith. If I am right about the role of creativity, however, that faith is unsustainable in its present form.

Despite the modifications and adjustments that have accrued since Plato and Aristotle wrote, the dominant system of philosophical belief rests on the distinction between appearance and reality that these Greek thinkers enunciated. That distinction has persisted as a mainstay of Western thought. The metaphysical import of this distinction was challenged by Hume's critique, but at a crucial point Hume failed to follow through and fully document the implications of his approach. As I have briefly mentioned, when he remarked about putting aside his analytical studies in order to join the company of his friends, he did not recognize that the nature of our being must be found *within* social realities rather than outside, beyond, and in another domain that only abstract reasoning can penetrate, either through dogmatic a priori speculation or, as in his case, through the skepticism of empirical analysis. It took another hundred years for thinkers of his stature to make a frontal attack on the distinction between appearance and reality, an attack that Hume would have commended but never accomplished himself.

Even if one appreciates the importance of this momentous effort, however, one must still explain our frequent assumption that at least *some* moral judgments are not simply subjective or idiosyncratic but have an objective basis in our reality. Throughout the nineteenth century, and to some extent more recently, romanticism captivated popular imagination by arguing that feelings, whether libidinal or otherwise, provide the requisite grounding for the ethical attitudes that impose their stringent demands upon us. Though much of his philosophizing was not Romantic in any sense, Schopenhauer has served as an intellectual father and then grandfather to this movement as it evolved into the present. But neither he nor those who digested his message could account for the fact that in themselves feelings are highly volatile, sometimes creative but sometimes not, and frequently an unreliable guide to what is really going on even in moral judgments that might seem to depend upon them.

Sartre's Partial Approximation

Among the many writers who have commented on the inadequacy of both reasoning in ethics and Romantic reliance upon feeling, I need cite only one who has spoken to the soul of many people in the twentieth and twenty-first centuries: Jean-Paul Sartre. His play *Les Mains Sales* (*Dirty Hands*) embodies pertinent thinking in this regard.

The play deals with the situation of a young man who gives himself to a Communist cause as a potential assassin. After having become acquainted with the political machinations of the leaders of this cause that he joined idealistically but naively, he decides not to carry out his orders blindly but rather to act only for whatever he truly feels to be right in each circumstance. He discovers, however, that he can never be sure what his feelings are, and this revelation then becomes the principal theme of the narrative.

In his prose writings Sartre explicitly argues that one cannot know what one feels except as related to what one does. In asserting that, Sartre undermines the entire Romantic approach to life. In *Les Mains Sales* the young protagonist, Hugo, has been sent to murder a regional Communist leader who has fallen out of favor in the zigzag policy within the

Party. But when Hugo meets and gets to know this person, he is filled with admiration for his courage, honesty, self-dedication, and manly wisdom. Hugo wavers wildly in his mission, hoping that his feelings will settle down and determine how he should act. He is married to a young woman, whom he has taken with him and who does not know what she really feels about him or their marriage. Hugo is correspondingly divided in his feelings toward her. The pattern completes itself when Hugo's wife becomes strongly attracted by the virility of the partisan leader. Seeing them in the preliminaries of lovemaking, Hugo impulsively takes action by killing the man he has admired so greatly. The denouement of the play consists in his experience of self-disgust because he still does not know what he actually felt or wanted to do. Feeling as well as reason has failed him. Concluding that he was motivated by sexual jealousy that he considers petty, unworthy, and totally unjustified in view of his ethical ideals, he refuses to let the Party treat him as a hero. He is then assassinated as a mere cipher who is now useless to the cause and possibly dangerous.

In his essay entitled "Existentialism Is a Humanism," Sartre enunciates a comparable perspective by telling an autobiographical anecdote. During the German occupation of Paris, a student visits him with a personal problem. The boy is old enough to enlist in the Resistance and feels that he ought to do so for patriotic reasons. But he is living alone with his mother, who dotes on him and has no one else to help her in life, her older son having been killed as an anti-German activist. Sartre listens quietly as the boy weighs his reasons pro and con for the different courses of action that he might follow. If he stays with his mother, his taking care of her will be a limited but clear and emphatic good. If he joins the Resistance, he can serve his country, but then there isn't any way of being sure of that since he doesn't know in advance how he will be assigned.

Recounting the details, Sartre emphasizes the futility of reasoning in such a situation, since every good argument can be countered by a good one that opposes it. He also points out that acting on one's feelings is no guarantee of anything: not only are we incapable of knowing what we really feel apart from how we act, but also our lack of knowledge often remains after we act on the basis of some feeling we thought we had. When Sartre does give a bit of advice to the boy, he simply says: "You are free, so choose, in other words, invent. No general code of ethics can tell you what you ought to do."[4]

Tantalizing as this comment may be, it nevertheless seems to be moving in the right direction. To invent is to take a step toward creativity, to being creative in selecting which among the contrasting reasons and relevant feelings you are going to take seriously, organizing them into a harmonious pattern that did not exist before, accepting as a genuine expression of yourself what will now be given prominence and so allow you to make whatever decision that may be meaningful in your life at the time. To invent in the sense that Sartre intends is to *transform and reconfigure* the situation one is in. Instead of wallowing indecisively, you creatively alter it in a way that causes you to take action despite the vagaries of both your attitudes and beliefs. Reason alone or feeling by itself cannot provide this culmination. It depends on a mode of practical imagination and serves as a propulsive force that can structure, or rather restructure, the immediate texture of your existence, though not necessarily in a single and uniform direction throughout.

Sartre's essay was based on a public lecture he gave shortly after the war. During the discussion period that followed it, a Marxist (Pierre Naville) criticized Sartre's final remark to the student. He claimed that Sartre was eluding the character of the boy's problem, and that a more commendable response to it would have involved searching for additional details about the facts in this case—further evidence about the relationship between mother and son, for instance, and in general any results of a more prolonged effort to discern what would be the likely consequences that might follow upon a possible decision. In merely telling someone that he is free and should therefore be inventive, Naville argued, Sartre shirked his obligation to help. Especially since Sartre was involved as the mentor to whom the student had brought this moral dilemma, Naville inferred that his refusal to give concrete advice could only be an example of bad faith.

Replying to this criticism, Sartre maintained that Naville misunderstood his relationship to the student. There were many others from whom the boy could have sought assistance, he claims, and his having turned to him, a left-wing supporter of the Resistance rather than a conservative priest or a collaborator with the Germans, indicates already what he wanted to hear and how he would decide. In a concluding statement that sounds somewhat cynical, Sartre says: "I knew what he was going to do, and that is what he did."[5]

I myself side with Naville to some extent. Without espousing what might be his correlative views about an objective order in history or the deterministic character of reality, I share his assurance that one who has been asked to give advice can be of service by encouraging the other person to think through the ramifications of the present problem. At the same time, I recognize the great though limited value in the Sartrean emphasis upon freedom and the need to create ideally a solution that cannot be deduced or otherwise discovered in the factual data alone. Though being inventive is less than being creative, it represents a quest for creativity that permeates the moral stratum of our species. This stratum extends from the social and political decisions in life to the affective attachments that constitute our intimate being at every level. If Sartre had been more creative in his attitude toward the youth and his ethical dilemma, their joint deliberation might have been more meaningful for both of them.

The Role of Compassion

Whether or not Schopenhauer was correct in treating compassion as the source of *all* ethics, he was surely right in seeing it as a moral disposition that is not reducible to rationality. Compassion is a largely unpredictable identification with a fellow creature whose suffering, or general difficulty in surviving, one freely takes upon oneself. Compassion is creative in that degree; and as an attachment that goes beyond purely cognitive ingredients, it exemplifies how feelings of oneness can be actively creative. Within the area of deciding morally and the attaining of a good life for the agent as well as others, it exemplifies the role of creativity in interpersonal behavior that we consider worthy of ethical approbation.

Compassion is a form of love, and it derives its dependence upon creativity from the pervasive role that creative imagination plays in all the varieties of love. At the same time, compassion has its own particular tie to creativity. By its very nature, compassion is capable of being extended to suffering or imperiled creatures of any kind, whether or not they are rational and entitled to the respect that every person should receive. As a matter of fact, however, most animate creatures exceed whatever desire we may have to be compassionate toward them, regardless of our eagerness to be creative with regard to them. I myself cannot feel compassion toward the organisms and even cells that live their lives within my body (or anyone else's). I do feel incipient but erratic compassion toward insects, even mosquitoes and other nuisances that wish to prey upon me. Rather than extinguishing them automatically, I would rather they just moved on and let me alone. But what about the trillions of animals and insects that are subjected to the destructive hazards of living on the planet that we human beings dominate? It is not impossible for me to feel significant compassion toward them, but I'm sure that in me it would occur only as a slightly creative but quite unreliable imitation of what I normally feel toward friends and family and sometimes other people.

The type of compassion that most persons elicit could not exist without the moral creativity that men and women are often able to summon up. Mass murderers are notoriously defective in this. Their victims are for them comparable to the vermin we exterminate either with disgust or without any emotion at all. Criminals like Hitler and Mussolini, or their recent replicas, are able to have great affection toward children and toward their dogs but obviously no compassion whatsoever for the hordes of innocent people they subject to ethnic cleansing for ideological reasons. In these monsters the requisite creation and activation of moral feeling and imagination does not exist. That is what makes them monsters.

In my earlier work I sought to clarify creativity's role in affective attachments, including compassion when it occurs, through the concept of what I called bestowal. From the start I realized that bestowal itself had to be analyzed in relation to imagination of one type or another, and that successful imagination has a close connection to a common form of creative impulse. Appraisal and the other responses that fit within the texture of affective life are also manifestations of creativity. Nevertheless bestowal and appraisal require their own separate analysis. They are not reducible to each other, and both of their modes of creativity have to be approached pluralistically in order for us to see how they operate in the diverse activities that belong to our species. But, as I have been saying throughout this book, that is true of creativity as a whole.

The Creative Pursuit of Meaning

In relation to what is native to our species, we must recognize that the ethical or religious systems that fill our lives are generically subsumed under a pursuit of meaning in which humankind is always engaged. We study a photograph of a galaxy and imagine that the rest of the universe is similar. We ask what can be the meaning of it all, and we are troubled by the fact that none is evident. The idea of a God or similar divinity may comfort many people, but it is secondary: we primarily want to feel that there is some kind of meaning that explains the cosmos and our place in it. Yet this kind of query is badly formulated, since we don't know what is meant by the notion of meaningfulness as applied to the astronomical world and worthy of either assuaging or possibly engendering the feelings of anxiety and dread that I discussed in chapter 1.

Even to say that we experience meaningful or meaningless events in our brief existence is unclear and in need of explanation. Everything we encounter, everything we know about, everything that is present to us and can be imagined by us, the totality that is *our* world as human beings, has a meaning for us. If a man dies because a boulder unexpectedly falls on him, we may say that his death had no meaning. That only signifies that the victim didn't die of what are usually called "natural causes" — for instance, an ailment related to the state of his body such as a cancerous tumor or a heart that finally stops pumping. But apart from that limited usage, the death by collision with a falling boulder is not devoid of meaning. We understand what happened and why, and we can account for the catastrophe by reference to the action of gravity on earth as it affects the precariously balanced rock as well as the unfortunately located man whose death results from his having been inescapably in its path.

All of science, learning, the acquisition of wisdom about our predicament and how to deal with it in practice is a summation of whatever meaning we are able to find in our surroundings and in the universe. The potentiality of this meaning is there, all about us, but apparent only in relation to what we are capable of making meaningful for ourselves. In their own way, cosmologists in science seek an explanation for everything, but it would be a mistake to think that the goal they have in mind, but may never attain, could possibly alleviate the ontological distress that most people feel. If all the pieces of the astronomical puzzle were in place, the impending sense of meaninglessness would still persist because we would not know why the universe should constitute just that puzzle and not another. We are dismayed in advance, and thereafter, because of the inscrutable pattern of the whole in addition to the ever-increasing hurdles for our getting the pieces into the correct position. Our malaise and dreadful fear that none of it has meaning cannot be altered by the developments in science, and would not be eliminated by any successes cosmologists might have.

So Deep Thought, the Galaxy computer in *The Hitchhiker's Guide to the Galaxy*, is right when it says that we don't really know what we hope to learn from our unrelenting questions about the meaning of everything. People who have the requisite religious faith, or who otherwise live systematically unencumbered by such questioning, avoid cosmic dread because they don't allow it to intrude upon their normal behavior. They survive without it either by relegating such matters to the clergy, who are thought to take the burden upon their own shoulders, or by surrounding themselves with the common preoccupations of living in nature and seeking the happiness of oneself and of those we care about. When Pascal called such modes of life "distractions," he meant that they prevent us from appreciating reality and loving God as we should. It is true that they are often trivial divertissements that people value even though they have little aesthetic or moral importance. They nevertheless belong to the human search for meaning.

Throughout this quest, there resides a single thread that unites the alternative behaviors that may satisfy it: they are all exemplars of creativity in practice. The doctors, lawyers, and other professionals burdened with decisions they must make each day resemble everyone else insofar as we all are engaged in fabricating some creative meaningfulness in what we do and think and feel. This applies to those who wonder about the meaning—or lack of it—in the universe just like those who do not. In all of us that mode of creativity propels our need to construct and enact an attitude toward life that consists, as much as possible, in finding aspects of our immediate world that are capable of *making* life meaningful to us. In that venture, all human beings become participants in a similar process of creativity, and to a modified degree the same may be true of other animate creatures in the nature we cohabit.

As an illustration of what I have been saying, I end by quoting a remark made by George Burns. He continued to perform as a comedian and one-man show until shortly before his death at a hundred. Coming out on stage once when he was in his middle nineties, he said to the audience: "I'm very glad to be with you tonight. At my age, I'm glad to be anywhere." He might have added, but not being a philosopher he did not have to, that the same is applicable however young or old one might be. It is a creative and very practical outlook that renders meaningful every span of life, regardless of its chronological duration. It is not an outlook that deludes us with false courage about our mortality, or that amounts to being merely resigned to our fate. Instead it empowers a person to go on living, and possibly remaining creative, without being tormented by worst-case scenarios of dread in a situation that can only warrant ineffable wonderment on our part.

9

Creativity in Science, Technology, and Mathematics

Interactions with Aesthetic Creativity

We normally think of science as an explicit quest for knowledge. Technology is thought to be the application of scientific theories that may be helpful to us as human beings who live in nature. By and in themselves, these conceptions may well appear correct and obvious. On inspection, however, we find they harbor ambiguities that need to be clarified. What is implied in the reference to "knowledge"? And in its reliance upon scientific theories, what does technology contribute? According to received opinion that we all have inherited, and for the most part repeat automatically, knowledge is a body of beliefs that faithfully represent the facts about something in the world or in ourselves, and even the universe as a whole. Technology would then exist as the implementing of such cognitive attainments, putting them to use for presumably worthy purposes. In this chapter I sketch a tentative and revisionist approach of mine in these areas as applied to the nature of creativity.

There is some undeniable truth in the assumptions I have just mentioned. But they also fall short. They leave us with reason to doubt that creativity has the role ascribed to it. In preparation for almost everything I will be saying, I offer two general and incomplete answers to the questions I posed. I suggest that science is not primarily dedicated to the acquisition of knowledge, and that technology is much more than just a mode of applying what is normally meant by the word *knowledge*. In mathematics it figures even less. I will be arguing throughout that science engenders a highly specialized type of creativity based on the theories and observations that comprise its subdivisions in physics, chemistry, biology, psychology, and so on, together with their various offshoots. For their part, technology and mathematics rely upon other, though related, forms of creativity. Their kinds differ from the creativity of science in accordance with alternate goals they seek independently of it. This bit of analysis may not tell us very much, but it can nevertheless serve as a reorientation that may lead to valid and fundamental changes in our thinking.

Having reached this far in the book, the reader will remember that I earlier broached the idea that most, and possibly all, creativity overlaps with aesthetic creativity to some degree. Scientific, technological, and mathematical creativity can therefore be treated as partly akin to creativity in art. Yet the disparate modes are also quite unlike each other. Those who reject the claim that science should be considered an art rightly state that the former is based on replication and purposeful objectivity while the latter expresses feelings and attitudes that artists impose upon subject matter they depict from some individual and personal perspective of their own. Sometimes this commonplace separation between art and science is modified by a recognition of how greatly science as well as technology consists in being an enterprise whose social mission is to pursue new ideas, which are sometimes creative yet nonaesthetic, that flourish in people who are trained as experts in the diverse scientific fields, or else as those who are able to apply what science discovers.

In this nuanced vein James D. Watson begins his book *The Double Helix* by saying that science "seldom proceeds in [a] straightforward logical manner. . . . Instead its steps forward (and backward) are often very human events in which personalities and cultural traditions play major roles."[1] Accurate as this statement may be, I am proposing something that is more radical. I wish to establish that the feelings and perceptions through which the "personalities and cultural traditions" play their roles in science or technology are themselves aesthetic and affective responses of a characteristic though special sort. Without such components neither science nor technology could amount to much, and only by combining them with relevant aspects of cognition can science or technology attain their respective types of creativity.

As I have mentioned, Einstein repeatedly said that since his theories were so beautiful he knew they had to be true. A jilted lover might grimace at that assumption. Einstein's adoration for what he discerned in nature would seem to be naive. All the same, his perplexing comment is more profound than one may have thought. He meant that the orderliness and symmetrical structure in his speculations as a physicist resemble the conditions under which we regularly refer to people or objects of any sort as being beautiful. His language was metaphorical, as it is when other scientists talk in a similar manner, and when mathematicians describe proofs as exquisite or elegant.

What I find most interesting, however, is the fact that Einstein was presupposing that the aesthetic interest one might have in symmetry and order as they occur throughout our daily existence can also pertain to explorations of the cosmic panorama beyond anything we experience in the tiny portion of the universe we inhabit. Nevertheless, Einstein's remark—suggestive though it is—can hardly suffice for understanding *how* science and technology depend upon their different aesthetic elements.

Einstein is famously known to have played the violin. In a thought experiment one might entertain, I envisage him sometimes doing so while he was thinking about his work and not playing in a group or as merely a pastime. More than some other instruments, the violin requires both keen musicianship and also a high level of concentration upon the sonic abstractions elicited by it. The beauty of the sounds Einstein was presumably making, or trying to make, may have seemed to him comparable to the abstract patterns that he sought to create, and did create, with his descriptions of imagined events that no one could actually experience—riding on a beam of light, for instance. Like music for the violin, Einstein's theories in physics were designed to disclose real phenomena in which we are embedded so thoroughly that they can be revealed only by unreal, but felicitous, constructions of the mind. Even so, Einstein's imaginings led to empirical observations that followed from them as validations of their truthfulness, which is not the same as the truthfulness of music though surely related to it, as I will later claim.

The violin playing of Sherlock Holmes is not the same as Einstein's. Holmes was scientifically inclined only in the sense that he pieced together observations of empirical data that might serve as clues to some causal network of facts that seemed to have virtually no theoretical value. The power of concentration that went into Holmes's playing of the violin excluded the type of revelations that Einstein sought, and that enabled him to make fundamental and fruitful generalizations in his science. Holmes may have recognized the beauty in his work as a detective—and most certainly, Dr. Watson did. Nevertheless in Holmes's case, as in Einstein's, it would be misleading to think that aesthetics alone explains much about the cognitive creativity they pursued. All the same, both men resorted to some notable interaction between feeling and reason, and that we must still elucidate.

Before turning to this issue, I want to linger a little longer on the image of an Einstein or a Holmes in the act of playing the violin. This instrument can be held in a hand while one walks about, as people sometimes do when they are deep in thought. It is like a pipe that some men smoke while meditating in a relaxed manner. In its form of musical abstraction, the violin is usually not conversational with an audience or with other instruments, as the playing of the piano or the drums often is. Like others in the string section, the violin can seem to move in a more ethereal realm, and it usually avoids effects that might resemble the touching of keys on a keyboard or the pounding of a taut surface. In his compositions, Igor Stravinsky occasionally emphasizes the violin's percussive possibilities, but he does that as a dramatic and even shocking violation of the norm. The violin's bow, and not the player's hand, most often strokes the instrument, and in its reflective mode the violin is quite able to sustain the mental processes in which an Einstein or Holmes can be simultaneously engaged.

Moreover, while soothing the player's spirit, the act of bowing establishes an intimate attachment with this material object that melodiously responds to being held almost cheek-to-cheek. In transmitting the artist's feelings, the bow expresses them indirectly. Since the violin has a curvature reminiscent of a human torso, the contact with it may be thought to have an erotic tincture. Even if it does, however, the abstract quality of the music precludes a libidinal or truly explicit sexual meaning. Violins also have the physical outline of a baby that a parent might hold with tenderness and affection. Men as well as women find that tactile relationship comforting. It is a consummation that many people cherish, and it can be wholly compatible with the experience of creative thinking that nevertheless remains quite distinct.

The Teachings of Poincaré

In the writings of Henri Poincaré (1854–1912), we find an approach that may be more helpful in our analysis of creativity than is Einstein's. Together with his great work in mathematics as well as physics and other fields, Poincaré published important speculations about the nature of scientific creativity. At one point, he depicts events similar to the one for which Kekulé is famous. In relation to a problem in mathematics that he was working on, Poincaré describes his frustration when, after sitting at his desk for an hour or two each day and trying to create various new combinations, he was unable to reach any results at all. But one evening, "contrary to my custom, I drank black coffee and could not sleep. Ideas rose in crowds; I felt them collide until pairs interlocked, so to speak, making a stable combination."[2] By the next morning, Poincaré tells us, he had only to write out, in a short time, the combinations that had come to him.

In another instance, Poincaré reports that he had put aside his mathematical studies while traveling through France. But when he was about to enter a bus in a small town, something happened that jolted him back to his work and led to unforeseen developments in his thinking that encouraged him to continue: "At the moment when I put my foot on the step the idea came to me, without anything in my former thoughts seeming to have paved the way for it. . . . I felt a perfect certainty." A single obstacle still remained, but it too evaporated a few days later. He was casually walking on the street when "the solution of the difficulty which had stopped me suddenly appeared."[3]

Almost everyone knows the experience of having "a bright idea" that pops up unforeseen and out of nowhere, at least nowhere that we can recognize. This terminology is sometimes used sarcastically, since a bright but shallow idea without substantial lineage may not have any reliable rapport with the nature of things. Yet more lasting and more fruitful kinds of bright ideas frequently occur in the lives of creative people. The brightness that issues from their creative moments is often luminescent rather than dazzling but to no avail. The rest of us, beset as we are by the nagging distractions of routine life, may have to settle for a mere glimmer of such creativity.

Because the brain can sometimes operate as a causal and originating agent, we tend to assume that the nowhere out of which an idea arises must be an unobtrusive but essential consequence of brain activity alone. That is not the case. When I walk over the bridge to my office at MIT, ideas often come to me surprisingly, at times novel in some respect though usually not. They are generated by the entire situation I am in, rather than by any single organ of my body. The act of walking, unlike running or being fast asleep, is gently conducive to the chemical processes that stimulate the living brain to entertain possibilities. It is a condition that is like, though not at all identical with, the state of dozing or being half-awake that Kekulé underwent.

A comparable effect may also result from our digestive and breathing systems when they perform their appointed duties with quiet efficiency. Creative ideas of the sort that Poincaré portrays emanate from the entire organism in some state of healthy functioning. That in turn belongs to both the immediate and more remote environment in which we live. The nowhere that fosters our bright idea is actually the everywhere of our existence.

The awareness in creative moments that arise without prior cogitation Poincaré calls "intuition." When the consequent product is gratifying to a mathematician who has had the requisite intuition, he says there results "the feeling of mathematical beauty, of the harmony of numbers and forms, of geometric elegance. This is a true esthetic feeling that all real mathematicians know, and surely it belongs to emotional sensibility."[4] In that vein Poincaré speaks of the "subconscious" as the source of all creative thought as well as the creative ideas themselves that he encounters when he has this experience.

In making these remarks, Poincaré means something very different from what Russell ascribed to the "unconscious" mechanism that responds to the commands he gives it by carrying out the work his conscious self cannot do. Far from imposing the Freudian concept of a hidden region of the mind that has laws and regulations native to itself (assuming that is what Russell was referring to), Poincaré limits the subconscious to individual thoughts that have not yet become articulate. They do not belong to a separate realm of any sort. His conception is thus more empirical and less mythological than Freud's. What he describes is what happens in ordinary memory when it eludes immediate recall but remains, as we say, on the tip of one's tongue until the forgotten name or fact bursts into consciousness like a deep-sea diver coming up for air.

It is this non-Freudian conception that I have been advocating throughout my writings. In some respects they presuppose a use of intuition similar to what Poincaré means while carefully avoiding any suggestion of superrational access to arcane, mystical truths hidden from daily consciousness. Intuition is more rapid and spontaneous than the intelligence or laborious problem solving that generally fills our lives, but it belongs to the same family of human ideation. When a tennis champ, covered with perspiration in a grueling moment of the match, hits the ball exactly as needed to score a point, he or she does not employ any special type of awareness that might be dignified by the word *intuition*. The champ has used a common means by which someone's thinking and behavior unite to effect a desired result, usually but not necessarily because that person has been trained for that purpose. From this, it follows that "the unconscious" is not a state of being that underlies and possibly subverts rationality or has some extralogical capacity as Freud or Russell believed. Instead it resides within the peripheries of ordinary consciousness in the way that unmindfulness does, or even absentmindedness, in situations where we act spontaneously and may not be wholly aware of what we have done.

David Bohm's Perspective in Relation to Poincaré's

In relation to questions about creativity in science, Poincaré's approach is coherent with the perspective that the physicist David Bohm presents in his book *On Creativity*. Bohm argues that the values of orderliness, symmetry, inner harmony, and beauty that scientists pursue are akin to those that motivate creativity in the arts. On the basis of this similarity, he claims that scientific truth is, in part at least, identical with aesthetic truth. He thinks they differ insofar as science must always adhere to some external factuality it tries to understand whereas artists can deviate from it to whatever extent they wish.[5] Though this idea may be defensible, as I believe it is, it leads to some of the questions that neither Bohm nor Poincaré adequately answer. Apart from those that pertain to aesthetic elements in science, to which I will presently return, we must decide how we should characterize the nature of that externality to which they are addressed.

In *Feeling and Imagination* I claimed that scientists who think that someday in the remote future science will attain complete knowledge about reality are deluding themselves. Why? Because we have no reason to assume that everything that is real in the universe as a whole will ever be accessible to us. Can we even be sure that we know what we are seeking? In his revulsion toward the deceptiveness and unreliability of our sensory existence, Plato believed there must be some absolute and preordained being, objectively "out there," that purified reason can penetrate. By emancipating ourselves from the limitations of sensate appearance, he thought, our cognitive faculties would have a pipeline to what is real and all-inclusive in the cosmos. But this egocentric supposition about our powers of cognition is just a flaw of human nature—human, all too human, to use Nietzsche's phrase.

In his formulation, Bohm stresses how greatly mistaken is the traditional belief that science strives to achieve, or at least approximate, absolute truth. That longstanding creed has continued, he says, "in spite of the fact that the actual history of science fits much better into the notion of unending possibilities for new discoveries, approaching no visible limit or end."[6] Far from supporting the common assertion that science can be conceived as marching toward total knowledge of all reality, however much time the fulfillment of this possibility may require, Bohm maintains that the massive progress science has made indicates something very different: "An indefinite and unending unfolding into a measureless unknown, rather than a better covering of some limited, measurable, and in principle completely knowable domain." He persuasively insists that no investigation into "the totality of the universe" can be "a meaningful or sensible thing to try to do."[7]

Bohm suggests that any such faith in absolute knowledge must be considered only as a worldview on the same footing as the myths that many societies fabricated before the advent of science. In the course of time, newer worldviews continuously erupt as a means of staying in tune with our species' constantly altered acquisition of knowledge. From that phenomenon, Bohm infers the following: "What is significant in this regard is not merely the *content* of these various world views, but, much more, *their proper function*, which is to help organize man's ever-changing knowledge and experience in a coherent way."[8]

It follows that we have been misled by those cunning words *real* and *reality*. These and related terms are very useful, but only in circumstances that demand a differentiation between particular and specifiable modes of cognition and expression. In various art forms, for instance, productions are called "realistic" insofar as their images and contrived effects resemble or somehow represent something we perceive in ordinary experience, what we call "real life." Theorists who belong to the school known as "realism" emphasize this component in aesthetic creativity. A person whose thoughts or actions remain faithful to the conditions of our existence as we normally encounter it in ourselves, and observe in others, is often considered to be "realistic."

None of this, nor the many cognate instances that one can easily summon up, implies an understanding of what transcendentalist philosophers and theologians designate as "ultimate" reality or "the" real as something unique unto itself. I will develop these ideas further in chapter 10, but here I wish to argue that creativity in science does not entail a search for knowledge about any objective situation vaguely referred to by this vagrant verbiage. In itself such talk denegrates scientific inquiry of every kind. As William James scornfully remarked about Spiritualist concepts of the "Soul": "Whatever you are *totally* ignorant of, assert to be the explanation of everything else."[9]

In answer to the question I raised about knowledge of "everything," we need only point out the hopelessness of thinking that science, or any other dedicated activity, can eventually disclose the truth about all there is. Such convictions founder not because of limited funding or the enormous difficulties of the project, but only because the conception of that goal is ill-formed and even indecipherable. Scientific creativity, which is a glowing achievement of the human spirit, requires a completely different explanation and analysis.

Motivations of Theories about Scientific Creativity

At the same time, I recognize the modes of creativity that motivate, in different ways, each of the alternate approaches I have been discussing. Bohm is clear-sighted in discerning the creative thrust that resides within the new perspective as he approvingly describes it. To accept the fact that the world is not a determinate entity completely available to scientific knowledge, and yet to organize one's findings into coherent structures that function suitably within their limited goals—that is indeed a creative attitude not only as a theory but also as an insight into the entirety of scientific creativity.

The older position, perpetuated still by the continued faith in it that many scientists doggedly retain, was also a creative reaction to the mysteries that surround us. Our daily experience, as well as the type of exploration that science undertakes in an attempt to make sense of it, is notoriously disorganized, scattered, and unclassifiable. There would seem to be little reason to believe that "the world" must have a single and discoverable nature. Nonetheless, and to some extent at least, most human beings feel that in a sense that may be the case. This frequent sentiment reverberates with the meaningfulness of "home" and "being at home" that most people experience in one form or another. We *habitually* think of the world as a fixed and single abode that surrounds us in all dimensions while also including us as part of the integral totality that is in principle amenable to rational clarification and emotional fulfillment.

But though we may live in close harmony with this way of thinking, we often fail to realize that it results from its own special kind of creativity as a comforting, even soothing, device that members of our species have constructed. It is not self-evidently true. It is just one of the transformations I have been talking about and will additionally discuss later in this chapter. Only human beings have conceptualized the faith in the objectivity and absolute ultimacy of what we seek to know in whatever way we can. The awe-inspiring character of this mode of creativity has the kind of mesmerizing effect that religions frequently cultivate. Unlike traditional creeds, however, this one is not a dogma we are usually aware of believing. For that reason alone, the creative courage that has finally begun to undermine the age-old and fruitless quest for any such certitude is worthy of our admiration.

Beauty and the Aesthetic in Scientific Creativity

Having established the presence of noncognitive elements in scientific creativity, and therefore in technological and mathematical creativity as well, we may still ask whence they arise. Here, too, the speculations of Poincaré can be of help. In an attempt to clarify his references to what he calls intuition, he delineates the role of the beautiful in the mentality of scientists and, above all, mathematicians: "The scientist does not study nature because it is useful; he studies it because he delights in it, and he delights in it because it is beautiful."[10] Poincaré says, more specifically, that he is referring to the search for intellectual beauty that is distinct from any quest for sensory beauty. Without disparaging the latter, he exalts the former's dedication to "the sense of the harmony of the cosmos, which makes us choose the facts most fitting to contribute to this harmony, just as the artist chooses from among the features of his model those which perfect the picture and give it character and life." In response to critics who might see in this description a turning aside from the truths of empirical observation, Poincaré affirms that "the real world" in all its simplicity and grandeur, its "simple facts, sublime facts," is more beautiful than any harmonious dreaming that might present itself as an alternative.[11]

That type of speculation is fraught with the same difficulties as occur in Einstein's claim that his theories must be correct because they are too beautiful not to be. Prima facie it seems plausible to think that if scientific creativity were to include aesthetic and affective components as well as others that are purely factual, the product of this quasi-artistic venture would be likely to deviate from the truthfulness about the world that scientists generally wish to attain. And what is the cash value of assuming that the cosmos is simple or harmonious in itself? Since we have no knowledge of that, and much evidence to the contrary, what can sustain such beliefs other than the joy and gratification that issue (creatively on their own) from the feeling that what we care about as homo sapiens on this planet indicates the nature of cosmic reality?

At this point I return to my questioning of terms like *real*, *unreal*, *reality*, and the realism that theorists have attributed to the ideal goals of either "realistic" art or of science. Throughout their history, both types of pursuit have recurrently defined themselves as a disclosure of how things are and, by extension, the reality of everything in its totality. I deny that this use of language is meaningful when taken literally, but I do not doubt its ability to express, in a metaphoric or even mythic fashion, extensive feelings and ideas that have had great importance in the lives of many people.

Physicists who assert that current knowledge of the Big Bang and the consequent evolution of the universe discloses basic truths about the world are prone to assume that their view provides rock-bottom information about reality. Questions about what there may have been before the Big Bang are readily dismissed as irrelevant, either because physics cannot at present, and never will be able to, accommodate such discourse, or else because there is nothing that we can truly imagine in this matter. But these assertions are themselves unverifiable, and all other demarcations of what may be known or conjectured are incapable of yielding authoritative beliefs about "cosmic totality." The mere utterance of these suggestions belongs to the mythmaking and metaphoric efforts that have been cultivated throughout the history of mankind.

Creative as such ideas may be, they manifest the workings of our aesthetic imagination and largely originate out of affect rather than reason. Though most or all of science issues from the propulsive search, and even passion, that motivates its craving for new discoveries, the quest for absolute closure is in a class of its own. It constitutes the form of quasi poetry that pervades the religiosity of science and of its derivatives, alike in that respect to most other religions that have been created on this planet.

Though we may infer that literal references to any final comprehensive reality are indefensible, one may still argue that we all do want to feel and believe that we are in touch with the realities of life, and that this particular need can even contribute to a type of creativity that underlies all the others. That will be the burden of my investigation in chapter 10.

Some Remarks about Technology in Itself

Thus far in the present discussion there has not arisen much clarification of the creativity in technology apart from its close relation to science. One might think of technology as the child of scientific awareness, since it is generally an application of what science has disclosed as feasible in the material world. At the same time, one could also say that technology existed long before science arrived. One might even maintain that technology called forth science capable of providing empirical knowledge that accommodated and greatly buttressed the pragmatic requirements of technology. As in most families, however, the siblings developed separately and have diversely sought what they each individually valued.

The detailed delineation of differences between creativity in science and creativity in technology I leave to those who are more learned in their acquaintance with both modalities.[12] For an adequate description to succeed, it must adhere to two fundamental principles: First, though all or most sciences—as opposed to the fine arts—dedicate themselves to the acquisition of precise and meaningful data through observation, inference, and replicatable experiments, they activate this noble aspiration in a variety of different ways. Even in the scientific discipline of physics, the creativity of a theorist like Newton or Einstein is not the same as the creativity of physicists who seek empirical confirmations of surmises and predictions that have been fed into the communal imagination.

Second, the many technologies are also systematically unlike each other in crucial respects. Whatever analyses future philosophers and theorists may someday formulate, such thinking about the technological application of scientific knowledge will be most convincing if it acknowledges their respective dedication to alternative goals and methodologies. The wholesome emphasis nowadays on interdisciplinary research in technology as well as science is predicated upon the likelihood of immeasurable advances that can result from uniting the *different* modes of creativity in new and often unforeseeable ways.

Further Explorations into the Role of the Aesthetic

With those aims in mind, we may make some headway in understanding some of the major questioning about which I have been hovering throughout this book, and particularly in this chapter. We must persist in wondering how science (or technology or mathematics) can merit the aesthetic terminology that, as we have seen, Poincaré, Einstein, and many others in this field consider essential for understanding the character of what they do. Elucidation of that will then give us a grip upon the distinctions that are often made between scientific truthfulness and aesthetic truthfulness in relation to the creativity of each.

Poincaré was right in suggesting that the intellectual beauty of science is not the same as sensory beauty, and therefore, by implication, scientific truthfulness is not identical with aesthetic truthfulness. An astronomer who perceives the sensory beauty of the aurora borealis on a clear night is not thereby enjoying an intellectual beauty relevant to his scientific mission. The sensory beauty of this visual event, and of the many others that occur in the experience of naturalists of every stripe, may serve to induce a scientist or mathematician to undertake and endure the laborious work that the search for knowledge entails. But that does not explain "intellectual beauty" and its role in scientific creativity. And neither does Poincaré's largely unsubstantiated claim that the feeling of mathematical beauty is "a true esthetic feeling that all real mathematicians know."

Like those who also make this affirmation, Poincaré cites the harmony of numbers and refers to geometric elegance. Yet he offers no defense against critics who might view terms like *harmony, elegance,* and *mathematical beauty* with a much colder eye. They could very well insist that such words are just metaphorical terms based on the more prestigious meaning of sensory beauty. We might add that when theorists of technology distinguish among production patterns that are considered beautiful or ugly in themselves, and not in terms of any sensory consideration, they too are mainly using linguistic jargon. Though the harmony of numbers and the elegance in a geometric proof or some graphic design may be as indubitable as the sensory beauty of a well-proportioned nude, we still need to learn *how* scientific or mathematical or technological creativity relies upon the nonsensory examples in a manner that embodies the aesthetic creativity that an artist's work may have.

Poincaré's ideas about intuition and the unconscious are proffered in response to such questioning. In his *Essay on the Psychology of Invention in the Mathematical Field,* Jacques Hadamard introduces an analysis that purports to explicate what Poincaré must have meant. Despite his discussion of various types of possible evidence for believing in the existence of what Poincaré calls the unconscious, however, Hadamard hardly detects anything more than what William James named as "fringe-consciousness." That term refers to our seeing what appears at the peripheries of our field of vision without our focusing on it.[13]

Hadamard also speculates about levels of consciousness, the lowest being subliminal and therefore unconscious though capable of harboring creative ideas that then appear in consciousness. As the faculty that supplements normal rationality, intuition is taken by Poincaré and Hadamard to be the feeling that expresses what is happening at the lowest level. This feeling presumably consists in the sense of beauty that Poincaré deemed fundamental in all creative work and that—in his estimation—all mathematicians recognize as such. But until that theory about scientific invention can itself be approached scientifically—through brain studies perhaps—I don't see how any speculation along these lines can be truly established.

In effect, we are left with the kind of puzzlement that many aestheticians have experienced in relation to a letter about his method of composition that Mozart may or may not have written. Though many scholars nowadays consider it a nineteenth-century forgery, the text is relevant because theorists like Hadamard refer to it as authentically depicting the nature of both mathematical and aesthetic intuition. While musical creation is not the same as creation in mathematics, what Mozart allegedly reports about himself might possibly illuminate both. The writer of the letter—let us call him Mozart here—says that he does not know where his musical themes

come from, but once one of them presents itself to him, others latch on to it and produce melodic fragments that will eventually enter into a composition. The account then continues as follows:

All this fires my soul, and provided I am not disturbed, my subject enlarges itself, becomes methodized and defined, and the whole, though it be long, stands almost finished and complete in my mind, so that I can survey it, like a fine picture or a beautiful statue, at a glance. Nor do I hear in my imagination the parts successively, but I hear them, as it were, all at once. . . . When I proceed to write down my ideas, I take out of the bag of my memory, if I may use that phrase, what has previously been collected into it, in the way I have mentioned. For this reason, the committing to paper is done quickly enough, for everything is, as I said before, already finished; and it rarely differs on paper from what it was in my imagination.[14]

Various commentators—Goethe and Heidegger, for instance—have interpreted the last lines as meaning that Mozart had intuitions of his musical works in their totality. And he does state that his imagination allows him to hear a piece "all at once." Even if this were taken literally, however, it would still not denote an unconscious event that anyone could properly identify as the source of an "intellectual sense of beauty."

For one thing, Mozart is not talking about something that is unconscious, but rather an overtly conscious process pertaining to his creative music making. Furthermore, he points out that what he hears in his imagination does not include the successive parts. This implies that he did not literally intuit the whole of the composition, even though he

speaks of hearing it in its entirety. The terms in his description are clearly being used metaphorically, since hearing in the imagination differs significantly from hearing the sounds that are processed through the ears.

What is literally heard in a musical composition comprises a temporal succession of auditory events, which Mozart explicitly precludes. Instead he likens his experience to the way his mind perceives in a glance a beautiful statue already finished and complete. John Keats elaborates a similar idea when he asserts, in his *Ode on a Grecian Urn*, that "Heard melodies are sweet, but those unheard / Are sweeter; therefore ye pipes play on; / Not to the sensual ear, but, more endeared, / Pipe to the spirit ditties of no tone."

In Mozart's case the metaphorical statement alludes to musical forms, aesthetic patterns, instead of toneless ditties, but the basic concept is comparable. Hearing in his imagination directly and in a glance, the real (or fake) Mozart probably did have an experience that differs from a purely sensory perception—as Poincaré says about mathematical beauty. But far from being unconscious, the composer would have been thoroughly aware of the absolute rightness that the particular beauty manifested. This sense of rightness is a feeling of how things *should* be: themes not left dangling or unconsummated, meanings not remaining incomplete, unresolved possibilities not being overlooked, opportunities for sensory or other goodness not squandered or unsavored. All this applies to scientific, and technological or mathematical, truthfulness as well as aesthetic truthfulness even though the relative weight of metaphorical versus literal language employed is noticeably diverse among them.

Image Making, Analogies, and Thought Experiments

While raising doubts about the meaning of what Poincaré calls intuition and the unconscious, I nevertheless agree that both of these, interpreted in a more commonplace and colloquial manner, play an important role in scientific and related creativity. Scientists and mathematicians have often attested to the utility of hunches and subtly suggestive feelings as a source of the reasoning that may lead on to challenging and sometimes valid conclusions. Moreover it is widely recognized that thinking can be bolstered by what seems to be a kind of intermittent blankness that does not belong to alert consciousness but nevertheless contributes to problem solving and the creative process. Poincaré's suggestions are worthy of attention because he goes further, and possibly deeper, in claiming that in mathematics "the useful combinations are precisely the most beautiful."[15] Yet he does not tell us why and how this should be the case.

Of greater import, I believe, is the presence in science and its related subjects of image-making, analogizing, and the construction of imaginative thought experiments. In his book, Hadamard inserts what he calls "a testimonial from Professor Einstein." It is a letter in which Einstein answers questions about the use of words in his work as a physicist. Emphasizing the occurrence of images and analogies that characterize his mentality, he says:

The words or the language, as they are written or spoken, do not seem to play any role in my mechanism of thought. The psychical entities which seem to serve as elements of thought are certain signs and more or less clear images which can be "voluntarily" reproduced and combined.

There is, of course, a certain connection between those elements and relevant logical concepts. It is also clear that the desire to arrive finally at logically connected concepts is the emotional basis of this rather vague play with the mentioned elements. But taken from a psychological viewpoint, this combinatory play seems to be the essential feature in productive thought—before there is any connection with logical construction in words or other signs which can be communicated to others.

The above mentioned elements are, in my case, of visual and some of muscular type. Conventional words or other signs have to be sought for laboriously only in a secondary stage, when the mentioned associative play is sufficiently established and can be reproduced at will.

According to what has been said, the play with the mentioned elements is aimed to be analogous to certain logical connections one is searching for.[16]

Frequently in the course of creative progress in science there has also been the use of thought experiments, for which Einstein is greatly renowned. They have special interest in his case because he seems to have reached his daring conclusions on the basis of them, leaving it to others to verify or reject his calculations through empirical observation and diligent testing. James Joyce's description of the artist standing apart from his creation, godlike and paring his fingernails, seems applicable to the Einsteinian mind. It reminds me of Babe Ruth pointing to right or center field and then, on the next pitch, hitting a home run there.

In the letter I quoted, Einstein's reference to the analogical use of images has current importance in view of the considerable attention that scholars have given to the general nature of scientific analogizing as it is connected with image making. One writer even asserts that "all knowledge is ultimately rooted in metaphorical (or analogical) modes of perception and thought."[17] Another expert in the field notes that through analogies scientists regularly re-represent an already accepted representation of something by means of a prior unrelated representation of something else. In scientific model constructions, analogy is said to be "a principal means through which people make inferences about novel experiences, phenomena, or situations, using what they already know and understand. It is, thus, central to understanding learning and problem solving."[18]

Among the many examples of scientific analogies often mentioned are those that unite water waves to sound and, then later, to light waves. As against Newton's particle theory of light, subsequent physicists favored the wave theory. When Bohr suggested that the wave and particle conceptions are complementary, not opposed, he was combining the two kinds of analogies that had been established previously. More telling for our present argument is the demonstration that scientific analogizing of this sort is in principle indistinguishable from that which occurs so often in all the arts. As Margaret A. Boden points out, in her article "What Is Creativity?," the most creative analogies in either art or science are not infrequently those that are most extreme, most surprising in their mode of unifying different domains, and therefore most innovative. Boden illustrates the creative audacity of such analogies with the passage in Shakespeare's *Macbeth* about sleep that knits up the raveled sleeve of care; but thought experiments by Einstein that envisage what would happen to a space traveler locked up in a chest could have served just as well.[19]

Relation between Scientific Truth and Aesthetic Truth

These links between art and science, technology, or mathematics support the foundational views of both Poincaré and Einstein. They reveal the crucial role of aesthetic elements in the modeling and apprehension of hypotheses that may then be empirically proven as elegant or beautiful representations of reality. The astounding leaps and fertile intimations function as integral parts of these creative productions on a par with the creativity in great works of art.

This brings us back to the questions about scientific truthfulness in relation to aesthetic truthfulness, and the possible credibility of thinking that all such creativity depends on the latter. In this context, the term *depends* may imply something too extreme under the circumstances. A weaker position, to the effect that science and the aesthetic overlap, would be more immune from criticism. In effect, that is what I have been exploring in the pages that immediately precede this one. If science, technology, and mathematics belong to one or more modes of creativity by virtue of image making, analogy, and imaginative thought experiments, this alone uncovers a significant interaction with artistic or quasi-artistic activities that, at their best, achieve aesthetic truthfulness. A moderate approach of that sort seems to me quite tenable while showing how science, technology, or mathematics is capable of being innovative, novel, inventive, and richly imaginative in ways that may well be called creative.

As an additional advantage, this view enables us to affirm that, despite their overlapping, scientific and aesthetic truthfulness are not identical. Scientists rightly pride themselves on discoveries about the facts of our existence to which their unique methodology gives them access. Artists, whether working in abstract forms or as realists portraying the details of ordinary life, may also claim that they purvey objective truths. But the objectivity is not the same in both. Discoveries in science, or the inventions of technology and mathematics, are generally impersonal, whereas in the arts there are few, if any, inventions or discoveries and the personal vision of the artist is both paramount and freely expressed beyond any preestablished limits.

One might reply that instrumentalists in music or chorus members in ballet, for instance, are required to follow the notated score instead of venting some individual vision of their own. But their artistic situation is ideally geared to the aesthetic truthfulness of what the composer, or choreographer, has created for them to perform, and his or her personality is always—though often subtly—present in what has been artistically created. By way of contrast, scientists, technologists, or mathematicians only rarely see their chosen subject matter as a mode of expressing their own feelings or individual longings, however much they are cognizant of the possibility that "subjective" attitudes may somehow underlie their work as well as their motivation for doing it.

Even so, we also know that this type of generalization does not hold for the great geniuses in any of these fields. They make enormous imaginative leaps and follow extraordinary hunches that lesser practitioners may consider a type of unprofessional gambling or impermissible risk-taking. When Einstein behaved in that way while formulating his theories of special and general relativity, he was finally vindicated by the later experiments that confirmed the truthfulness of his theorization and the brilliance of his creativity. But when he thereafter persisted, in his usual fashion, to ignore the in-determinacy of quantum mechanics and stubbornly spent decades on a unified field theory that most physicists now consider hopeless, his great creativity would seem to have dwindled.

The example of Einstein's lifelong efforts yields crucial facts about the nature of creativity: particularly that it is contingent upon ongoing cognitive success in the areas to which it belongs as the energizing force within a creative process. Moreover, even if creativity is a propensity in the life most people aspire toward, and possibly a manifestation of whatever reality we find meaningful, it operates in strange and frequently haphazard ways that augment our sense of mystery and confusion about what that reality may be. Chapter 10 continues this path of reasoning.

10

Creativity and Reality

In my previous chapters I suggested that much of our thinking about the nature of reality is confused or erroneous. At the same time, I suggested that there are types of creativity that accompany virtually all our statements or beliefs about reality. In this chapter I want to establish at least three things: first, that what in our familiar language is called reality is a compendium produced by vague but common *feelings* about reality; second, that there are different kinds of comparable and interrelated feelings of this sort; and finally, that the inherent modes of creativity in this area exist within a particular dimension of their own and that even without our attempting a thorough analysis a preliminary outline of it may help us understand these aspects of human consciousness.

William James and Recent Science

Not much effort along these lines has been made by philosophers in the last hundred years, but in *The Varieties of Religious Experience*, written by William James at the beginning of the twentieth century, we find a paragraph that may get us started:

It is as if there were in the human consciousness a *sense of reality, a feeling of objective presence, a perception* of what we may call "*something there*," more deep and more general than any of the special and particular "senses" by which the current psychology supposes existent realities to be originally revealed. If this were so, we might suppose the senses to waken our attitudes and conduct as they so habitually do, by first exciting this sense of reality; but anything else, any idea, for example, that might similarly excite it, would have that same prerogative of appearing real which objects of sense normally possess.[1]

Elsewhere James remarks: "*In its inner nature, belief, or the sense of reality, is a sort of feeling more allied to the emotions than to anything else.*"[2]

James's position is not entirely clear. Sometimes he speaks of the phenomenon as a sensing of reality, and at other times he calls it the "perception of reality." A chapter in his *Principles of Psychology* has that title. Occasionally, as we have just seen, he refers to it as the "feeling" of reality. He does not seem to consider this variation of terminology significant. But throughout his work the words *sense, perception,* and *feeling* are differently defined and differently used. The former two are distinguished with respect to the relative simplicity of their objects or contents. The function of sense or sensation "is that of mere *acquaintance* with a fact. Perception's function, on the other hand, is knowledge *about* a fact, and this knowledge admits of numberless degrees of complication."[3]

I suggest that none of these formulations is adequate. If the "sense of reality" were indeed a sense (a form of sensation), albeit a sense more deep and general than any specific sensation, it would have to follow that it consists in the acquaintance with an entity or fact that is thought of as "real."

To have a sensation of hardness is to experience contact with an actual something taken as "hard." But the same cannot hold for the alleged sense of reality. There we are not engaging with anything in its *self* that is deemed real: we are instead having an overall experience, barely conscious, that seems to indicate the reality of some object or circumstance.

Similarly, the sense of reality cannot be a perception of reality. For then, it would have to occur as the property of an individual content, the knowledge of which would depend on its relations to other things. Such a description can be adequate for explaining how it is that we distinguish illusory objects from those that are nonillusory. It tells us the conditions in which something that is real can be expected to occur. It does not, however, tell us what any *sense* of reality is.

Finally, as a last resort, we may understand and even accept James's surmise about a "feeling of reality." But then we need to learn exactly what kind of feeling that might be. It is not enough to present it as a "general" or "sort of" feeling allied to the emotions. At the same time, there has been some impressive support for James's vague idea in the current speculation of brain and cognitive theorists. Though usually couched in professionalistic caveats about the nascent character of scientific research in this area, it yields a refreshing departure from purely physicalistic thinking about human consciousness.

For instance, in an article entitled "Emotion and Consciousness," Kathleen Wider argues that "it is not the thinking activity of the mind alone that produces the most basic level of self-awareness. It is the affective nature of consciousness, which usually includes a cognitive element, that does." Wider amplifies this statement by claiming that "there is always something it is like to be a subject of consciousness, to be me at this moment, here and now, and that 'something it is like' is constituted by a feeling."[4]

I see this as a promising, though partial, elucidation of the Jamesian reference to a feeling of reality underlying or circumvenient to our sensing of the world. Wider sustains the forcefulness of her suggestion by citing the work of brain theorists such as Jaak Panksepp and Antonio Damasio, who tentatively remark not only that all consciousness is rendered self-conscious by ingredient aspects of feeling and affectivity as a whole but also—in Panksepp's words—that "every moment of our conscious life is undergirded by feelings."[5]

Wider brilliantly illustrates this phenomenon by showing how emotions, as representative of other feelings, orient and control the varied contents of her consciousness: "The driver who has just moved into my lane has *purposively* cut me off. My children have the volume on the television turned up high to irritate me; even the carpet I trip over has, I feel, tripped me. Everything of which I am aware is present to me in a certain way in part because of my emotional state."[6] After further descriptions about feelings of romantic love causing a heightened sexualization of the world as we experience it, Wider concludes: "It is in virtue of the affective quality of consciousness that whenever I am conscious, I am pre-reflectively conscious [of *myself*], of how it is with me now."[7]

Taking this as a guiding principle that cognitive and brain science may soon develop much further in the empirical and creative work it does, I suggest that this notion of an affective and self-referential underpinning of all consciousness may lead us to a proper interpretation of the generic feeling of reality. To get there, we need to supplement the ideas about a prereflective awareness of oneself with other ideas that appear in Aristotle's *De Anima*. Having noted that the self receives information about the world from the five senses of sight, hearing, touch, taste, and smell, Aristotle puzzled over the fact that we also have a broader and more comprehensive sense of the fact that we are such that the five senses operate in the ways that are familiar to everyone. Aristotle concluded that an inner agency supervenes upon the outer ones. In a recent translation, he asserts: "There is a common faculty that accompanies all the senses, by which one senses [for example] that one is seeing and that one is hearing. For certainly it is not by sight that one sees that one is seeing. . . . It is, rather, thanks to a certain part of the soul that is common to the sense organs."[8]

In the history of philosophical speculation about the self, this inner aptitude has been named and interpreted in many ways.[9] To me it seems plausible to think that it belongs to one's feeling of oneself as the being that has whatever consciousness one may have at any time. Sensory experience is a part of that. It serves as the intermediary between us and what we receive as possible information about a world that we are sensing. Since the senses perform this function within a prereflective context that is shaped and somewhat controlled by the gamut of feelings with which we identify ourselves, the intermediate experience creates a varying complexity of notions about what is real in us as well as outside in some external reality.

From this, it follows that the feeling of self, of "oneself" — whatever it may be for each person at any moment—is deeply rooted in our consciousness alongside the individual contents of our experience, including the sensory data that seem to come from the world in which we live. The feeling of reality is therefore actually a conglomerate of *feelings about* one or another event or circumstance that we recognize as supremely outstanding in our life at that time. Upon it we have rendered the valued category of being real that may in itself ascribe greater meaning for us than other, lesser, aspects of existence. Therein lies the creativity in the feelings of reality that we have. Like all the rest of human creativity, they sustain inventive and imaginative gestures, acts, and attitudes that bestow a special importance upon sensations and all else of consciousness that occurs within the self that is ourself.

The great nineteenth-century psychologist and psychiatrist Pierre Janet described "le sentiment du réel" (the feeling of what is real) as attention or attentiveness: "To hold a perception or an idea with the feeling that it is quite real, that is to say, to coordinate around this perception all our tendencies, all our activities, this is the very work of attention."[10] That suggestion is worth exploring further, but first I want to consider some relevant views of David Hume, the founder of modern empiricism.

Humean Intimations

Hume devoted a great deal of space to the issue we have been discussing, although he never uses the exact same words as James. His terminology is idiosyncratic and his approach is clearly different from James's (or mine), but still it is an equivalent feeling of reality to which he referred in his *Treatise of Human Nature*:

'Tis evident, that whatever is present to the memory, striking upon the mind with a vivacity which resembles an immediate impression, must become of considerable moment in all the operations of the mind, and must easily distinguish itself above the mere fictions of the imagination. Of these impressions or ideas of the memory we form a kind of system, comprehending whatever we remember to have been present, either to our internal perceptions or sense; and every particular of that system joined, to the present impressions, we are pleased to call a *reality*.[11]

This kind of reality is for Hume "the object of the memory and sense." The next step takes him to "the judgment": "But the mind stops not here with the system of memories. For finding, that with this system of perceptions, there is another connected by custom, or if you will, by the relation of cause or effect, it proceeds to the consideration of their ideas; . . . it forms them into a new system, which it likewise dignifies with the title of *realities*."[12]

From this point of vantage, we can better appreciate the import of Hume's assertion that belief "consists not in the nature and order of our ideas, but in the manner of their conception, and in their feeling to the mind."[13] In this context he is surely referring to the feeling of reality. Without analyzing what in particular is accepted as real, he states:

This operation of the mind, which forms the belief of any matter of fact, seems hitherto to have been one of the greatest mysteries of philosophy: tho' no one has so much as suspected, that there was any difficulty in explaining it. . . . An idea assented to *feels* different from a fictitious idea, that the fancy alone presents to us: and this different feeling I endeavour to explain by calling it a superior *force*, or *vivacity*, or *solidity*, or *firmness*, or *steadiness*. This variety of terms, which may seem so unphilosophical, is intended only to express that act of the mind, which renders realities more present to us than fictions, causes them to weigh more in the thought, and gives them a superior influence on the passions and imagination.[14]

The Feeling of Reality

For us in the twenty-first century, what remains essential in Hume's position is the underlying assumption that the feeling of reality present in the operation of belief consists in the kind of powerful response that still needs to be explained. Unlike any ordinary belief, I wish to argue, this feeling is not something that automatically issues from the mere occurrence of consciousness but rather embodies a separate act of creativity on our part.

Janet's identifying "le sentiment du réel" with attention or attentiveness, as we have seen, takes us a step closer to the truth. Incomplete as this suggestion may be, it implies, at least, that the feeling of reality has a being that is independent of perceiving or bodily sensing and consequently is not itself having a perception or sensation but rather exists as an affective mode or disposition. Even so, we may ask: what kind of attention or attentiveness is the feeling of reality to which Hume and James might have been alluding?

James skirts my kind of probing by asserting: *"Any object which remains uncontradicted is* ipso facto *believed and posited as absolute reality."*[15] He reaches this conclusion, and even emphasizes it as in my quotation, after considering the state of a "new-born mind, entirely blank and waiting for experience to begin."[16]

Similar remarks are made by Alexander Bain, whom James quotes. "The leading fact in Belief, according to my view of it, is our Primitive Credulity," Bain says: "We begin by believing everything; whatever is, is true.... The animal born in the morning of a summer day proceeds upon the fact of daylight; assumes the perpetuity of that fact."[17] But how can one know that a newborn animal "assumes the perpetuity" of *anything*? The animal may not make provision for surviving after nightfall; it may accept the givenness of daylight without ever seeming to ponder about it; and yet one cannot conclude from these premises that it is entertaining beliefs about perpetual daylight or anything else. At best, the most one could say is that the newborn *is incapable of believing in nightfall*. From this, it does not follow that "the animal" has acquired the beginnings of feelings about reality, as James and Bain suggest.

I do not wish to question the close relation between belief and the feeling of reality. Rather, like Hume, or at least my interpretation of him, I view the feeling of reality as a unique phenomenon in all human experience, even when there is no belief. Apart from belief, the feeling of reality reduces to the submissive and minimal acceptance by someone of an explicit circumstance with which that person is involved. With the advent of a vital problem and the search for its solution, the feeling of reality pervades one's belief and thus transforms the original acceptance into a more complex situation.

Suppose I wish to know what time it is. That is the problem— the time. I undertake an inquiry: I look at my watch. If I have reason to doubt its ability to keep correct time, I carry the inquiry further. If I trust my watch, however, I leave matters there, and, in so doing, manifest my belief that the time is whatever it says it is. But the situation will have changed once my investigation arises and is geared to the motivating problem I have described and its possible solution. This new situation is more than merely perceptual, for now the feeling of reality is intermeshed with it as the basis for beliefs I may then have.

In daily experience and throughout our attitudes toward various things, the feeling of reality often burns with a low intensity, with a cool, if steady, pilot light. The ordinary world is habitual, and generally seductive to our consciousness, precisely because it occurs without any need for a massive display of affect or cognition. When awareness is fervidly aroused, however, and our perception of objects is as keen as Hume could allow any impression to be, then the incandescent quality of our feeling of reality may approach the kindling point. As James puts it: "One of the charms of drunkenness unquestionably lies in the deepening of the sense of reality and truth which is gained therein. In whatever light things may then appear to us, they seem more utterly what they are, more 'utterly utter' than when we are sober. This goes to a fully unutterable extreme in the nitrous oxide intoxication, in which a man's very soul will sweat with conviction, and he be all the while unable to tell what he is convinced of at all."[18]

The Feeling of Unreality

When a person is disposed to reject an experience or mode of feeling, the situation is often permeated by a tone of dissatisfaction with oneself and with respect to one's involvement in this experience. That is the setting for the "feeling of unreality." Undergoing it is not the same as believing that some things or events are in fact unreal. For instance, once I have awakened, I recognize my dream of last night as having been only a dream. But while I was actually having it, my dream may have smacked of reality as much as any part of my waking life. One should therefore say that during the dream experience I had the feeling of reality in relation to the dream itself, and as a vibrant occurrence authentically just as it was. Once I am awake, I still experience a feeling of reality, but now the conscious condition I am in is something richer than the dream itself. What currently exists is my belief that the dream really happened last night, that it had a content that my memory imperfectly reports to me, and that it may possibly be interpreted in one fashion or another. Thus the dream, that fanciful and fleeting kind of nocturnal event, may be characterized as something whose ingredients were "unreal" without their necessarily arousing in me a feeling of unreality. The latter is an unwelcome state that many people undergo, and its troubled character is not at all unreal.

The feeling of unreality can also be a specific component of our dreams. As the dream progresses, we may feel that the events in it are somehow not what they seem and not true to life as we know it. This intimation that what appears differs from what is real is, however, not the same as actually having a feeling *of* unreality, which would serve as a somewhat unpleasant repudiation of the dream experience in its entirety. Squeamishly going through the dream, we would refuse to treat it as any account of what does or might exist. We reject it as such; we do not take it as even a plausible representation, terrifying though it may be.

Persons who are tormented by the feeling of unreality have a panoramic problem. All of life may seem to them unsettling and unreliable. Nevertheless, for some of these people, the experience is a transitory dislocation that passes after a brief shudder. It then borders on what Freud calls the *unheimlich,* or "uncanny." In his article with that title, Freud refers to this as "purely an affair of 'reality-testing', a question of the material reality of the phenomena."[19] And then there are the familiar psychiatric reports of people who feel they are living in a dream: "I live in a dream, in empty space"; "I feel none of the things of this world"; "I see everything through a veil and within a fog"; "I hear people speak as if in a dream"; "I don't really distinguish between what I've lived and what I've dreamed." And so forth.

This condition resembles what Janet treated as "the sentiment of unreality." He took it as the symptom of a debilitating mental disease. Some of his patients insisted that everything in their life was unreal, and even that the world itself had no true reality. They were not talking as philosophers, Platonic or otherwise; they were not formulating some version of the distinction between appearance and reality. They were instead describing the feelings of unease or even of psychological pain that they experienced throughout daily life. When Janet asked these patients whether they thought the chair they were sitting on was not real, they answered as normal people would. "Of course it is," they said, "but it doesn't *feel* real to me."

More recently, Oliver Sacks has documented the frightful condition of "The Disembodied Lady" who suffered a loss of her body's feeling of its own muscular activity. "Something awful's happened," she exclaimed. "I can't feel my body. I feel weird—disembodied."[20] In her case, her feeling of unreality resulted from a neurological affliction coupled with the horror of no longer having the feelings that used to put her in touch with her physical reality.

One might possibly interpret such utterances as, in part or on some occasions, a characteristic form of creativity in relation to the variable feeling of reality that most people have without always being aware of its existence. One can even take the verbal locution of Sacks's patient or Janet's as an artful cry for help, a quasi-metaphoric effort that poetically calls attention to the agonizing feeling of homelessness in the world the patient inhabits, and an extremely anxious alienation from it.

Even so, we must always remember that, whatever its vividness of expression, the feeling of unreality reveals a *deficiency* in potential creativity of a sort that a healthy feeling of reality makes available to people who enjoy being alive. Those persons engage in purposive behavior, they relish the beauty and goodness they are lucky enough to experience, and, to some degree or other, they fulfill both artistic and nonartistic ideals that matter greatly to them. Creative though the feeling of unreality may be in its limited and perverse way, it defeats that triumphant and life-enhancing aspect of human nature. Here, again, we may find reason to believe that— benign and wondrous as creativity often is—it remains capable of being harmful and perhaps dangerous beyond all expectation.

The Function of Creativity

If only because the feelings of either reality or unreality contain these affective as well as innovative dimensions, they each contribute to a mode of creativity that is irreducible to any others. The feeling that the perceptual world we encounter is real rather than a fantasy of our imagination is unlike the feeling of pain that strikes us when someone pricks our finger. The latter occurrence is a separate and unwelcome reality. We have not created it; what caused that sharp effect is the physical act of being stabbed in this manner. If, however, on another occasion, we simply open our eyes and feel that what we see is really there, and nothing that might be considered an illusion like the nonexistent oasis in the desert, the circumstance is quite different. This much of the overall experience results from a creative device that we ourselves have imposed upon the visual appearance. The underlying disparity shows itself in the affective tone of our feeling that we are "at one with reality," as the phrase goes, and fully alive rather than drifting aimlessly in a vapid and dreamy condition, whether awake or asleep.

This particular type of creativity is so evanescent, albeit pervasive in ordinary life, that it is easily taken for granted, as if it were a routine response like turning off the gas before you leave a kitchen. It does indeed resemble a pervasive habit, but one that we all acquire in our earliest days. At birth, the infant's mind may be characterized, in James's famous saying, as a "booming, buzzing confusion" (a phrase he sometimes varied as a "blooming, buzzing confusion"). We have no reason to think that feelings or ideas about reality have a place in that amorphous state, but like creativity of any sort, they develop gradually and possibly very quickly. The feeling of reality that can eventually operate creatively in a person's life occurs without his or her giving much thought to it on most occasions.

This is not to say that the experience is uniform at every moment. When, out of the corner of your eye, you detect a glimmer of light behind you as you cross the street, you intuit that it results from the headlights of an approaching car. You know that the danger of being hit is real and you react accordingly, but you don't fully perceive either the lights or the car as the real objects they must be. If you did, you would be attending to them *as* realities—forcefully present in your experience of them, clearly etched in your mind. You would actively *realize* what they are.

In much of our conscious life we voyage through the perceptual world taking notice of the objects we encounter but not being fully aware of their reality. Even if we look at them directly, they may resemble the glimmering lights in my example. We see the cityscape as building blocks that crowd out the horizon but are hardly distinguished from one another. The shrubbery and other vegetation outdoors mainly serve as markers on our route, or even obstacles to be avoided in our trajectory. The people we pass are frequently indiscernible as individuals though clearly human. We know them to be real, and that alone can be a creative occurrence that we enact, but if, as happens very often, we scarcely fixate on their individual properties, we are not attending to them as the realities that they are. Until that happens, our feeling of reality is hidden or present only imperfectly; in any event, it exists as a circumscribed version of the creative potentiality in us.

Many years ago I enjoyed watching Norbert Wiener, the founder of cybernetics, walk through the Infinite Corridor at MIT reading a book that he held in his left hand while keeping himself on course to wherever he was going by means of a finger of his right hand, which guided him along the wall on that side. He was intentionally obliterating anything in his environment that might compete with the reality in which he was engrossed. I see that as an iconic image of what I have been describing as often characteristic of us all as we wend our way through the world.

The Augmenting of Felt Reality

My discussion thus far may help elucidate the fact, which I have been examining in much of my writings, that love is creative by its very nature. The beloved becomes extraordinarily, and sometimes unmatchably, real to the lover because of the attention that has been creatively bestowed upon her or

him. The sense of that person's indefeasible reality is a product of the creativity that is manifested by the bestowal needed
for love to occur and develop. The same can be said about
the concomitant appraisal, without which there could be no
bestowal. To the shrewd and fixated appraiser who intently
eyes some commodity (or person being treated like a commodity), nothing could be more real at the moment. Unless
this concerted act of appraisal is transformed into the different
type of value creatively bestowed upon a person, thing, or
ideal as it is in itself, there will not be love but only a professional
interest and perhaps acquisitiveness or greed. At its best, the
feeling of reality may also be present and glowing with an
all-inclusive ardor that results from joining the alternate
attitudes that love creatively unites.

Many philosophers have offered advice about how to
move beyond the meager and largely diminished feeling of
reality that people experience most frequently. All of Plato's
metaphysics can be read this way. On the assumption that
everyday perception is always illusory, as it sometimes is,
Plato devises means by which one can transcend the unreality
of that world we naively accept as it appears. Through purified
reason, more abstract than even mathematics and the reaches
of scientific speculation, he discerns the universal properties
that comprise the definition of everything in our language that
alludes to absolute reality—above all, the good and beautiful
as they instill meaning to whatever comes into existence.

At the top of the ladder of his analysis, the Platonic
philosopher envisages these principles of goodness and
beauty, the highest Forms, as they permeate the existence of all
that is and all that is possible in the cosmos. Though Plato calls
this intuition purely rational, it is offered as an expressive and

transcendent disclosure about a realm of being that shows itself more exactly and more explicitly in feelings of reality than in anything else that belongs to the lesser condition of mere appearance.

The idea of God that later theologians in the Judeo-Christian tradition depicted, and that millions of people have believed in, renders the Platonic views about the final intuition into articles of religious faith that make the underlying mythology more accessible to devotees. In the process, the dogma also declares the importance of affective elements such as creative love and the giving of oneself. In loving God, who is also designated as the embodiment of what is real in the being of everything, the true believer has a feeling of reality that completely exceeds the distorted experiences of ordinary life. I see the search for such a feeling as a momentous, though highly questionable, event in the history of human creativity.

As part of its program, Romantic ideology of the nineteenth century sought to unify the realms of appearance and reality. Earlier thinkers who were pantheists had long since claimed that God and nature are the same, and therefore that the absolute reality of the former is indistinguishable from the developmental reality of the latter. For the Romantics, many of whom were not themselves pantheists, this meant that there must be a way of experiencing nature that includes that greatest and most encompassing feeling of reality. The vehicle toward it was sometimes identified as the aesthetic attitude, not only in the making and appreciating of works of art but also in feeling love for oneself, for other persons, for nature as a whole, and in short for everything that exists. Though Nietzsche is not representative of all romanticism, this view about the culminating feeling of reality reaches a pinnacle in his notions about *amor fati* to which I previously referred: the love of both the good and the evil in the world.

In earlier books I have documented the faults in both the Romantic outlook and the philosophy of Nietzsche. Their alertness to the aesthetic is, however, a saving remnant that redirects our modern mentality away from the stultification inherent in Platonic metaphysics as well as the governing rationalism that evolved out of it and that still remains in current scientistic theory. As a way of seeing the world, the aesthetic pervades the mode of creativity that underlies our feelings about reality. Attending to something or someone as truly real, rather than fictitious or hallucinatory or the product of idle dreaming, is a creative act in itself. It is not instinctive or innately programmed as concomitant to our having an experience. If that were so, all there is in our consciousness would appear to us as equally and most fully real.

That is not the case, though everything is what it is and not another thing, and so even the most elusive sensation has a reality as just the datum that it is. But this does not mean that every sensation induces a feeling of its own reality. Any such response is superimposed by us upon the bare sensation or perception as an artifact of our creativity in *experiencing* it as real rather than illusory or a figment of our imaginative powers. Though imagination also belongs to the aesthetic, it results from a compartment in it that differs from any other reality.

Types of Feeling of Reality and Unreality

There are three kinds of feeling of reality, and correspondingly three kinds of feeling of unreality. There is an existential, a moral, and a valuational aspect of each. The existential is an attentiveness with respect to the instantiated being of any sensory or perceptual aspect of consciousness, and by extension any judgment, belief, theory, or worldview that purports to give descriptive information about the way things are, phenomenologically or otherwise. Most of us have this type of feeling of reality when we consider the everyday world of material objects to be real. It is also the feeling the daydreamer has insofar as he rests content within his rainy Sunday world of seductive fantasy.

The existential feeling of reality can also be illustrated by an extreme type of self-delusion like hallucination. This is often defined as an experience, sensory or perceptual, of some object that seems to be real but is not. One patient reported having what he called "thoughts-out-loud," which he recognized to be voices that were hallucinatory but that affected him as being real. We can denigrate any such response by calling it a cognitive aberration, but the semipoetic character of its depiction nevertheless alerts us to an imaginative element within this mental state. That may be what makes the condition so invidious to persons who feel its allure.

The moral aspect of the feeling of reality consists in its ability to influence one's entire affective life—the feelings about right and wrong, about what we should do in some situation, and generally how to live for the sake of attaining adequate happiness and a pattern of meaningfulness that matter to oneself as well as others. Though, in *The Principles of Psychology*, James provided a lengthy and sophisticated analysis of what he calls the sense of reality, he allowed himself to wander in *The Varieties of Religious Experience* through a quagmire of dubious reports fed to him by people who claimed to have undergone strange but very powerful intuitions in relation to what they considered extranatural "presences." The force and apparent acceptability of such visitations often had a great effect upon these individuals, sometimes even convincing them that life is worth living after all, in one system of morality or another. James's manner of investigation into these statements is quizzical and uncertain throughout, but his willingness to treat them seriously reveals at least a modicum of possibly unwarranted sympathy with the beliefs that issued from them.

For me what matters most is the way that the feeling of reality in situations like those can alter the quality and direction of a person's subsequent existence. The examples show how basic views about value and evaluating may come into play as a result of sensings of this sort. Particularly, and most obviously, if the moral reorientation leads to some religious conversion or lifelong commitment, the valuational result may be earth-shaking to the individual as well as devastating to members of the family or society whose past intimacies or meaningful attachments are now dismissed and radically devalued.

For people whose cosmic awareness has thereby been intensified or even initiated—as the scribe alleges to have happened to Saul of Tarsus (Saint Paul) on the road to Damascus—the momentous impact can include a wholly new configuration of attitudes toward the world as a whole. But instead of concluding that the existential feeling of reality can have this type of moral and valuational consequence only for religious people who respond in this way, I see these creative results as essential to merely having a feeling of reality as it exists creatively in every person. The experience of Paul was an extreme and very dramatic occurrence, comparable to being struck by lightning and never being the same again. Yet it is what happens continuously, though unobtrusively and usually without the grandiose spectacle of Paul's religiosity, when we feel that we are most solidly in touch with what seems to us to be reality. However gradually, our feelings about how one should live in order to have a happy or meaningful life, often sustaining our actual ability to live accordingly, progressively change throughout the moral and social modes of creativity.

Aesthetics of Reality and Unreality

Much of these changes in the tone and quality of our feelings of reality is consciously willed by human beings, at times artificially produced by them. For instance, consider the successive periods in the reception of television images. When they were first introduced several decades ago, audiences were fascinated by the realistic spectacle of live people and real life situations being filmed and recorded with some degree of verisimilitude. Viewers watched the images with a feeling of reality that was unaffected by their grainy appearance and lack of color in the early days. As the technology advanced, all that gave way to sharpened images, resulting from greater definition of the pixels, and colored in approximation of what people take to be normal perception. This effect was, and is still, much preferred because it provides a feeling of reality that most audiences value exorbitantly.

The school of realism in all the graphic media has always held aloft this effect as a source of aesthetic truthfulness. In fact, however, it is often the case that an accentuated feeling of reality is created at the cost of lessening the accuracy and authenticity in some representation of a person or circumstance being filmed. Whether in a painting or a television image, the high definition and exquisite precision of the perceptual outcome may in fact deviate from what people ordinarily see. Unless they wear eyeglasses that "correct" their vision to make it as sharp as possible, the world as they see it is usually quite different. Far from being true to the nature of our visual field, the representations thought to be realistic often sacrifice the utter truthfulness of that in order to attain a preferential feeling of reality as more suitable for whatever is being portrayed. This paradoxical trade-off is caused by the unavoidable dependency upon the techniques necessitated by a particular art form as the grounding of its chosen mode of creativity.

To an accomplished artist such dependency is scarcely an impediment. For one who has an adequate talent in his art, the imposed constraints become creative opportunities, much as the poet Richard Wilbur suggested when he said that the genie gets his power from having been in the bottle. Moreover, versatile artists find alternate ways of coping with the paradox I have mentioned. For example, in order to convey through their moving images alone the chaotic and ambiguous state of modern urban life, the New Wave filmmakers of the years just after World War II intentionally made black-and-white movies that were grainy, disjointed, and sometimes unfocused. Instead of increasing our perceptual feeling and awareness of reality, they sought to augment our sociological or even political sense of it. These directors were relying upon gritty cinematic effects as a way of commenting about contemporary life.

As another mode of coping creatively with this situation, poets like Robert Frost and William Carlos Williams overtly attempted to use their verse as a means of what Frost called "realization." They described affective realities and portrayed events in daily existence with a desire to induce in their readers some deepened feeling of reality that pervaded their experience, which the audience would otherwise have treated as commonplace or routine. The imagistic poetry of the early T. S. Eliot and Ezra Pound, as well as many others in the twentieth century, was designed in a similar fashion. Those who were properly attuned to this form of creative writing would not perceive something new but instead they would savor the newness in whatever might now present itself forcefully to their imagination.

In the pictorial arts, that kind of endeavor goes back to the time of Giotto and even the Roman portrait painters of the first century AD. In neorealistic films like *The Bicycle Thief* we do not see reality itself (assuming for the moment that we know what that is), but rather we are shown images of realities in a way that enables us to recognize them while captivating our interest and involvement through familiar, even clichéd, feelings *about* their reality.

In the thinking of creators like Schopenhauer and Walt Whitman, who were quite different in other respects, this project of realization overlapped with other philosophical ideas they had. Whitman believed that his poetry could vividly bring to view the normally ignored sensing of commonplace things and events in our joint experience. This quest for augmented social and communal realization was itself inherent in Schopenhauer's belief that all of us, and everything else, constitute "the Will," which he calls metaphysical Being in itself. In this view, the compassionate response that Schopenhauer considered basic in the formation of any ethical system results from the implied intuition that all existing creatures are realities that we must creatively identify with our own reality.

While this doctrine is not the same as religious pantheism, it nevertheless originates from Eastern as well as Western conceptions of divinity as not only the underlying reality of everything but also the supreme *realization*, the most creative and wholly real manifestation, of the reality that everything has merely in being what it is. I think this is what propels the Nietzschean notion of cosmic love, the love of everything that exists. All things and persons and events in the universe would then be accepted as the realized reality that invariably belongs to them and that occurs in the empirical world under the rubric of appearance.

Concluding Remarks

In view of the approach I have been sketching, we may be able to clarify, and now extend, the notion of transformation that has entered into my recent ideas. The "reality" that theologians, scientists, artists, and laymen curious about the meaning of life have sought turns out to be a synoptic term for referring to the endless ways in which everything is what it is because of its being a transformation of whatever has preceded it. Far from duplicating any earlier reality that caused it, or somehow brought it into being, the new entity transforms its forebears. This partial or radical transfiguration is not only novel but also, in varying degrees, a creative phenomenon that is usually unpredictable and unpremeditated. In seeing each thing or person as a member of the whole, and inseparable from the entire world that we experience and imagine, we enclose it within whatever feelings of reality that are with us always.

From this it follows that the orthodox conceptions have indeed misled us. To adapt something Wittgenstein says in a related context: We have been deceived by a picture of how the world is. It is not only that language cannot correspond to some fixed and definite reality out there, but also that no such reality exists as assumed. All that occurs in our conception devolves from our *feelings* of reality, which we have creatively molded into a palpable category that structures whatever we can even comprehend. In Bohm's notion of "assimilation" I find an intimation of the idea of transformation as I perceive it. To assimilate, as he understands the process, is to integrate new data with what is already known. That takes us part of the way, but beyond it there is the element of alteration, changing through some flexile process a preestablished pattern that is rendered malleable by superimposed imagination and creativity. The concept of transformation accommodates that dynamic and interactive possibility.

To say that our common parlance and assumptions about a state of being that we call "reality" is fundamentally mistaken, and is itself a form of verbal creativity, does not imply that all of human existence is creative. Much of it is platitudinous, dull, boring, and all too often dreary. We revere men and women of genius not because we hope to attain their level of creativity but rather because we wish to become *like* them, though we know full well that we are not their equals in this regard.

❁

Discussing transformation in relation to creativity, I sought to show how each eludes the perfectionist creed that most philosophers have either affirmed or taken for granted in their reasoning. My thinking about the nature of love entered into these deliberations because that disposition is predicated upon a combination of the two valuational phenomena that I have studied for many years: affective bestowal and appraisal. In love, bestowing value is generally based on some appraisive value, which is never absolute even though the language of bestowal may be. The lover sees his beloved through linguistic or gestural or physical acts toward her or him as if that person were appraisively perfect, which neither believes literally. Bestowal is not forgiveness or illusion but rather a metaphoric tribute to the human search for perfection within a context of inevitable imperfection. The enactment of that is a preeminent mode of practical and aesthetic creativity.

As a part of his attack on perfectionism, Jean Renoir quotes someone who said that a genius is a person who tries to do what everyone else does, but fails. The notion that the important thing in art is perfection, Renoir continues, is "an unfortunate idea": "Perfection is an insane joke." In their fixation on copying details like the appearance of a hand or foot, academic paintings may be "perfect," but that is why they are so boring. In art and all of creativity, Renoir insists, "what matters is human contact." The creative person will not be concerned with attaining perfection of any sort but rather with reaching an audience, however small, through making products whose limited goodness he and others can savor. This concept of human contact is enunciated in Renoir's film *The Rules of the Game* when Octave laments that he has never made "contact with the public." As a culmination of his thought, Renoir remarks: "The most important thing in life is love," which is never perfect, he rightly says.[1]

One reason that creativity is also never perfect, either in itself or in its achievements, is its dependence throughout the creative process upon our fateful immersion in the temporality of life. In its constant aspiration, creativity seeks to transcend some looming future as well as the past. As a springboard of this effort, creative persons do often want to live in the future. As in science fiction, they envisage what coming generations might create someday through novel technologies or lifestyles. But in present and actual reality the future is always a fiction to a large extent. We cannot know with any accuracy what will happen and, at best, we can only respond to this unknowability by imagining what is probable or merely possible, and then create some indication of what we hope or fear that the future will be. If we live in the past, as some stultified scholars do, we cannot create much, if anything. And yet the present in which we always live perforce is itself an emanation out of the past. As a result, we cannot truly foresee what is likely in the future, or address it creatively, unless we live at least partly in some previous reality. This is a paradoxical aspect of the human predicament and a challenge to the very being of creativity.

In addition to the modes of creativity that I have focused on in this book, those that are primarily social or biological are also worthy of our attention. Making new life through germination or parturition or artificial insemination, and in ways that vary greatly though uniformly in some respects, is a mode of creation without which no species could continue to exist. Every life-form is programmed to be creative in this manner. In all organisms the process of biological creativity can be defeated by the effects of environmental hazards as well as innate restraints that undermine it. In human beings these include emotional and intellectual components of our nature that are sometimes essential for nonbiological creativity. Social and interpersonal factors of that sort are prevalent throughout the affective and cognitive dimensions of our species. In recent years much work in this area has been done by writers in both psychiatric and cognitive psychology. I have felt no need to discuss it in this book, but a great deal of the research in that field is entirely congruent with the reflections I have been offering as a humanist philosopher.

In relation to childbirth, which is an example of "ordinary creativity" that Andreasen's discussion neglects, we must ponder the following question: Just what is the mother, or the mother and father, creating when they have a baby? They have not and cannot literally *create* their offspring: they can only give it the possibility of having life—hopefully a good life— and, in doing so, ideally help humankind go on profitably, to survive at least a while longer than any individual can. Schopenhauer considers the latter of these creative acts more important than the former. I disagree. They are equally important.

Finishing this book as I have, I am aware that its subject matter warrants and deserves much further investigation—by others as well as myself. The blossoming research in neurobiology and cognitive science is on the brink of discoveries about creativity that every philosopher or other theorist in the humanities must attend to, whatever his or her specialty may be. Moreover, as I have been arguing for some time, these and other scientific ventures can benefit immeasurably *as science* through inter-disciplinary cooperation with the humanistic approach in areas that pertain to the expertise of all alike. My text, here and in its prequels, was written with that as its goal. If only as a blueprint that others who have a similar vision can apply in one way or another, my world picture—which I also see as a would-be work of conceptual art—will have fulfilled its mission.

I recently had a long and very fruitful (for me) conversation with a scientist who received the Nobel Prize for his cell research. He rejected the idea that humanists and investigators like himself could benefit from interdisciplinary work between them. He said: "We stand on opposite shores of an enormous river. The bridge you want to construct cannot be built. The river is simply too wide." He may be right about some of the sciences and some of the humanities. But the neurologist Vilnyanur S. Ramachandran mentions in one place that his studies of the brain may some day explain the nature of linguistic metaphor and even provide a "very phrenological view of creativity."[2] The suggestions by Andreasen and others about neuron plasticity and the brain's constant creativity I interpret as promising concepts that now require humanistic input for their further development.[3] Psychiatrically inclined scientists—for instance, Kay Redfield Jamison—who try to decipher the relation between artistic creativity and manic-depressive or related illnesses are also fashioning parts of the bridge I have in mind.[4] Nor are theirs the only pursuits where such constructive efforts have already begun.

We shall see in time whether the comprehensive span from shore to shore can eventually be achieved as a creative reality in itself. I look forward to the new disciplines that the search for it will generate.

Appendix: On Creativity

Moreland Perkins

In the dictionary you might find something like this as a definition of the verb *create*: cause to exist, bring into existence. From this one might for a moment suppose that what is needed in order to be creative is merely to spend one's time bringing things into existence. This idea, one quickly realizes, can seem to say both too much and too little. On the one hand it suggests making something out of nothing, which God is said to do, but we cannot. We can create only by making something out of something, or, as in musical performance, by making something with something. So for human beings as creators we have to understand the phrase "bring into existence" as implying that one works upon or with some material so as to change it, and thereby to make something new.

However, were we to stop with that idea about how to be creative, we should of course say too little. For by that idea, anyone busy changing the form of something is being creative: I could be creative by filling an hour tearing paper into strips. Or I could walk through a school building breaking windows in the classrooms: that would be creative. Indeed by this idea of creativity, it's even easier to create. If I change my position in my chair, or roll over in bed, then I have worked with the material that is my own body so as to change its form. I've created a new position of my body, hence been creative. And the mistake here is not because of the material chosen, my own body. For dance is one of the creative arts, and it involves no more than working with one's own body as material and causing changes in its shape and motion. Obviously something important is not yet included in our description of a creative act. Something we all implicitly understand about being creative is missing. Not just any working upon or with material so as to change its condition counts as being creative.

Do we, then, apply that term *creative* if, and only if we judge that what a person makes has value for us?

Well, surely having value is not enough. Think of a man who uses a machine to stamp and cut silver dollars from large sheets of silver. For eight hours he does just that, and perhaps makes a million dollars a day. We do not say he is a creative person because of his daily making of things of value—though he is, of course, judged to be a productive worker. Productive, yes; creative, no.

Making things of value is not enough to count as being creative. Is it, however, necessary? If what you make has no value for us, does your making it fail to be creative? I suggest that it does: we do not call a person creative if we judge that what he makes has no value. To create, in the sense of this word that counts for a person's being creative, what one makes must have value.

If I judge, concerning a given professional philosopher, that his book has no value, then I will not count him as having been a creative person in writing that book. In my judgment, his time will not have been spent creatively in writing it. If another philosopher judges the same book to have solid value, he will consider the man to have been creative in writing it. So, too, an adult who, to imagine the absurd, thinks schools are an evil institution, hence their destruction a work of value, might judge the breaker of school windows to have put in a creative hour or two.

I do not mean to raise here issues about the objectivity of judgments of value, and hence of creativity. I mean only to affirm that all ascriptions of creativity to a person's activity are evaluations. They are always assessments that assign positive value to what the person has made. To be creative, what one makes has to meet certain standards of value. Merely making something new is not enough. However, the case of the silver-dollar cutter illustrates the point that making something of value is also not enough to make one's activity creative. Making something of value is necessary, but not sufficient for creativity. What more, then, is involved in our idea of being creative?

Perhaps one will think that there is a richer sense of the word *new* according to which in order to be creative it is enough to make something both new and of value. A new silver dollar is merely a new instance of a kind of thing that's been around a long time, more or less exactly like all the others of its kind. But what if the objects the man was making were, each one of them, "new" in the sense of unique, each quite unlike any other of its kind. Suppose that with his machine he produced an array of silver snowflakes. Suppose each flake was of an interesting and attractive design and each different from the others in significant ways—perhaps even unpredictably different ways. Well, whether predictably or unpredictably different, if all he does is operate a machine that someone else so designed that this result is achieved mechanically, then in making these valuable silver snowflakes he is not being creative. In order to be creative it is not enough to make something new, unique, and valuable.

By now it should be evident what we need to say. The idea for what a creative person makes must be her own. Or, as we might put it, if she is to get credit for being creative, she must not merely make what she makes, she must invent it. Being creative, we might say, is inventively working upon or with some material so as to make it into something new and valuable. The new form taken by the old stuff originates with the creator. The explanation for the thing made having the form it has is not to be found in some circumstances antecedent to or external to the thought and action of the maker. The explanation stops with her. It is, as we say, her conception that is embodied in the thing she makes.

Or—we must note—her conception may be embodied in the action she performs, for of course actions themselves may justly be found to be creative. The material transformed in such a case is the agent's behavior and the conception of the action—or perhaps at least the responsibility for it—is hers. The qualification about responsibility suggests a possible difference in regard to our criteria for creative actions. As contrasted with making things, there is a difference in criteria that will merit some attention later. For a writer or a painter or a philosopher to be credited with creative work, the conception must be hers. For a leader of men and women to be credited with creative action, it may be that the conception need not be hers, only the responsibility for injecting her action into a particular situation. For the moment, however, we can ignore this possible peculiarity of creative actions and consider only the creative making of things. That the conception of what she makes must be the maker's, that she must in effect invent what she makes, entails, in turn, that creative work is purposeful, deliberate, intentional. The agent intends to make a certain kind of thing; what she makes is the kind of thing it was her purpose to make. I say the kind of thing, because it won't do to say of creative work that always the worker intended at the start to make exactly the specific thing she succeeded in making. For this suggests that she knows ahead of time exactly how it is to come out, which is often—perhaps usually—not true. But the kind of thing she makes she must be engaged in trying to make if she is to be credited with creativity. This much is implied by the condition that the conception must be hers.

"Kind of thing" must here be understood as very specific. It's not merely a portrait of a man before her this painter means to be making. She has specific ideas of the sort of portrait she's aiming for, ideas about character, spirit, emotional condition of the painting's subject, as well as ideas about color and patterns of color, use of paint, and so forth.

Yet this reference to guidance by concepts may seem sometimes to be an overstatement, or seem somewhat mis-leading. It is not immediately clear that it always applies, for example, to creative work in painting, say, or expressive dancing, or even always to poetry or fiction. Of course concepts must be at work in poetry and fiction since the material is linguistic. Yet one might not be quite certain that the fashioning of the whole is guided always by a conscious idea. This raises, I think, a question of fundamental importance. We want, on the one hand, to say the conception must be his even of the jazz musician, or of the expressive dancer or painter, yet we may not be prepared to say that forming the product is explicitly guided by a conscious idea. How do we reconcile these two elements in our notion of creativity? How can we say better exactly what we mean, here? I think the answer has some important implications.

Work is judged creative, at least by knowledgeable judges, only when it presupposes in the creator three attributes: first, a complex awareness of a problem presented by certain material; second, mastery of methods of setting to work on that material to solve the problem; and third, talent for generating the kinds of patterning of the elements of the material that constitute satisfactory solutions of the problem.

A creative person making the thing she makes presupposes concentration upon a problem, mastery of a discipline and a medium, and practical appreciation of successful forms of resolution of similar problems. In consequence, the solution she fashions cannot fail to be perceived by a knowledgeable judge as inventive, as intelligent, as expressing a conception of her own, whether or not she can at the moment of creation articulate a conscious idea that guides her in fashioning the work.

The creative worker at the end of her work has perceived a complex pattern of elements, which she perceives as providing a resolution of her artistic problem—and we agree in this perception, judging the work valuable. We cannot in these circumstances fail to perceive the work as embodying an original conception, whether or not the artist acknowledges having a conscious idea prior to her producing it. Whether or not the conception ever existed disembodied in the artist's mind apart from her actually working out the material resolution of her artistic problems, it is embodied in the material and she fashioned—she invented—that embodiment. Hence its conception is hers.

If the resolution of the problem presented by the material is not a product of disciplined mastery of the medium, it is luck. In that case, no doubt there is a sense in which something is created, but the person cannot truly be said to have been creative. The concentration involved in creativity is concentration upon the possibilities, the potentialities of the medium, the material. The only way this concentration can be effective is in consequence of knowledge gained from working in the medium, with the material. This in turn requires that work is carried out with concentration upon, and hence knowledge gained of the standards required of successful work in that medium. In short, there has been a disciplined appreciation of good work.

Nor must we be prevented from recognizing this presupposition of disciplined mastery of medium and training in appreciation of standards by our observations of apparently sudden and very early displays of creativity in children. For example, the production of wit or humor is creative work. And it may sometimes seem that a child shows a talent for this kind of creation that is suddenly simply there, as if he were born with it. But that is an illusion. Behind his first production of wit or humor are years of most intensive concentration upon the disciplined mastery of the use of words to accomplish desired effects.

Moreover, such a child gives a selective attention, quite distinctive and different in degree and kind from the attention of another child in a similar environment, attention to the production of wit and humor whenever he encounters it. No doubt there is some innate proclivity and ground of talent in this initial selectivity of response and attention. However, this innate talent can yield creative power only in virtue of what will have already been, by the time the child shows creative wit or humor, some years of training in appreciation. It may be quite voluntary, or virtually involuntary, it is so natural. It may go unnoticed by his parents, but a silent study that is quite as much an assimilation of a sophisticated tradition as is the painter's deliberate study of earlier masters. It is equally a tutelage in the standards of this art.

What is more, there will have been too a period of trial and error, of training in the use of words for this particular effect. This also may not have been much noticed by parents, partly because it is not successful as wit or humor, hence less noteworthy, partly because its intent may not always be fully clear.

Indeed, another reason why such a child's apprenticeship in method and standards may be overlooked by adults is because it may in no small measure constitute a nuisance. This adult attitude may show itself, for example, in the classroom, where (sadly) even successful humor or wit is often perceived primarily as a disruptive tendency. This posture in, say, a boy's second-grade teacher is scarcely conducive to noticing that he is serving an apprenticeship in a creative art. Also, much of the child's freest experimentation in humor and wit will go on with other children in the absence of the more alien and mysterious standards of adults. Again, it may go unnoticed by adults.

Similar remarks hold, I believe, for another child who starts out writing exceptionally good stories. She will have had by then years of training both in the telling of stories and in a special kind of attention to other's telling and reading of stories. This may be the attention of the apprentice born, with the talent to aspire to mastery of that art. She appreciates stories as not merely something to consume but something to produce. She gives a kind of attention to the how of the art of making stories that another child does not give. She shows a disposition to begin imitating such performances with a child's seriousness that is distinctive.

A creative person, then, sees in the resolutions of certain problems of a particular medium by the production of certain effects not merely something to be enjoyed or used or consumed but an invitation to participate. She sees in them an intimation of a method to be acquired, a vision of a medium to be mastered, a deployment of standards of good work to be imitated. So she makes the problems her own, she makes the method her own, she makes the medium her own, and she makes the standards her own. Then either she does or does not show invention, display imagination, and create something of value.

Should we say that having made all these things her own, she either does or does not show a creative impulse for working to resolve the problems? Or should we say that if she succeeds in making all these things her own, then, by definition, she has become creative? I am inclined to say the latter. The person who fails, under conditions of apparently similar training and motivation, to become creative has either failed to make the method her own, failed to make the medium her own, failed to make the standards of performance her own, or failed to make the problems her own. If all this can be done and is done then one will have begun to create. For in truth the only certain evidence that a person has made all these things her own is that she creates in that field!

Of the four things I have suggested that it is both necessary and sufficient that a person make them her own if she is to be counted as creative—namely, method, medium, standards, and problems—is one more central or essential than another? Yes and no. No, because if only one is present, without the other three, then there will not be creativity. If any three conditions are fulfilled but the fourth is not, creativity will be impossible.

However, there is one sense in which one of the four is more central. One may think to oneself about a person making these four things her own and find oneself perhaps wondering, "Still, isn't there something missing, namely the drive to create?" When one thinks that, and thinks, therefore, that these four conditions are not enough, then I believe that this factor, what one might call the creative drive, is included in one of the four elements I have mentioned.

Which one? Making the problems, or some of the problems of this particular field of action, one's own. For to say that one has made these problems one's own is to say that one has invested some significant portion of one's energy in the task of solving these problems, or some of them, or at least one of them.

The sense in which one makes the problems one's own is not that one has acquired a certain anxiety or emotion about some situation, or feels cornered or beset by some difficulties or circumstances. One makes the problem one's own in the sense that one becomes in some degree preoccupied with finding a resolution to a problem, with working out a solution, with producing one solution. Now, since if there is a mechanical method for producing a solution, we do not count the work as creative, this means that a person has become preoccupied with solving a problem for which there is no mechanical solution. Therefore, of necessity, she has become preoccupied with inventing the solution.

And what is that but being possessed of a creative drive? That's exactly what it is—provided that the mastery of method is there, the mastery of medium is there, the appreciation of standards is there. Then we can speak of the commitment to resolution of the problem as possession of a creative drive. For we cannot call the drive properly creative unless it is within the power of the person to create; and this requires these other three factors. Without these other three, mastery of method, medium, and standards, we might speak of a wish to create, but not of the creative drive. But with these three present, making the problem one's own is being possessed of the creative drive.

Has perseverance been left out? I think not. For this is also included in the idea of making the problems one's own, remembering that this is not a way of speaking of an emotion or an anxiety or a concern, but a way of speaking of a commitment, a preoccupation, a determination to resolve the problem. And this, properly understood, entails perseverance. Otherwise it is not the problem itself that one has made one's own but merely a feeling of the problem, or a concern about the problem, or an anxiety about it. To make the problems one's own is to make oneself into a person engaged in, committed to, resolving the problem. Both the drive and the perseverance needed to create are, therefore, contained within the making one's own of problems within the field.

Of the four elements in creativity that I have suggested for your consideration I want especially to speak of two, and of connections between these two, with a view to what is involved in becoming creative. I pick these two not because they are more important than the other two but because I am inclined to think that, in thinking of creativity, educators are perhaps somewhat more inclined to overlook certain interrelationships between these two than between the other two. I may be wrong in this suspicion but even if so, some selective emphasis is needed here, and I do feel reasonably confident that this selection will be as useful as any other. The two elements I mean are the training in appreciation of standards and the orientation toward problems of production and toward making these problems one's own. More or less buried in my earlier remarks is one that, from the point of view of an interest in what is involved in becoming creative, is perhaps the most important. This was the idea that a mark of the creative person, whether child or adult, amateur or professional, is that she responds to the product that is the end result of some particular region of creative endeavor with an interest in how it is made, how it is done. Her consumption of the product, as we might call it, her appreciation of it, her enjoyment of it, or her use of it is always in part comprised of a sensitivity to and interest in how it is made, how it is done.

I think everyone who thinks at all about creativity is aware of the importance of this productive orientation in the creative person. But what I think is not always so regularly recognized is the importance—as it were within the attention to how the thing is made—the importance of attention to the standards realized in the production, or performance. A productive orientation must, to yield creativity, become a discipline in critical appreciation of standards for the production of good work in this area.

In some respects even more interesting is this fact: that the surest way of developing a critical appreciation of standards of excellence in some area of production or performance is to take up a productive orientation toward work in this area.

Ours is a society much oriented toward mechanical methods in production, and toward consumption of others' productive work in our own leisure time. I think one of the most valuable aspects of a productive orientation is the development of a form of critical appreciation of creative work. A productive approach can make one's participation as consumer of such work an exercise in intelligence, in appraisal, even, in some measure, a sharing of value, of interests, of skills, of ends, of methods with a large community of interesting human beings. Orienting onself to making the product, one's life is enlarged, the community of persons with whom one shares creative work is enlarged, and the human meaning of the works that one enjoys or understands or uses is appreciated more nearly from within. One's life acquires some of the values that those who create these objects acquire in creating them.

In this respect one cannot help thinking of that all-pervasive form of all-too-passive consumption of a product of creativity, watching television. I imagine that more than one parent wishes this could be stopped altogether—but of course it cannot be. It's here to stay. And of course one hears a good deal of the educational use of television.

I think the idea of educational use does not very often mean what it might mean. It might mean not the consumption of educational films, but training in creative appreciation of television productions, whatever their character. If a school works out ways of developing a productive orientation toward television, this is the truly educational use of television. This is treating television not merely as an educational product to be consumed, but as a model of creative work to be understood and participated in, a field for productive orientation, for asking the question, How is it done? and trying to find the answer. Indeed one could seek this answer for every aspect of television production, including even the technical part (the broadcasting of images, or how this is done) and the production of every kind of "show"—the news show, the comedy hour, the children's show, the dramatic work, the commercials, the talk show, and so on.

Even failures can be illuminating, because the recognition of what it takes to meet the standards of successful production are helped by the experience of the difficulty in meeting those standards when one attempts it oneself. Television watching could in some measure be changed from mere passive consumption into intelligent, analytical, even creative participation in production. Even though most persons would never join the television industry, indeed would do no more than watch it, their watching could itself become a creative participation.

I think very similar opportunities present themselves in children's books, both novels, or stories, and textbooks—for example, history books. Children should look at them with a productive orientation, asking how it is done, and asking whether and how it could be done better. Scarcely anyone has failed to look at some children's book, storybook, or textbook at some time and noticed some way it could be done better. Why shouldn't children be encouraged to do this themselves? Even here it is too unfortunate to be mere consumers. It is better to develop some sense of community with the producers of the work from which one is learning. And this can only be done by taking up a creative orientation toward the books one studies. How are they made? What are the pitfalls, the possibilities of failure, and what is presupposed in successful production of such works?

The only way to understand the writing of history is to write history. How many schoolchildren ever get assigned the task of writing the history of something they can do original research on—for example, their own school, the town library, their neighborhood?

Finally, some words on creativity in action, which was mentioned earlier, an area where, too, history and biography can be employed. Perhaps we could speak here of creative leadership. I remarked earlier that we do not in this area demand of creativity that the conception of the creative action be the leader's own. She may get her ideas from advisors, for example; but the responsibility for choosing the context of action, and the very concrete form of its execution needs to be hers. And of course the criterion of inventiveness in resolving a problem applies here as elsewhere. I think one of the most interesting studies in this area is of the standards for excellent performance, and how they vary in different political contexts. Perhaps most interesting, or anyhow most relevant, to us, are the peculiarly complex standards that apply to creative leadership by a political leader in a democratic country.

I remember, for example, in reading the long, multivolume biography of George Washington by Douglas S. Freeman, finding that one of the most creative things that Washington did as military leader of the Revolution was the following. He insisted, time and time again, upon showing the fullest respect and deference to a body of men—the Continental Congress of what was not yet even a nation—who, time and time again, seemed to deserve nothing but contempt, and cry out to be ignored.

Now the idea that the man with executive power, even one with charismatic popularity in a time of extreme crisis, should always defer to the body that represents the people was not Washington's own idea. Politically, Washington was not an original thinker. He got his ideas about the nature of a democratic republic from others (and from experience in Virginia politics). However, taking responsibility for showing this deference throughout six years of revolutionary war, under the most trying conditions, when the needs of action seemed desperately to call for one man to take the power into his own hands, this was creative leadership. For he was insisting under these circumstances on bestowing respect on a body of men who found it often enough virtually impossible to respect themselves, who scarcely yet existed as an institution. And he was thereby creating a democratic tradition, creating, in part, a republic, where before there had been only the aspiration for a republic.

To compare and to contrast the standards that had to be met for creative work by a military leader operating in the political environment of a Washington with those of one operating in the very different political environment of a Napoleon would be instructive.

Indeed we have a useful example of this complexity of standards for creative leadership in a republic exhibited just far enough back in time to be treated in schools as history. President Richard Nixon's creativity in certain areas of leadership in foreign affairs struck many at the time as indisputable. That achievement looked quite secure. Yet suddenly, in his second term, it appeared that he had not taken responsibility for certain standards being met in the process of leading a democratic government. This failure undermined his capacity to lead and diminished the effectiveness of the nation on the international scene. In the end, his creativity was stultified by his failure to appreciate the standards of performance required of excellence in leadership in this special political context, that of democracy.

Certainly one wants to encourage in students a critical appreciation of such criteria of creativity in political leadership. One way to do this might be to read enough to set a problem of leadership in some interesting case, and then ask students to figure out how they would act in that situation. Then read on and find out how the person did in fact act. Some of President George W. Bush's responses to 9/11 could be used in this way. Even more challenging would be the case of Franklin D. Roosevelt.

Even here the power to appreciate the historical examples may be enhanced by real-life action, actual practice in school at taking responsibility for inventive solutions to problems of group direction, under conditions that determine complex standards, hence restrictions upon performance.

One correction: I just now described these standards as restrictions upon a leader's actions. That was because I had in mind Nixon's example. Yet if one brings to mind Washington's example, were these democratic standards restrictions or opportunities? Leaving aside felicitously creative innovations that may contribute to improved standards in a field of action, in general, to find the standards of excellence in performance to be restrictions is an indication that one has not made the appropriate problem one's own. To make one's own the problems native to the medium—the problems inherent in democratic political leadership—is to find in its standards one's own opportunity for creativity. Washington's opportunity for creativity was Nixon's obstacle to it.

Notes

Preface

1. For a comprehensive outlook on creativity from various perspectives, see Wikipedia entry "Creativity," http://en.wikipedia. org/wiki/Creativity, 18 November 2009; see also Jeffrey Maitland, "Creativity," *The Journal of Aesthetics and Art Criticism* 34, no. 4 (Summer 1976), 397–409; essays in *Creativity in the Arts*, ed. Vincent Tomas (Englewoods Cliffs, NJ: Prentice-Hall, 1964); essays in *The Nature of Creativity*, ed. Robert J. Sternberg (Cambridge: Cambridge University Press, 1988); Stevan Harnad, "Creativity: Method or Magic?," http://cogprints.org/1627/1/harnad.creativity.html; essays in *Creativity and Affect*, ed. Melvin P. Shaw and Mark A. Runco (Norwood, NJ: Ablex, 1994); essays in *Creators on Creating: Awakening and Cultivating the Imaginative Mind*, ed. Frank Barton, Alfonso Montuori, and Anthea Barron (New York: Penguin, 1997); Mihaly Csikszentmihalyi, *Creativity: Flow and the Psychology of Discovery and Invention* (New York: HarperCollins, 1996); Abraham Maslow, "Creativeness," in his *The Farther Reaches of Human Nature* (New York: Viking, 1971), 57–100, and also Abraham Maslow, "Creativity in Self-Actualizing People," in *Creativity and Its Cultivation*, ed. H. H. Anderson (New York: Harper, 1959); Berys Gaut, "Creativity and Imagination," in *The Creation of Art: New Essays in Philosophical Aesthetics*, ed. Berys Gaut and Paisley Livingston (Cambridge: Cambridge University Press, 2003), 148–173; Berys Gaut, "Creativity," in *A Companion to Aesthetics*, ed. Stephen Davies, Kathleen Higgins,

Robert Hopkins, Robert Stecker, and David Cooper (London: Wiley-Blackwell, 2009), 207–210; Marvin Minsky, *The Emotion Machine: Commonsense Thinking, Artificial Intelligence, and the Future of the Human Mind* (New York: Simon and Schuster, 2006).

1 Prologue: Reversing Mistakes about Creativity

1. Charles Hartshorne, *Creative Synthesis and Philosophic Method* (La Salle, IL: Open Court, 1970), 3.

2. Alfred N. Whitehead, *Modes of Thought* (New York: Macmillan, 1938), 168–169.

3. Whitehead, *Modes of Thought*, 174.

4. Henri Bergson, *The Two Sources of Morality and Religion*, trans. R. Ashley Audra and Cloudesley Brereton, with the assistance of W. Horsfall Carter (New York: Holt, 1935), 245–246.

5. Bergson, *Two Sources of Morality and Religion*, 240.

6. William Shakespeare, *Twelfth Night*, act 4, sc. 2.

7. William Shakespeare, *King Lear*, act 1, sc. 1.

8. William Shakespeare, *Hamlet*, act 1, sc. 1.

9. Albert Einstein, "What I Believe," *Forum and Century* 84, no. 4 (October 1930), 192–193.

2 The Creative Experience

1. On Renoir's methodology, see Jean Renoir, *Renoir on Renoir Interviews, Essays and Remarks*, ed. Carol Volk (Cambridge: Cambridge University Press, 1989), 46ff. See my chapter on Renoir in *Three Philosophical Filmmakers: Hitchcock, Welles, Renoir* (Cambridge, MA: MIT Press, 2004), 147–219, and 221–257.

2. On this, see David N. Perkins, *The Eureka Effect: The Art and Logic of Breakthrough Thinking* (New York: Norton, 2001); see also his *The Mind's Best Work* (Cambridge, MA: Harvard University Press, 2001).

3. Bertrand Russell, *The Conquest of Happiness* (London: George Allen & Unwin, 1936), 76–77.

4. Arthur Koestler, *The Act of Creation* (London: Hutchinson, 1964), 178.

5. Koestler, *Act of Creation*, 185–186.

6. Mary Shelley, *Frankenstein*, ed. Johanna M. Smith (Boston: St. Martin's, 1992), 23.

7. *The Creative Experience*, ed. Stanley Rosner and Lawrence E. Abt (New York: Grossman, 1970), 74.

8. Russell, *Conquest of Happiness*, 76–77.

9. Alan Lightman, *A Sense of the Mysterious: Science and the Human Spirit* (New York: Pantheon, 2005), 16.

3   The Creative Process

1. Renoir, *Renoir on Renoir*, 39–40.

2. Renoir, *Renoir on Renoir*, 40.

4   Three Myths of Artistic Creativity

1. Sigmund Freud, "The Relation of the Poet to Day-Dreaming," in his *On Creativity and the Unconscious: Papers on the Psychology of Art, Literature, Love, Religion* (New York: Harper, 1958), 44–54.

2. Konrad Lange, "Illusion in Play and Art," in *A Modern Book of Esthetics*, ed. Melvin Rader (New York: Holt, Rinehart and Winston, 1960), 5–14.

3. Freud, *On Creativity and the Unconscious*, 47.

4. Freud, *On Creativity and the Unconscious*, 52, 53.

5. Sigmund Freud, "Wish-Fulfillment and the Unconscious," in *A Modern Book of Esthetics*, ed. Melvin Rader (New York: Holt, Rinehart and Winston, 1960), 129.

6. Freud, *On Creativity and the Unconscious*, 51.

7. Richard P. Feynman, *"Surely You're Joking, Mr. Feynman!":
Adventures of a Curious Character* (New York: Norton, 1985), 174.

8. William Shakespeare, *The Tempest*, act 4, sc. 1.

9. Carl G. Jung, *Modern Man in Search of a Soul* (New York: Harcourt,
Brace and Company, 1934), 194.

10. Jung, *Modern Man in Search of a Soul*, 195.

11. Jung, *Modern Man in Search of a Soul*, 197.

12. Jung, *Modern Man in Search of a Soul*, 198–199.

13. Leo Tolstoy, *What Is Art and Essays on Art*, trans. Aylmer Maude
(New York: Hesperides, 2008), 123.

14. See Irving Singer, *The Nature of Love*, vol. 3, *The Modern World*,
with a new preface by the author (Cambridge, MA: MIT Press, 2009),
in particular 49–66.

15. Henri Bergson, *Laughter: An Essay on the Meaning of the Comic*,
trans. Cloudesley Brereton and Fred Rothwell (New York: Macmillan,
1914), 150.

16. Bergson, *Laughter*, 153.

17. Bergson, *Laughter*, 157.

18. Bergson, *Laughter*, 161.

19. Bergson, *Laughter*, 171.

5   Aesthetic Creativity

1. *The Dialogues of Plato, Vol. 3: Ion, Hippias Minor, Laches, Protagoras*,
trans. R. E. Allen (New Haven: Yale University Press, 1996), 13–14.

2. George Santayana, *Reason in Art*, vol. 4 of *The Life of Reason: Or the
Phases of Human Progress* (New York: Scribner's, 1946), 230.

3. Quoted in Walter Lippman, *A Preface to Morals* (New York: Macmillan, 1929), 98.

4. *The Whistler Journal*, ed. E. R. and J. Pennell (Philadelphia: Lippincott, 1921), 137.

5. Gustave Flaubert, Letter to Louise Colet, *Correspondence*, vol. 2, ed. Louis Conard (Paris: Conard, 1926), 461.

6. Oscar Wilde, *The Picture of Dorian Gray* (New York: Charterhouse, 1904), viii.

7. James Joyce, *A Portrait of the Artist as a Young Man* (New York: Bantam, 1992), 209.

8. *The Whistler Journal*, 137.

9. See R. G. Collingwood, "Art as Expression," in *Artistic Expression*, ed. John Hospers (New York: Appleton-Century-Crofts, 1972), 26–50. In the same volume, see also John Hospers, "The Croce-Collingwood Theory of Art," 51–71. For further discussion, see *Neoplatonism and Western Aesthetics*, ed. Aphrodite Alexandraks (Albany: State University of New York Press, 2002); Noël Carroll, *Philosophy of Art: A Contemporary Introduction* (London: Routledge, 1999; *Routledge Companion to Aesthetics*, ed. Berys Gaut and Dominic McIver Lopes (London: Routledge, 2005).

10. John Dewey, *Art as Experience*, in *The Works of John Dewey, 1925–1953*, vol. 10, ed. Jo Ann Boydston (Carbondale and Edwardsville: Southern Illinois University Press, [1934] 1987), 52.

11. For the history of this concept, see James Engell, *Creative Imagination: Enlightenment to Romanticism* (Cambridge, MA: Harvard University Press, 1981), 172–183.

12. Monroe C. Beardsley, *The Aesthetic Point of View*, ed. Michael J. Wrean and Donald M. Callen (Ithaca, NY: Cornell University Press, 1982), 260–262. See also Vincent Tomas, "Creativity in Art," in *Creativity in the Arts*, ed. Vincent Tomas (Englewood Cliffs, NJ: Prentice-Hall, 1964), 97–109.

6   Creativity in Expression, Metaphor, Myth

1. Dewey, *Art as Experience*, 55.

2. Dewey, *Art as Experience*, 58.

3. Dewey, *Art as Experience*, 110.

4. Quoted in John Hospers, *Meaning and Truth in the Arts* (Chapel Hill: University of North Carolina Press, 1946), 101. See also John Hospers, "Art and Expression," in his *Understanding the Arts* (Englewood Cliffs, NJ: Prentice-Hall, 1982), 192–227.

5. Oscar Wilde, "The Decay of Lying," in his *Intentions and the Soul of Man*, quoted in *A Modern Book of Esthetics*, ed. Melvin Rader (New York: Holt, Rinehart and Winston, 1960), 22.

6. Aristotle, *The Poetics of Aristotle*, ed. and trans. S. H. Butcher (New York: Macmillan, 1902), 77.

7. On this, see Arnold Modell, *Imagination and the Meaningful Brain* (Cambridge, MA: MIT Press, 2003), 25–48.

8. See Irving Singer, *Feeling and Imagination: The Vibrant Flux of Our Existence* (Lanham, MD: Rowman and Littlefield, 2001).

9. Karen Armstrong, *A Short History of Myth* (Edinburgh: Canongate, 2005), 3–5.

10. Armstrong, *Short History of Myth*, 147.

11. Armstrong, *Short History of Myth*, 149.

12. On this, see Irving Singer, *Reality Transformed: Film as Meaning and Technique* (Cambridge, MA: MIT Press, 1998), and also *Cinematic Mythmaking: Philosophy in Film* (Cambridge, MA: MIT Press, 2008).

7   The Prosaic and the Absurd in Their Creative Context

1. Nancy C. Andreasen, *The Creating Brain: The Neuroscience of Genius* (New York: Dana, 2005), 26–27.

2. Albert Camus, "The Myth of Sisyphus," in his *The Myth of Sisyphus and Other Essays*, trans. Justin O'Brien (New York: Vintage, 1951), 124.

3. William Shakespeare, *A Midsummer Night's Dream*, act 3, sc. 2.

4. On philosophical or quasi-philosophical discussions of joking, see Berys Gaut, "Just Joking: The Ethics and Aesthetics of Humour," *Philosophy and Literature* 22 (1998), 51–68; Ted Cohen, *Jokes: Philosophical Thoughts on Joking Matters* (Chicago: Chicago University Press, 1999); Jim Holt, *Stop Me If You've Heard This: A History and Philosophy of Jokes* (New York: Norton, 2008).

5. Thomas Nagel, "The Absurd," in his *Mortal Questions* (Cambridge: Cambridge University Press, 1979), 11–23.

6. William Shakespeare, *Twelfth Night*, act 5, sc. 1.

7. Arthur Koestler, *Insight and Outlook: An Inquiry into the Common Foundations of Science, Art, and Social Ethics* (Lincoln: University of Nebraska Press, 1949), 417.

8. Koestler, *Insight and Outlook*, 419.

9. Koestler, *Insight and Outlook*, 421.

10. Bergson, *Laughter*, 170–171.

11. Friedrich Nietzsche, *The Gay Science*, trans. Walter Kaufmann (New York: Random House, 1974).

8   Creativity in Practice

1. Ludwig Edelstein, *The Hippocratic Oath: Text, Translation and Interpretation* (Baltimore: Johns Hopkins University Press, 1967), 6.

2. Louis Lasagna, "Would Hippocrates Rewrite His Oath?," *The New York Times Magazine*, June 28, 1964.

3. On this, see Anthony Weston, *Creative Problem Solving in Ethics* (New York: Oxford University Press, 2007); Tom L. Beauchamp and James F. Childress, *Principles of Biomedical Ethics* (New York: Oxford University Press, 2008); Robert M. Veatch, Amy M. Haddad, and

Dan C. English, *Case Studies in Biomedical Ethics: Decision-Making, Principles, and Cases* (New York: Oxford University Press, 2010).

4. Jean-Paul Sartre, *Existentialism Is a Humanism* (New Haven, CT: Yale University Press, 2007), 33.

5. Sartre, *Existentialism Is a Humanism*, 72.

9   Creativity in Science, Technology, and Mathematics

1. James D. Watson, *The Double Helix: A Personal Account of the Discovery of the Structure of DNA* (New York: Atheneum, 1968), i.

2. Henri Poincaré, "Science and Method," in his *The Foundations of Science*, trans. George Bruce Halstead (Lancaster, PA: Science Press, 1946), 387.

3. Poincaré, *Foundations of Science*, 388.

4. Poincaré, *Foundations of Science*, 391. On this, see Seymour Papert, "The Mathematical Unconscious," in *On Aesthetics in Science*, ed. Judith Wechsler (Cambridge, MA: MIT Press, 1981), 104–119; and also Judith Wechsler's introduction to that volume, 1–7.

5. David Bohm, *On Creativity*, ed. Lee Nichol (London: Routledge, 1998), 32–36 and passim.

6. Bohm, *On Creativity*, 71.

7. Bohm, *On Creativity*, 71–72.

8. Bohm, *On Creativity*, 72.

9. William James, *The Principles of Psychology*, vol. 1 (Cambridge, MA: Harvard University Press, 1981), 329.

10. Poincaré, *Foundations of Science*, 366.

11. Poincaré, *Foundations of Science*, 367.

12. On this, see essays in *Inventive Minds: Creativity in Technology*, ed. Robert J. Weber and David N. Perkins (New York: Oxford University Press, 1992).

13. Jacques Hadamard, *An Essay on the Psychology of Invention in the Mathematical Field* (New York: Dover, 1954), 142–143.

14. Quoted in Neal Zaslaw, "Mozart as a Working Stiff," in *On Mozart*, ed. James M. Morris (New York: Cambridge University Press, 1944), 109. See also Peter Kivy, "Mozart and Monotheism: An Essay in Spurious Aesthetics," *The Journal of Musicology* 2, no. 3 (Summer 1983), 322ff.

15. See Poincaré, *Foundations of Science*, 392.

16. Quoted in Hadamard, *Essay*, 142–143.

17. David Leary, *Metaphors in the History of Psychology* (Cambridge: Cambridge University Press, 1990), 2.

18. Nancy J. Nersessian, *Creating Scientific Concepts* (Cambridge, MA: MIT Press, 2008), 135ff.

19. Margaret A. Boden, "What Is Creativity?," in *Dimensions of Creativity*, ed. Margaret A. Boden (Cambridge, MA: MIT Press, 1994), 98ff. In this collection, see also David N. Perkins, "Creativity: Beyond the Darwinian Paradigm"; Howard Gardner, "The Creators' Patterns"; Colin Martindale, "How Can We Measure a Society's Creativity?" See also Margaret A. Boden, *The Creative Mind: Myths and Mechanisms* (London: Routledge, 2004).

10   Creativity and Reality

1. William James, *The Varieties of Religious Experience: A Study in Human Nature* (London: Longmans, Green, 1941), 58; italics in the original.

2. William James, *The Principles of Psychology*, vol. 2, 913; italics in the original.

3. William James, *The Principles of Psychology*, vol. 2, 652; italics in the original.

4. Kathleen Wider, "Emotion and Consciousness," in *Self-Representational Approaches to Consciousness*, ed. Uriah Kriegel and Kenneth Williford (Cambridge, MA: MIT Press, 2006), 63.

5. Jaak Panksepp, "The Periconscious Substrates of Consciousness: Affective States and the Evolutionary Origins of the Self," *Journal of Consciousness Studies* 5 (1998), 567.

6. Wider, *Self-Representational Approaches to Consciousness*, 73–74; italics in the original.

7. Wider, *Self-Representational Approaches to Consciousness*, 74; italics in the original. For a neurological theory of the self in terms of memory and body image, see Israel Rosenfield, *The Strange, Familiar, and Forgotten: An Anatomy of Consciousness* (New York: Vintage, 1993).

8. Aristotle, *De Anima*, quoted in Daniel Heller-Roazen, *The Inner Touch: Archaeology of a Sensation* (Cambridge, MA: MIT Press, 2009), 37.

9. Heller-Roazen, *Inner Touch*, passim.

10. Pierre Janet, *Les Obsessions et la Psychasthénie*, vol. 1 (New York: Arno, 1976), 478. My translation.

11. David Hume, *A Treatise of Human Nature*, ed. L. A. Selby-Bigge (Oxford: Clarendon, 1968), 107–108.

12. Hume, *Treatise of Human Nature*, 108.

13. Hume, *Treatise of Human Nature*, 629.

14. Hume, *Treatise of Human Nature*, 628–629.

15. James, *Principles of Psychology*, vol. 2, 918.

16. James, *Principles of Psychology*, vol. 2, 917

17. Quoted in James, *Principles of Psychology*, vol. 2, 946.

18. James, *Principles of Psychology*, vol. 2, 914.

19. Freud, "The 'Uncanny,'" in his *Writings on Art and Literature*, ed. Warner Hamacher and David E. Wellbery (Stanford, CA: Stanford University Press, 1997), 225.

20. Oliver Sacks, *The Man Who Mistook His Wife for a Hat, and Other Clinical Tales* (New York: Simon and Schuster, 1985), 44. See also Rosenfield, *Strange, Familiar, and Forgotten*, 57.

Concluding Remarks

1. Renoir, *Renoir on Renoir*, 251.

2. Quoted in John Colapinto, "Brain Games," *The New Yorker*, May 11, 2009, vol. 85, no. 13, 85; see also V. S. Ramachandran and William Hirstein, "The Science of Art: A Neurological Theory of Aesthetic Experience," in *Journal of Consciousness Studies* 6, nos. 6–7 (1999), 15–51. See also Semir Zeki, "Neural Concept Formation and Art: Dante, Michelangelo, Wagner," in *Neurology of the Arts : Painting, Music, Literature*, ed. F. Clifford Rose (London: Imperial College Press, 2004), 13–41; Hideaki Kawabata and Semir Zeki, "Neural Correlates of Beauty," *Journal of Neurophysiology* 91 (2004), 1699–1705; Gerald M. Edelman, *Wider Than The Sky* (New Haven, CT: Yale University Press, 2004); Francisco J. Varela, "Neurophenomenology: A Methodological Remedy for the Hard Problem," in *Explaining Consciousness—The 'Hard Problem,'* ed. Jonathan Shear (Cambridge, MA: MIT Press, 1997), 337–357.

3. Andreasen, *Creating Brain*, 146–158.

4. Kay Redfield Jamison, *Touched With Fire: Manic-Depressive Illness and the Artistic Temperament* (New York: Free Press, 1994). See also her *An Unquiet Mind* (New York: Knopf, 1995). See also *Poets on Prozac: Mental Illness, Treatment, and the Creative Process*, ed. Richard M. Berlin (Baltimore, MD: Johns Hopkins University Press, 2008), particularly the editor's introduction, 1–11.

Index